Dade's Last Command

DADE'S
Last Command

Frank Laumer

Foreword by John K. Mahon

University Press of Florida

Gainesville / Tallahassee / Tampa / Boca Raton

Pensacola / Orlando / Miami / Jacksonville

00 99 98 97 96 95 6 5 4 3 2 1

Library of Congress Cataloging-in-Publication Data
Laumer, Frank.
Dade's last command/Frank Laumer.
p.   cm.
Includes bibliographical references and index.
ISBN 0-8130-1324-0 (acid-free paper)
1. Dade's Battle, 1835.   2. Seminole War, 2nd. 1835–1842.
3. Dade, Francis Langhorne, 1793?–1835.   I. Title.
E83.835L36   1995
973.5'7—dc20   94-26086

The University Press of Florida is the scholarly publishing
agency for the State University System of Florida, comprised of
Florida A & M University, Florida Atlantic University, Florida
International University, Florida State University, University of
Central Florida, University of Florida, University of
North Florida, University of South Florida, and University of
West Florida.

University Press of Florida
15 Northwest 15th Street
Gainesville, FL 32611

To my wife, my friend,
Dale Anne Laumer

"The war in Florida was conducted largely as a slave-catching enterprise for the benefit of the citizens of Georgia and Florida."

GRANT FOREMAN, *Indian Removal*

Contents

Illustrations

Foreword

John K. Mahon

Dade's Last Command supersedes *Massacre!* as the definitive account of the march and annihilation of Maj. Francis Dade's column of 108 men in December 1835. Except for the fact that *Massacre!* is nearly sold out, and that Laumer has since 1968 continued intensive research on the men and the land, the original would not need to be replaced. *Massacre!* is as gripping an account of a march and a battle as can be found in American military literature. It embodies impeccable research, and as far as the historical record makes it possible, every detail of the action is perfectly accurate. The same literary grace and precise research carry over into *Dade's Last Command.*

Laumer writes of the events of the march and battle in a way that allows readers to feel they are there. He and others made the march themselves, stopping each night where the doomed column bivouacked. The reader shares the rain and shine with the soldiers and the Seminoles because Laumer made use of weather records, a resource not often used in military narratives.

Much knowledge of the soldiers, the Seminoles, and the terrain is woven into the text, and the author uses great skill in interpolating this material without interrupting the central story. Based on the author's research since 1968, *Dade's Last Command* makes use of additional detail on the backgrounds of men and officers, on the Seminoles, on the much-maligned Louis Pacheco, on weapons and clothing, on the mistake made by the military commanders in ordering the march of Dade's command through hostile territory, and on Dade's decisions as commander of the ill-fated column.

There does not exist a more vivid but at the same time more historically accurate account of a single action in U.S. military literature.

Preface

My home is on the north bank of the Withlacoochee River. Through research I found the site of Fort Dade on the south bank of the river and a half mile upstream, now a field empty of all but pine and palmetto. The fort had been named for Bvt. Maj. Francis Langhorne Dade, killed in the Second Seminole War.

In 1962 I first visited Dade Battlefield Historic Site, fifteen miles north of my home. Strangely, only a handful of articles had been written about this man, his command of one hundred men, why they had come here in December 1835, why they had died.

With some reluctance (the Fort Dade research had taken two years), I took up the task of searching for answers to my new questions. Five years later I thought the task was fairly over, most of the facts in. I wrote a book, a history of the battle, and called it *Massacre!*

Research is a hard habit to break. I continued writing letters, making phone calls, traveling here and there. Now, twenty-five years after *Massacre!*, it is time to bring the story up to date. But this is no longer simply the story of a battle. It is also a glimpse into a lost world, a world in which men sacrificed other men's lives in order to maintain the slavery of yet other men. It is a story of this land, these men.

Talisman
March 1994

Acknowledgments

No pursuit is more dependent than research upon the kindness of strangers. In thirty years of searching for information relating to this battle, I have been privileged to deal—through letters, calls, and visits—with hundreds of people across the United States, in Europe, and in Australia. Almost without exception my inquiries have been received with patience, understanding, and courtesy. From files, diaries, and archives have come arcane details relating to these men, their states of mind, their weapons and clothing, the weather, and the state of the world at the time of Dade's battle. This search has been a wonderful journey of discovery, not only about the facts relating to my subject but about the kindness of men, women, and children, many of whom I have not had the pleasure of meeting. I extend to each of them my deepest gratitude.

The search began with the bones of these men. Work of the last quarter century has begun to flesh them out through height, age, complexion, medical records. Pictures of four have been found, and others are known to exist. Glimpsed through pictures, letters, military records, and recollections of friends (and enemies), we have tried to reveal them, not as a collection of bones, buttons, weapons, and numbers, but as men of flesh and blood, fears and hopes, courage and despair, victories and defeats.

Carolyn Watson, teaching a sixth-grade class at Pine View Middle School in Land O'Lakes, Florida, learned of my quest and marshaled her students on behalf of Dade's command. They found newspaper descriptions of the battle published in 1886, 1892, and 1924, none of which I had seen. One of the two papers of 1892 carried a long interview with, and even a picture of, Louis Pacheco. The children also found a report to the House of Representatives of 1862 relating to a petition by Caroline Clark (Pvt. Ransom Clark's daughter) for a pension, thus advancing the search for direct descendants of this remarkable man. The generous and intelligent assistance of the children, under Carolyn's inspiration and direction, has helped the world remember.

John Papworth, a friend and attorney in Syracuse, New York, obtained a court order in December 1977 allowing me to exhume the remains of Ransom Clark. A few days later, my wife, Dale Anne, our daughters Amie and Jodi, my son, Chris, and my brother, Marsh, flew to Syracuse, rented a car, drove to Greigsville, bought a pick and shovel, and drove to the little cemetery. While opening the grave I was told that someone in the group that had gathered wished to speak to me. Ruth Fitz Simmons, a lovely lady in her eighties, introduced herself as the great-great-great-granddaughter of Henry Clark, Ransom's brother. At her home in nearby Pifford she brought out the family Bible, and for the first time I saw the names of Ransom's parents and those of his four brothers and five sisters. This information, in turn, has led to a correspondence with descendants of Ransom's siblings across the country, among them Ruby Williams of Manhattan, Kansas, Carl and Margaret Henry of Floral City, Florida, Shirley Schoenleber of Spokane, Washington, and Ralph Ransom Clark of Havana, Florida. Each has offered information, leads, and encouragement. My son-in-law, James Punch, painstakingly made a handscript of the will and related papers of Benjamin Clark, Ransom's father. My daughter Suzanne put this in typescript and thus produced for me details of the Clark family relationship, which I believe affected directly the personality and constitution of Ransom Clark. (Benjamin bequeathed to his then-disabled son the sum of one dollar.) Lois Flynn of Wadsworth, New York, another stranger, volunteered her heated garage for Dr. Djavaheri's use in his examination of the remains of Ransom Clark.

Jack Friend of Mobile, Alabama, provided maps and other information regarding Mobile Bay at the time of Clark's boat accident in January 1835. Jane McDonald, museum aide at Fort Morgan, scoured that fort's records and found helpful mention of Clark, Chandler, Belton, and Dade. She further provided me with yearly reports for the month of January, giving temperature for both air and water in Mobile Bay. Each of these has been a brushstroke, large or small, in painting the picture of this land, these men.

A dear friend, Joni Herzog of Largo, Florida, took up the search for Pvt. Joseph Sprague. A year of calls and correspondence produced a wealth on Spragues generally but only tantalizing hints about Joseph. Through her perceptive correspondence she reached Ruth Pearson of St. Albans, Vermont, owner of the letters of a man totally unrelated to the Dade search—Capt. Joseph Swearingen, killed in the battle of Okeechobee on Christmas Day, 1837. In addition to some forty letters, Mrs. Pearson has an oil portrait of Captain Swearingen and several artifacts relating to him, treasures for those searching for the history of *that* man, *that* battle. Mrs. Herzog persuaded Mrs. Pearson of the need to have photocopies of the letters brought to Florida to add clarity to the career of one more man whose life was given in the Florida struggle. Without Mrs. Herzog's efforts, there is hardly a doubt that these letters would never again have seen the light of research. Now they are under the able care of Elizabeth Alexander, librarian at the P. K. Yonge Library at the University of Florida in Gainesville.

I am indebted to Lee Farnsworth of Winter Garden, Florida, for a copy of an 1823 requisition for officers' hats that included Dade's head size. Carl Allison of Adams City Hatters in Tampa translated the measurement (twenty-four inches) into the current measure (7 3/4–7 7/8), along with the information that this was the largest size men's hat within the "standard" range. Hence, my description of Dade's head as "large." Mr. Farnsworth also provided me with the report of a military court proceeding in 1820 in which Dade was a supernumerary member, thus pinning down one more date in my Dade chronology.

At West Point I discovered that Capt. George Gardiner's brother, John, was also a graduate of the academy (1828). Subsequent research in John's records provided much new material on the family, which in turn shed new light on the personality and character of George Gardiner. James Stancil of Tampa provided me with photocopies of several letters of Lt. John Gardiner written in Key West in January 1836 describing the reaction of Mrs. Gardiner to the news of her husband's death and mentioning in passing the need to have her furniture shipped from Fort Brooke to New

York. This latter information I have used in an attempt to re-create the Gardiners' quarters at Tampa.

Rumor had it that a Dr. Joseph Cushman at the University of the South in Sewanee, Tennessee, had a portrait of Francis Dade. "No, not Dade," he told me, "but I do have an oil painting of Captain Fraser." He explained that his wife was a descendant of Fraser's brother. The Cushmans kindly had a color photo made of the painting, the first likeness I found of any man with the command. Sadly, the room in the Cushmans' home where the painting was displayed later caught fire and the work was destroyed. The only likeness now in existence is the photo so fortuitously made.

Dr. James Covington, Emeritus Dana Professor of History at the University of Tampa and a prolific author on Native Americans and Florida history, brought to my attention the strange story of the "removal" of Captain Fraser's remains from the Fort Brooke cemetery. In addition, Dr. Covington's unparalleled and generously shared knowledge of the Seminole people and their history has given me whatever understanding I have of these invincible people.

Early in my research I had found excerpts from a privately bound work titled "The Personal Reminiscences of William Starr Basinger 1827–1910." The author was a nephew of Lieutenant Basinger, son of his brother Thomas. Through correspondence and phone calls with various Basingers I found that Richard Bateson of Blusston, South Carolina, had a full typescript of the "Reminiscences." With amazing generosity and trust, Mr. Bateson recently mailed the book to me, whom he had never met. From its nearly five hundred pages, several more details of Lieutenant Basinger's life and death emerged that have helped tell his story. Mr. Bateson also granted permission for the P. K. Yonge Library, University of Florida, to copy the manuscript, thereby making it readily available to all. In addition, he suggested that I might contact Gen. Sterling Wright (retired) of Virginia, who just *might* have some sort of likeness of Basinger. General Wright returned my call and said calmly, "Yes, we have an oil painting on glass which we believe to be a portrait of Lieutenant Basinger. The understanding in the family is that it was painted soon after his graduation from West Point, though the young man is in civilian clothes." General Wright generously provided me with a photograph of the painting, included here. And finally, I had the good fortune of meeting Mr. Bateson and his wife. Where? Dade Battlefield, of course.

Charles Hines of Clearwater, Florida, loaned me a copy of *Lenoir County (N.C.) Heritage*, which covers Kinston, home of Dr. Gatlin. This contained a map of the town and information on conditions and circumstances during the years of the doctor's life there. I was particularly thrilled when I found on page 14 a daguerreotype captioned "John Slade Gatlin, killed in Florida Territory at the battle of Dade's Defeat." My pleasure in the discovery was allayed by the knowledge that the earliest known photographic process was not invented until 1839, four years after the death of Dr. Gatlin. A likely assumption is that the likeness is the doctor's brother, Richard. Close, but no cigar.

For background medical information that would likely have been known to Dr. Gatlin, I asked for help from Dr. Ashby Hammond of Gainesville, Florida. With his customary kindness, Dr. Hammond provided me with obscure reports submitted by army surgeons in the field during the period of the Florida wars. These reports include descriptions of climate and terrain, location and condition of forts, and, most important for my purposes, methods employed by army doctors in the field. Also invaluable was the *Statistical Report on the Sickness and Mortality in the Army of the United States* for the period (1819–39). Added to these uncommon records were equally important observations by Dr. Hammond himself, based upon his own years of study of medical conditions in Florida during the period. In short, I am indebted to Dr. Hammond for virtually every medical reference in the present work.

In the search for information on Lieutenant Mudge, I found my way to John K. Mudge in Las Cruces, New Mexico. Mr. Mudge had a history of the Mudge family published in 1868. He generously photocopied and sent me pages of pertinent information and, wonderfully, a photograph of an engraving of Lieutenant Mudge. Then, several years later, of the Mudges living in Florida, George Otis Mudge of Port Richey approached me at the conclusion of the annual reenactment. He handed me a wrapped package which could only be a copy of the very rare Mudge history. He told me the book was mine. Mr. Mudge died in 1992, but I will always remember our meeting and his gift.

John E. White, reference assistant with the Wilson Library at the University of North Carolina, helped me puzzle out questions relating to the Richard Keith Call papers which describe the meeting between Call and Clinch at Fort Drane and also contain recollections concerning Francis Dade from one who had known him. I particularly recall conversations with late Governor and Mary Call Collins (she is the daughter of Mary Call, youngest daughter of Richard Call), owners of the Call papers. Always gracious and helpful, the Collinses gave permission for the use of this rare and unpublished material, now a part of the Florida State Archives.

After establishing the exact route of the old Fort King Road from Fort Brooke (Tampa) to the battlefield, as well as the location of Dade's nightly encampments, I walked the road in December 1963. By 1988 the Dade Battlefield Society had supplied me with a complete and exact reproduction of the full uniform of a private soldier of 1835, including musket and accoutrements. I had learned a great deal of the rigors of the march in 1963, but now I would actually be able to experience the wear, the weight, the fit and misfit of clothing and equipment, just as every man of Dade's command had. In December 1988 I made the journey again. Many reenactors in full uniform, as well as "civilians," joined me this time—twenty or so in all—as we gathered at the Little Hillsborough River crossing just north of Tampa. Through the next five days our ranks swelled and thinned as we hiked, camped, slept, and hiked again. Overall planning, registration, and arrangements were superbly handled by the Dade Battlefield Society, particularly Marsha Woodard, Sheila Mann, and Ginger Bell. Local historical societies, Friends of Hillsborough River State Park and Fort Foster, with the cooperation of citizen support organizations along the route, provided meals; the Florida Highway Patrol and county and city police assisted with highway crossings and traffic control. Cooperation and assistance in every phase of the planning and the journey itself were given without regard to time or trouble by the entire staff of Dade Battlefield Historic Site, particularly then-manager Jeff Montgomery and rangers Jim McCann and Jim Sparks. Among reenactors who took part in portions or all of the march were Dr. Ray Giron, Steve Abolt, Frank Hamilton, Jerry and John Morris, Dan Marshall, Dave Leonard, Marsha Woodard, Sheila Mann, Jean McNary, Andrea Carlson, Debbie Richter, Jan Glidewell, Steve Perkins, Earl Ferguson, Craig Villanti, Bruce Howie, Clyde Southern, and Don Pennay. All were good comrades. In addition to making the entire sixty-mile march, Jan Glidewell, columnist for the *St. Petersburg Times*, awakened interest in at least one period of Florida's history for countless readers by his thoughtful and almost daily articles from the field.

My son, Chris, joined me again (he had hiked the second day, fifteen miles, in 1963, when he was eleven), and for the entire march this time. My daughters Jennifer, Amie, and Jodi were strong and cheerful companions through all the days and nights when school or domestic duties permitted. Their love and support in this, as in so many things, is a cornerstone of my life.

Betsy and Vince Ruano now own "the round clay sink" where Dade's command spent their last night on earth. They gladly made the pond and surrounding grounds available to our considerable group for our encampment near the end of our march. And Kenneth Strait of Spring Hill, Florida, invited me aboard his ancient Piper Cub in August 1988 for a low-level flight the length of the Fort King Road and back. This provided me with a clear sense of the continuity of the road as the route unfolded below us, stretches of the actual road often clear when the path crossed pine barrens and hammocks. The interest and generosity of the Ruanos and Mr. Strait are deeply appreciated.

I take this opportunity to express my appreciation again to Dr. Raymond E. Giron of McIntosh, Florida, an expert on period firearms and edged weapons, choreographer of the Dade reenactment (as well as those of Olustee and Natural Bridge), author, artist, and holder of fourteen film production credits. In addition, Dr. Giron is surely the most knowledgeable and accomplished reenactor in the country. Any knowledge I have acquired concerning the types of muskets of the Seminole War period, their mechanisms, and firing procedure are due principally to Dr. Giron's tutelage. He has responded to a hundred calls for details of weaponry over the years, and always with patience. My debt to him is great.

The discovery that someone has the odd document or book that holds some fragment of Dade's story has been a delight. My daughter Suzanne, while visiting a friend one evening in Lockport, New York, chanced upon a small, leather-bound volume among others on the mantle. She found it was a near mint-condition copy of Samuel Drake's *Tragedies of the Wilderness* (1839). Always on the alert for anything that might relate to my quest, she was delighted to find that one of the "narratives" was by Ransom Clark. The friend, Sandy Church, not only gave Suzanne permission to send this rare volume to me but said that I might keep it on semipermanent loan until he asked for its return.

Others who were equally generous in sharing rare and valuable material with no thought of reward other than the author's thanks are Richard Ferry of McClenny, Florida, who loaned me a copy of *General Regulations for the Army of the United States* for 1835, and, again, Ray Giron, who later gave me a bound photocopy of the same regulations. With this volume in hand, it seems unthinkable that I could have attempted the present work without it. Steve Abolt of Fort Worth, Texas, provided me with a copy of Winfield Scott's *Infantry Tactics* for 1835, a volume that he was instrumental in republishing from an original. All who are concerned with American military activities during this period are indebted to Mr. Abolt for making this rare work available. Joseph Rubinfine of Pleasantville, New Jersey, a dealer in historical Americana, had an original letter from Clinch to Dade of October 17, 1835. At my request, Mr. Rubinfine promptly and generously provided me with a photocopy of the letter, a document vital to understanding Dade's move from Key West to Fort Brooke. Dan Cohn of Kenneth Rendell, Inc., in Beverly Hills, California, provided me with a copy of a previously unknown letter of Dade that had been offered as a prize on the *Wheel of Fortune* television program. And David Girdy of "One of a Kind Collectibles" (autographed memorabilia) in Miami, Florida, sent me a copy of a Dade letter from 1818 describing Dade's first arrival in Florida. Another important letter is Dade's to Jones of December 14, 1835, a copy of which was given to me by Gordon Bleuler. This letter is a part of Mr. Bleuler's collection of postal history and, like that of Mr. Rubinfine's collection, clarifies the circumstances surrounding Major Dade's final months. Bill Dayton, a friend, historian, and attorney in Dade City, Florida, gave me *A French-English Military Technical Dictionary* (1917), which was a valuable tool for understanding French terms in the diary of Lt. Henry Prince and other documents bearing upon this work. Each of these men contributed to whatever value or interest the present work may possess.

In October 1978 I received a call from Winnie Murphy, museum guide at Dade Battlefield State Historic Site. A visiting couple, Mr. and Mrs.

Ralph Coggleshall, claimed to have an original diary kept by a West Pointer, Henry Prince, during the Second Seminole War. I spoke to Mr. Coggshall and invited him and his wife to our home. After seeing photocopies of a few pages, it was clear that this was a work unknown to research. The Coggeshalls eventually made a decision to sell the diary in order that it be returned to Florida. Over a period of several years a group worked to produce a typescript of some 350 diary pages, and through it all bits and pieces about Dade's march and battle emerged: the fact that the white man, Stafford, was the original interpreter; the horse that would have saved Gatlin's life, though it would have cost Dr. Nourse his. The diary of Henry Prince is one of the most important original documents on the Second Seminole War to be found in recent years. Florida's history can be more fully understood as a result of the interest and kind disposition of Mr. and Mrs. Coggeshall, the ongoing interest of my friend Bill Goza, who made available the financial help of the Wentworth Foundation for the final purchase of the Prince diary, and the uncounted hours of work over a period of three years by the volunteers who were instrumental in preparing first a legible handscript, then the typescript, and through it all, proofreading, proofreading, and more proofreading. I am grateful to them all.

To understand at least a little of the natural phenomena that had a bearing on Dade's command, I turned to experts in various fields. In order to comprehend the nature of sinkholes (Mudge's "round clay sink") as they may have been perceived in the early 1800s, I turned to John Watson, hydrologist with the Southwest Florida Water Management District in Brooksville, Florida. Mr. Watson supplied me with enough reference material on the subject for me to become an expert myself if I had the ability to understand even a fair portion of the contents. And in the planetarium of the University of South Florida, Dr. Jack Robinson presented me with the night sky over central Florida from December 23 through December 28 as it would have appeared in 1835. Alas, Dr. Robinson felt that Halley's Comet, though visible to the naked eye from Washington, D.C., would probably not have been visible to the men of Dade's command. Another detail I wondered about concerned the matter of the rapid and certain damage to logs or lumber allowed to remain in contact with the earth during the construction of forts, causeways, or bridges. The southern climate is far more conducive to termite damage than the early road and fort builders would probably have known. What effect might this lack of knowledge have had on Dade and his men? The palisade surrounding Fort Brooke, as well as the log structures within, would have been infested within months, perhaps necessitating an almost continual labor of repair and reconstruction, while the causeways laid over marshy areas would have turned to mush. Dr. L. A. Hetrick, Emeritus Professor of Entomology at the University of Florida in Gainesville, suggested to me that "if designations [for termites] were used, they probably were 'white ants' or 'wood lice,'" and I have referred to them as such in the text. Small points, these, with finally a great deal of time and information reduced to a single phrase, even one word, but at least a superficial understanding of them has been critical to the author. I am indebted to Mr. Watson, Dr. Robinson, and Dr. Hetrick for sharing their understanding.

Dr. Gary Mormino, Professor of History at the University of South Florida and author, has found and shared with me several important writings on and by the black interpreter with Dade's command, Louis Pacheco. Tony Pizzo, historian, author, and teacher, brought to my attention obscure pictures and descriptions of Fort Brooke, progenitor of his beloved "Tampa Town." The help and encouragement of these two men, and their friendship over the years, are deeply valued. Tony's recent death has been a heartfelt loss and a loss to Florida history. Virginia Bergeman Peters, author of the wonderfully written *The Florida Wars*, shared with me an issue of the *Army and Navy Chronicle* (June 15, 1837), which contains a medical report of Private Clark's condition given by Dr. John Cuyler, as well as one of Clark's several accounts of the battle. This generosity by a fellow researcher is one of the enduring satisfactions found and deeply valued by the author in preparing the present work.

Knowing nothing of oxen, I turned to Leroy Ford of Dade City, who has a long familiarity with the handling of these animals gained from his work for a logging company whose principal source of labor was oxen during the early years of this century. I am indebted to Mr. Ford for sharing with me his knowledge of their needs, capacities, and nature in several interviews over the past six years.

The living history drama that brings this story to the public through the annual reenactment of Dade's battle is under the overall direction of

Dr. Ray Giron, who is also choreographer and actor (Captain Gardiner). Dr. Giron is also responsible for the soldier reenactor encampment, while Paul Morrison (a white man) is leader of the reenactors who portray Seminole Indians. Under these men, hundreds of reenactors, some of whom come from as far afield as Illinois and Texas, devote more than spare time each year to bring the public the most accurate presentation of this tragic battle that can be imagined. With meticulous attention to every detail of their uniforms and equipment, these men and women strive to present this event in America's history with total authenticity.

As an overall source of original material on this or any event in American history there exists nothing to compare with the National Archives. In knowledge and courtesy the staff cannot be surpassed. In the search for Florida-related material specifically, the P. K. Yonge Library of the University of Florida in Gainesville is without equal. Librarian Elizabeth Alexander and archivist Bruce Chappel collect, preserve, and can provide virtually any printed material relating to Florida's history, from the mundane to the miraculous. Without Ms. Alexander's help there is simply no use in attempting to write of Florida's history.

Gerry Jones, library assistant and senior supervisor of the Hugh Embry Library of Dade City, has assisted the author hundreds of times over the past thirteen years. On interlibrary loan she has brought me nuggets from across the country. Her help, her courtesy, and her patience have been endless. I am very grateful.

Bill Goza, Dr. John Mahon, and Dr. Giron read all or parts of the manuscript and annotated the work, correcting errors and suggesting technical changes based upon their particular expertise. Only one who has done this type of work can appreciate the time, thought, and knowledge given by them.

Without the help of four fine women this book would never have made it past a typewriter. Kitty Szaro, computer specialist, taught me how to turn the machine on, move within the document, delete, and save. All I'd known how to do was type. She saved portions of the present manuscript time and again from the mindless ravages of this machine. Eunice Nefe has taken over most of my business burdens for nearly five years to give me time to write. Clare Verelli saved me for one vital year. Donna Clark was instrumental in coordinating hundreds of references and compil-

ing the bibliography and index. All are intelligent, infinitely patient, understanding, and dear to me.

Dale Anne Bowman and I were married twenty-one years ago. There
has probably not been one day of those fine years that the name of Dade
has not come up. At the battlefield, in the National Archives, by a snow-
covered grave in New York, towing children, and making notes, Dale has
been with me at every step, encouraging, digging (in the files and in the
field), covering all the bases I was too busy with Dade to cover, holding
my hand. In case I haven't said it as often as I might, I thank you. And
I love you.

Introduction

The Battlefield

February 20, 1836

Seven companies of U.S. infantry, commanded by Lt. Col. William S. Foster, marched north on the Fort King Road, a twenty-foot-wide path through the Florida wilderness. One hundred yards west of the road, five hundred Louisiana volunteers under Col. Persifor F. Smith pushed their way through palmetto and tall grass. East of the road Capt. Francis S. Belton, Second Regiment Artillery, led the right-hand column, four companies of artillery outfitted as infantry. The advance guard formed the point; a heavy guard brought up the rear. Seventy-seven Creek Indians acted as guides, scouts, and hunters. Lieutenant Colonel David E. Twiggs, acting brigadier general, was in command of the brigade. In overall command was Bvt. Maj. Gen. Edmund P. Gaines. All in all, a good thousand men.[1]

Captain Belton, for one, thought they were none too many. For the past two months, as commandant of Fort Brooke on Tampa Bay, he had allowed himself to be immobilized within the pickets by the Seminole threat. His one decision, made in obedience to orders but against all reason, had ended in disaster. "In expectation of an attack [upon the fort] every night," he had nonetheless sent eight officers and one hundred soldiers on a march through the Seminole Nation. Within the hour he and the others would reach the spot where the detachment had been destroyed nearly eight weeks before—a spot, he wrote, "which a melancholy imagination had often depicted."[2]

The story was they had done their best, but against a thousand Seminoles it had not been enough. Clouds of buzzards filled the morning light above the pines. Belton and the others were far too late for rescue. The only thing they could provide now was a decent burial.

Gaines's army had left Fort Brooke eight days before to force a passage through to Fort King, one hundred miles north. There had been no regular communication between the forts for nearly three months. The command was traveling light—ten days' rations for each man (half of it carried on their backs) and only twelve horses divided among staff and regimental commanders to carry rations and subsistence. Each night they had surrounded their encampment with logs stacked three feet high, "within which the entire command slept on their arms." This was Seminole country.[3]

It had been a good march as marches go: officers and men tense, expecting attack, particularly at the four river crossings; bridges half burned, some men in the water with the rest strung out on both banks. Three days earlier the sound of firing had come back from the advance guard; it turned out they had come on ten or fifteen wild hogs. They had burned a few Seminole towns, nothing more than clusters of palmetto huts. A private in Belton's company had deserted (God only knew where he ended up), the volunteers had threatened to quit, Lt. Isaac Reeve had accidentally shot himself in the hip back at the Hillsborough—since then he'd been hauled in the cart. On approaching the Big Withlacoochee River the Creeks had warned that a Seminole attack was imminent and insisted they be allowed to return to Fort Brooke. "A half hour's talk, however, reassured them, and they moved on without evincing any further timidity."[4]

One day was about like another—up at 6:30 to the drumbeat of reveille, then roll call, coffee, hard biscuits and bacon, muskets fired at a signal from the bugle, march as many as eighteen miles, entrench, eat, each man rolled in his blanket near a fire by the time tattoo was beaten.

Yesterday had been cold, a light rain falling. They'd had the good fortune to cross the Little Withlacoochee, their last river, on a log instead of fording. Less than a mile north of the river they had put the torch to another Seminole village, caught a couple of horses. Another mile and they'd come upon some stray cattle, slaughtered them, distributed the meat. At day's end they had reached the last earthly encampment of the men who now lay beneath the buzzards up ahead. Francis Belton had not slept well.[5]

Now he led his men through "long tough grass, as high as one's head, of the color and texture of hedge grass." Green shoots thrust up from charred clumps here and there. Scorched palmetto gave little cover. Belton stared across the burnt and desolate field, left, right, dreading what he knew he would find. A pond covering an acre or two was visible ahead on the right. To avoid the marshy ground he angled his column to the left, toward the road. "The first indications of the disaster, . . . such as shoes, parts of clothing, and then, two bodies, partially stripped, were discovered in the marsh grass, perhaps one hundred yards to the right of the position, being first observed by myself. . . . These remains were probably those of men who were shot down, or who fell, overcome by fatal wounds, after escaping from the breastwork."[6]

Second Lieutenant James Duncan, twenty-three years old, described a scene that could have come from the pen of Edgar Allan Poe, a classmate at West Point: "The first indications of our proximity [to the battlefield] were soldiers shoes & clothing, soon after a skeleton then another! then another!! [S]oon we came upon the scene in all its horrors. Gracious God what a sight. [T]he vultures rose in clouds as the approach of the column drove them from their prey, the very breastwork was black with them. [S]ome hovered over us as we looked upon the scene before us whilst others settled upon the adjoining trees waiting for our departure, in order to return to their prey." The smell was appalling.[7]

Captain Ethan Allen Hitchcock, West Point class of 1817, was a member of Gaines's staff. "Our advanced guard had passed the ground without halting, when the general and his staff came upon one of the most appalling scenes that can be imagined." The columns were halted, a strong guard thrown around the entire field. In an uneasy silence the heavy beat of vultures' wings could be heard as they reluctantly left their prey to settle impatiently on the pines. General Gaines, tall, white-haired, his face covered with fine wrinkles, vain in spite of having only one tooth left in his mouth, led his staff the last few yards, passing a dozen or so pine stumps, their trunks gone to form the small enclosure ahead. Hitchcock pointed out a supply wagon off to the right, "the two oxen of which were lying dead, as if they had fallen asleep, their yokes still on them." The remains of horses still harnessed for a cannon lay nearby.[8]

"We then came to a small enclosure, made by felling trees in such a manner as to form a triangular breastwork for defence." Another staff member, 1st Lt. George A. McCall, noted that "the logs composing the breastwork, none of which were over eight inches at the butt, were filled on every side of the exterior with rifle-bullets of small size." The bark had begun to loosen and fall here and there; for the most part it still clung tightly to the trunks. Pinesap had leaked like tears down the flaking bark, but the pungent odor could not smother the stink of death. The general and a dozen officers gathered along the wall, waist high, twenty yards long. In silence they stared down at a sight that would haunt them as long as they lived.[9]

"The interior of the breastwork was covered with the bodies of the slain as they had been left by their savage foe. [B]roken guns, bayonets & accoutrements lay scattered around, a gun here, a bayonet there, a box in this place, and a belt in that." Lieutenant Duncan had graduated from West Point only one year ahead of two officers whose blackening corpses lay before him.[10]

Hitchcock saw "within the triangle, along the north and west faces of it, . . . about thirty bodies, mostly mere skeletons, although much of the clothing was left upon them. These were lying, almost every one of them, in precisely the same position they must have occupied during the fight, their heads next to the logs over which they had delivered their last fire, and their bodies stretched with striking regularity parallel to each other." Near the center of the enclosure lay the remains of a short, stocky man whom McCall recognized as an officer who "had command of the company of bombardiers, sappers and miners at West Point, when I was admitted as a cadet." He continued, "There were but three or four of the men that had fallen backwards into the interior of the little work; the rest lay . . . regularly at right angles to one or other of the three faces of their little fort, the head lying on the top log . . . or immediately below it, as if they had been toy-soldiers arranged by a child in his sport."[11]

Gingerly, McCall and the others entered the little barricade. "As revolting as the task was," they moved carefully among the bodies, attempting to identify the men they had known. Though little more than skeletons were left of some, with others "the flesh had shrunk, but the skin remained whole, dried, smooth, and hard." One man was recognized by the terrible glitter of a gold filling in his ravaged mouth, another by the grey in his hair, another by his size. Captain Belton recognized one man by a pocket

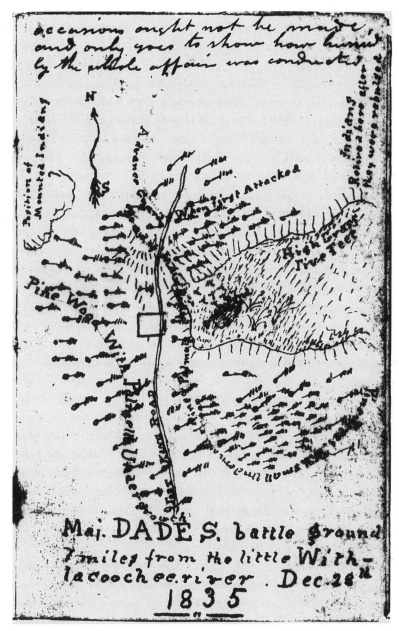

"Maj. DADES battle ground 7 miles from the little Withlachoochee river Dec. 28th, 1835." From the diary of Lt. James Duncan, February 20, 1836. U.S. Military Academy.

pistol still on the body. Henry Lee Heiskell, assistant surgeon, recognized another man by his beard. He cautiously searched the man's pockets, found a silk handkerchief, some letters. He cut a lock of hair, removed a red leather money belt—sad remembrances for the young officer's widow. McCall "carefully examined our poor dear fellows, both officers and men, either kneeling or extended on their breasts, the head in very many instances lying upon the upper log of their breastworks; and I invariably found the bullet-mark in the forehead or the front of the neck. The picture of those brave men lying thus in their 'sky blue' clothing, which had scarcely faded, was such as can never be effaced from my memory."[12]

The limber and chest for the cannon squatted among the dead. The chest was empty. Every round but one had been thrown, only one charge unfired. "The proof how well our men fought," wrote McCall, "was seen by us in the dozens of musket-balls crowded into single trees in the sides that faced the little breastwork. . . . These shots had been fired at particular Indians who fought from behind these trees." In a wide semicircle through the woods to the west the trees were "much torn with musket and grape shot." Another officer "noticed that the pine trees were cut by cannon ball and grape shot in every direction for a mile." The gun had evidently been positioned outside the north wall, where the carriage lay forlorn, barrel gone, axle and wheels partially burned.[13]

Enlisted men in small groups were allowed to walk over the ground, "to examine the position our men had so nobly defended, and to ponder on the sad sights there presented to their view." One of three white survivors of the battle limped slowly, painfully about the field, his right pelvic bone shattered, a Seminole bullet in his right lung, a hole through his right shoulder that was never going to heal. One arm useless, one leg unable to bear his weight, without food, and half naked, he had crawled sixty miles back to Fort Brooke.[14]

Assistant Surgeon John M. Cuyler had given the wounded man an emetic, and in the resulting choking and vomiting a small piece of his coat had come up. The ball that had carried it into his lung was impossible to remove. Cuyler described him as being "totally disabled from obtaining his subsistance [sic]." There was talk he might be discharged with a pension. Right now he was just another soldier, not in the best of shape but still on his feet.[15]

"Massacre of Major Dade and His Command." From *Incidents in American History* (New York: Coolidge, 1847).

The carnage was particularly appalling to Francis Belton. Having made it clear that he would resign his commission rather than "face what he considered certain death for himself and his men," he had allowed, had *ordered*, another to lead those same men against the same odds, and it had come to this. "The best in the army lie bleaching in the air, defaced by Negroes and torn [by] obscene birds," was Belton's haunted declaration.[16]

Once the officers and men had done the best they could at identifying the remains, the bodies within the barricade were moved aside and the digging of graves begun. Officers and men wandered the field trying to identify half-ruined remains scattered up and down the road. Regulations called for the regimental number, branch of service, company letter, and soldier's number and name to be clearly marked inside the right sleeve of the jacket near the shoulder. Under the circumstances, finding this information in those jackets left on the dead was a gruesome task. Strangely, there had been little if any looting of the bodies. In addition to a great quantity of ornamental jewelry, pins, brooches, rings, and gold watches, they found upwards of three hundred dollars in paper, gold, and silver in the soldiers' pockets, and more paper money, some partly burnt, scattered over the field. "Around, and at various distances from the entrenchment, lay many bodies, particularly on the E. & N.E. and along the course of the Fort King Road," wrote Belton. "The clothing was more entire, as well as the bodies, than expected; many skulls were broken in, and the greater number lay supine, and the limbs stretched apart, marking the agony with which life ceased."[17]

Two hundred and fifty yards beyond the barricade, Belton came to another cluster of bodies, "stricken down, as if one blow had been death to all & that blow a bolt from heaven!" This was the advance guard, two officers at the rear, another in front. One man could be identified only by a ring still on his finger, another by a miniature in the bosom of his shirt, the third by his silver infantry buttons and his vest. This was the officer who had volunteered to lead the detachment, a man who "would not have been here, but for the highest and noblest impulses," Belton wrote. "He stepped forth to save a husband's and a parent's feelings, nay a wife's life, he himself standing in all those dear relations. . . . Here were the noblest sacrifices combined; first for his country, and then for humanity & friendship." For several days after the command had left Fort Brooke,

Belton had been in touch with this man by courier, and had closed one note with the question, "Shall you keep on?" Perhaps not a reasonable question to put to a man under orders to lead a detachment through enemy country. Should he have *ordered* him to turn back? Would he have turned back if he had? Should he never have allowed them to leave Fort Brooke in the first place?[18]

Within the barricade two graves were dug, each five feet wide, thirteen feet long, four feet deep. Enlisted men did their best to gather the remains (they could hardly be called bodies) of ninety-eight fellow soldiers, putting them in the graves two and three deep. Outside the northeast corner, close to the wall, a third grave was dug and the eight officers interred. "Your agonized limbs were decently adjusted by affections [*sic*] unrevolt[ed] hands, and with reverence, as if your spirits were around," Belton wrote. "And although the pomp of the Soldiers laurelled here, was absent, yet sympathy mourned & sorrow wept." The cannon, a six-pounder, spiked with a ramrod by its crew and torn from its carriage and thrown into the pond by the Seminoles, was dragged from the water and inverted over the officers' grave. "This, become their monument, till country or comrades shall proudly place their fame in full relief in the frequented paths of men . . . or perhaps near the Shrine, where devotions [*sic*] eye may dim for the fate, and petition for the souls of these unshriven dead."[19]

In his distress Belton approached General Gaines and urged "that everything that could be done should be done in the best manner possible, that the funeral service should be read and every little ceremony attended to that might come in our power. [H]e represented it, not only as due to the officers themselves, but as due to the feelings of their friends, who could not but be desirous that the last earthly tribute should be paid them." Gaines concurred, then turned the details over to Twiggs, who, according to Duncan, "acquitted himself horribly." This could only have added to Belton's anguish. Burial done, the troops were quickly formed in columns of companies. With the Fourth Infantry band leading, "the men, with arms reversed and with sad but stern countenances, at a slow pace, marched round the entire ground." To Belton, "the notes of martial music, wailing 'Welcome to the Glory Bed' [and] 'Bruce's Address' . . . never before had . . . touch[ed] American hearts with such pathos." In half an hour the columns were in motion toward the enemy.[20]

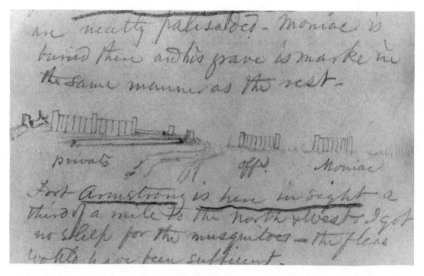

Drawing by 2nd Lt. Henry Prince of the graves of Dade's command, showing
the enlisted men on the left, the officers in the center, and the grave of Lt.
David Moniac (killed in battle on November 31, 1836) on the right. From the
diary of 2nd Lt. Prince, March 1837. P. K. Yonge Library.

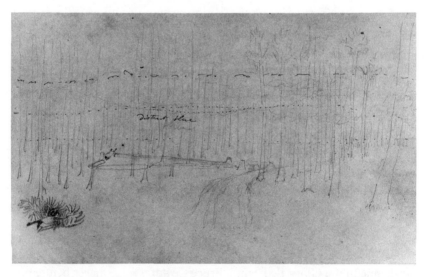

Drawing by 2nd Lt. Prince of the Dade battlefield and Fort King Road. From
the diary of 2nd Lt. Prince, March 1837. P. K. Yonge Library.

The territory of Florida was an unknown land to most Americans in 1836; remote, hot, infested with insects, snakes, and hostile Indians. The few soldiers stationed there generally felt more sympathy than hostility for the Seminoles, attributing most of the scattered violence to slave hunters and whiskey peddlers. Now 105 soldiers were dead. It no longer mattered whether the orders that had sent two companies on a march through the Seminole Nation had been an attempt to bluff the Indians or whether the soldiers were simply bait on the government hook. The bluff had been called, the bait taken. From Key West, Florida, to Portland, Maine, the papers cried "Massacre!" The men whose bodies filled the hasty graves had not died in vain. Now America could go to war, Florida could be taken, Indians "removed," blacks brought to slavery.

Chapter One

The First Day
Wednesday, December 23, 1835

A hell of a way to spend Christmas. In two days they'd be partway to
Fort King, squatting in a pine barren and hoping they could keep their
scalps till New Year's. For Pvt. Ransom Clark, Company C, Second
Regiment Artillery, the year had begun with a capsized boat in Mobile
Bay. He was the only survivor. How would it end?[1]

One hundred soldiers—two companies of the U.S. Army—formed a
double column strung the length of the parade ground of Fort Brooke,
Florida Territory. Since yesterday's warm rain the temperature had
dropped to a cool fifty-four degrees and brought a clear dawn sky, redolent
of orange blossoms on the salt air of Tampa Bay. Other soldiers, half a
dozen officers, a crowd of civilians, and a few friendly Seminoles separated
themselves from the column and faded back, leaving the detachment to
stand alone. Final instructions had been given, goodbyes said. It was time
to go. One officer had assured his wife that he would be gone for "a couple
of weeks at the farthest." If hostile Seminoles had their way, it would be
forever.[2]

Captain George Washington Gardiner, Company C, Second Regiment
Artillery, was in command. The ninety-first graduate of West Point, he
had ranked first in the class of 1814 in spite of his "stunted appearance
. . . and not standing much higher than five feet." Now he was forty-two
years old and had grown "almost as thick as he was long," but he was
"full of judgment . . . most manly and determined." If judgment and
determination counted for much, this was the time and the place. In a
moment the gates would swing open, and through them he would lead
seven officers, one hundred men, one Seminole, and a civilian interpreter

named Stafford. Gardiner's orders were to take the detachment north one hundred miles to the relief of Fort King. Their path lay straight through the Seminole Nation. If fighting was to come, well, that's what soldiers were paid for. Stafford could do the talking.[3]

Gardiner's company had come down from Fort Pickens on November 27. Francis S. Belton, captain in command of Company B, Second Artillery, had finally arrived on December 11 after a difficult thirteen-day passage from Fort Morgan in Alabama. Two other companies were already on hand, one commanded by Maj. Richard Zantzinger, the other by Capt. Upton Sinclair Fraser. Orders from Bvt. Brig. Gen. Duncan Lamont Clinch at Fort King had been waiting when Belton arrived, addressed to "The Officer in Command." Zantzinger, the ranking officer, had commanded the fort until October 11, when Fraser had been given command, but upon Belton's arrival, "from an agreement among the officers themselves, Belton was considered the commander." There wasn't much choice. The responsibility could only fall on Belton or Zantzinger, since Gardiner and Fraser were already under Clinch's order: "On the arrival of Capt. Belton's and Capt. Gardiner's Companies at Fort Brooke, you will order Captn. Fraser's and Captn. Gardiner's Companies, to proceed to this Post as soon as practicable." Perhaps the responsibility for carrying out this astonishing order—sending one hundred men on a march through hostile territory—had made it simpler for Zantzinger to decline the position of commander.[4]

Fraser had been at Fort Brooke for a year, in command off and on even before October. In turning over command to Belton he reviewed orders and reports on hand and explained their position. Hostile Seminoles had become more violent every day, smashing and burning, driving settlers into the protection of the fort. Just three days ago a Mr. Simmons had come in on the run, his home and crops twenty-eight miles out gone up in smoke. The sutler's place up at the Big Hillsborough had been plundered, one of his white people fired on. More than one hundred refugees, many of them women and children, were inside the pickets every night, crowded in with four companies of soldiers. On paper this could look like plenty of men for defense, except that two companies were undermanned, and of 207 men on the roster a good many were on sick report with fevers and inflammatory diseases. Three more companies should come in any time, but there wouldn't be much help there—Fraser's and Gardiner's companies had only been awaiting Belton's arrival to move out, and two of those expected were to follow them. When all was said and done, Belton would be left with perhaps ninety effectives to defend the fort against an attack that could come at any moment.[5]

Fraser had done his best to place the fort in a state of defense. The entire garrison had been working for weeks with "great energy and perseverance," soldiers and civilians working together with "extraordinary effort." They had stood pine logs shoulder to shoulder surrounding the camp, built block houses at opposite corners. Ditches had been dug around the fort—except at the entrance—three feet wide and eight feet deep to slow an attack. Sharpened stakes had been set in the bottom and covered with straw. Some thirty civilians had volunteered as rangers, furnishing mounted patrols to keep approaches under observation during the early morning hours and anytime there was any suspicion of an attack. Even in the dead of night the alarm drum frequently sounded.[6]

As to supplies, well, they didn't look good. Provisions were low but might hold out; more serious was the scanty supply of ammunition for muskets and the two six-pounders. Fraser pointed out the insufficiency of ordnance stores; less than twenty thousand musket ball cartridges and more than half of them unserviceable, fit only to be made into musket ball canister for the cannon. Clinch's order had specified that Fraser and Gardiner take thirty rounds per man. That would leave Belton perhaps six thousand for defense. In addition they had fifteen kegs of rifle powder and a small supply for the cannon.[7]

But in spite of all this, and even with communications with headquarters at Fort King entirely broken up, "without any instructions—authority or means," spirits were good and "great confidence [was] felt by all that an attack if sever[e]lly meditated must fail and by such a result, materially aid the interest of the government." In other words, if Seminoles attacked the fort—if they made war on women and children—then certainly the government policy of Indian removal would be seen by the American people as being not only reasonable but essential.[8]

The real problem here in the fort was that defense had not been a circumstance anticipated when "Cantonment" Brooke had been established eleven years before. It had been built more as a symbol of American authority than as a military fort. Ten years earlier there had been rumors of a possible attack and the camp had been hastily stockaded, but a month later the rumors had passed and the pickets had been pulled up and stacked. Since then attack had never been anything more than a rumor. Seminoles had been looked upon as a responsibility, a nuisance rather than a threat.[9]

The United States had acquired Florida in 1821. No longer would the area be a haven for escaped slaves, a trapdoor in the bottom of the nation through which they could drop out of Alabama and Georgia and land in freedom. A year after the acquisition, President Monroe had stated flatly that the Seminoles "should be removed . . . or concentrated within narrower limits." To those who owned them, slaves were a capital investment; to the Seminoles they were men and women. Among the Seminoles they were scattered, absorbed, difficult to find. And the larger the Seminole land, the more difficult the search. In 1823 the limits of Seminole land had been defined in the Treaty of Moultrie Creek as a tract in the middle of the Florida Territory some sixty miles wide by one hundred and twenty miles long. One week after the signing of the treaty, the three commissioners had written to Secretary of War John C. Calhoun, "It is indispensable for . . . the future security of Florida that all intercourse with foreign Countries or Individuals exercising an influence over [the Seminoles] be cut off, and that an exclusive control be obtained and maintained by the American Government. This is only to be effected by the immediate establishment of Military posts at the Bay of Tampa, Charlotte Harbor, and . . . near Cape Florida on the Eastern Coast."[10]

The Seminoles would be isolated within the area reserved for them by the treaty, the reservation surveyed, and a few posts of observation built to oversee the isolation. For three hundred years, off and on, Europeans had been sailing into Tampa Bay and trading with the inhabitants; they got food, mostly, and gave in return beads, mirrors, and disease. Under American control there would be no more coastal trading with Indians, no more foreign flags on Tampa Bay. "To embody such a population within prescribed limits . . . will require in some degree the exercise of authority, with the presence of a military establishment adequate to enforce it." The Seminoles would be fenced in with surveys and paper and a few soldiers stationed on the perimeter to see that they stayed within the fence.[11]

Within a year, four companies of the Fourth Infantry Regiment, under
Lt. Col. George Mercer Brooke, had landed on the east shore of Tampa
Bay. "Perhaps, apart from its military advantages, a more beautiful spot
could not have been found in the whole southern country, the place being
covered by a large number of live-oak trees, on a gentle slope extending
to the bay." Work was begun on barracks, quartermaster and commissary
storehouses, stables, a hospital, bakehouse, and guardhouse. Boards were
sawed for flooring, logs notched down for walls, spaces between the logs
chinked with split pieces of pine and daubed with clay. Shingles were
rived from pine, scarcely a nail used to secure them, instead hung on the
rafters with wooden pegs. "We are situated on the Northeast bank of the
Hillsborough river immediately on its entrance into the Bay of the same
name," reported Colonel Brooke. "We were . . . influenced by the quantity
of cleared land which was at once adapted to gardens for the officers and
men."[12]

Colonel Brooke failed to mention that the land had recently been cleared
and a home built by men employed by a Robert Hackley in the belief
that his family owned the site, as well as eleven million other acres in
Florida. Hackley's father had bought the land in 1819 from the Duke of
Alagon, who in turn had received it in a grant from King Ferdinand VII
of Spain. Claiming that Hackley's title was invalid, Brooke arrested the
men, sent them off to Pensacola to stand trial, and confiscated the house
as well as four to five thousand dollars worth of ship's timber the men
had cut. He wrote to Secretary of War Calhoun to ask if the timber could
not be sold and the money used for "a library, Musical instruments . . .
and such other things as may add to the comfort and convenience of the
troops."[13]

"Ft. Brooke . . . is situated immediately on the water's edge in the
corner of one of the most beautiful and regular groves I ever saw," wrote
a soldier. "The grove is of Live-oak and Orange trees, and resembles more
an ornamented College Green, than the encampment ground of [an] army."
Sparing the trees, the soldiers enlarged Hackley's clearing to include some
fifteen acres, nine already in garden. "The only defences then made were
two block-houses at two of the angles of the parallelogram, the line of
men's quarters making the exterior line of defence." Thought was given
to shade and beauty. "Our camp extends under a canopy of the most

superb trees I ever beheld," wrote Lt. George McCall. "These giant live-oaks throw out their huge limbs at a distance of six to ten feet from the ground; these enormous limbs, as large as the trunks of common trees, extend in an almost horizontal direction for ten or fifteen feet, then spreading and rising to the height of fifty or sixty feet, form a dense round head that is a perfect parasol. [They] are hung with long pendants of the Spanish moss, and with festoons of the yellow jessamine . . . with clusters of bright-yellow flowers." Only the garden was fenced.[14]

Boredom, not danger, was a problem. "I fish or ride whenever I am not on duty," Lieutenant McCall had written in those peaceful days. "On return of the fishing detail, the boat . . . is unloaded and the fish laid out on the wharf. The fish-call is sounded, and the orderly sergeants appear with two men and a handbarrow, and carry off as many as they want for their companies; and Indians that may be about are then allowed to help themselves; and the remnant is then taken by the Colonel's boat's crew, and buried to make compost for that officer's garden." Thus in 1824—a fort that needed no walls, and Seminoles who stood somewhere between the soldiers and the compost heap when it came to welfare.[15]

Through the years the "narrower limits" had been grudgingly expanded, and expanded again, but no buffer zone, no treaty, no danger would keep the slave hunters out of the reservation. The lion might (and in fact did, by and large) stay in his den, but when intruders persisted in bearding him there he was quite capable of clawing them to death. Stealing (even when the subjects stolen are human beings) is not inherently a violent crime; stopping the thief often necessitates violence. Slave catching was legal; thwarting slave catchers was not. Through the years there had been plenty of intruders, plenty of violence, plenty of death. John Quincy Adams, no friend of slavery, had succeeded Monroe and was convinced that the "narrower limits" had failed, that it was indeed time for removal. As long as an Indian remained in Florida, shielding blacks, there would be trouble. To remove blacks—protect them, in fact, from slavery—they (and the Seminoles) must be placed beyond the reach of slave catchers. Then Andrew Jackson, slave owner, nemesis of all Indians, succeeded Adams. At his insistence the Indian Removal Act became law in 1830, but rather than protecting blacks, sending them west as "property" of the Seminoles, he made sure that when the Seminoles were put through the

screen of removal all blacks would be caught in the mesh. The act was
implemented with the Treaty of Payne's Landing in 1832. Clearly the
Seminole presence was no longer going to be tolerated. Even the progeny
of slaves escaped a hundred years ago or more would be brought into
bondage.

And now it was 1835. Fort Brooke had walls, and Seminoles were no
longer waiting around for secondhand fish. It was true that some had
agreed to give up their land, go west. For them emigration was to begin
on January 1, 1836—nine days away. And Fort Brooke was the point of
embarkation. But an ever-growing majority of Seminoles, the "Nation,"
threatened war.

So much for the fort. What about this order to send two companies to
Fort King? Fraser brought out the maps. The western boundary of the
Seminole reservation was about eight miles inland from the bay. The Fort
King Road angled northeast from the fort into the reservation, then headed
pretty much due north one hundred miles to Fort King. The detachment
would have no support—once it left Fort Brooke they would be on their
own. But if Belton felt that he could wait for the arrival of the two
companies coming from New Orleans and a third from Key West, he
could double the strength of the detachment, give it something like a
fighting chance if trouble came.

Clinch had specified that Fraser and Gardiner leave for Fort King "as
soon as practicable," to be followed by two more companies that were
presumably on the way to Fort Brooke. What was more practicable than
sending all four together? Clinch had directed that the detachment "will
come prepared to take the field." As far as Fraser knew, Clinch already
had four companies on hand. In other words, he wasn't in trouble, under
siege, calling for rescue. Sounded like he simply meant to gather a force
sufficient to make a move against the hostiles. If that was the case, delay
would be more reasonable than the risk of sending two companies alone.
Of course, it was true they had no way of knowing if Clinch's circumstances
had changed since he sent the order. Had he been cut off by the hostiles,
isolated, as they were here on Tampa Bay? Was his order just a routine
movement of troops, or a cry for help? He had written on November 13,
when the hostile faction among the Seminoles had already been causing
trouble for months, striking out at soldiers, civilians, sometimes even their

own people who had agreed to emigrate. Since then few messages had come through, none since the first of the month. As far as travel *north* from Tampa Bay, Maj. John Lytle, paymaster, had left for Fort King the last week in November with a few men, then a black runner had been sent on December 5. No way of knowing if they had made it through. And if Clinch had thought the Seminole threat so serious that he needed two hundred additional men in order to move against them, how could one hundred men expect to cross the land of those same people?[16]

One look at the map made the problem appallingly clear—it was understood the hostiles were gathered like a nest of hornets in the Great Swamp, an area some twenty miles wide by fifty long, the floodlands of the Withlacoochee River. The swamp started here, a couple of miles west of the military road where it crossed the Big Withlacoochee, then followed the river north another seven miles or so to where the Little Withlacoochee joined. There it became the Wahoo Swamp and began to bend west with the combined rivers as they headed for the Gulf of Mexico, an area known as the Cove of the Withlacoochee, "a Cretan labyrinth, held from the knowledge of the white man, as the sacred groves of the Druids were never entered except by the initiated." The whole area was trackless—in dry weather a morass swarming with snakes, alligators, and insects; in the rainy season it flooded out for miles, putting the whole swamp underwater. Here and there were hammocks, small, rounded knolls or hillocks where the Seminoles made their camps. Since the trouble started they'd been moving their families into the swamp, taking all they had with them. They could live there for years—forever, maybe. And they could slip out, attack, and disappear back in the swamp. Impossible country. "In short, all the difficult parts of Florida were, to the whole army, one *terra incognita*. Government gave . . . no topographical information, nor had any to give; and the bookseller's maps only afforded outlines filled up with unlucky guesses."[17]

As for Gardiner and his command, here—where the military road crossed the Big River—was where the real danger began, between the two rivers, what was called the Forks of the Withlacoochee. Tines, really. Two of them, coming in from the east, draining the central part of the Florida Territory, feeding the swamp. The Fort King Road crossed the Big Withlacoochee here, about fifty miles north of Tampa Bay, then ran

nearly due north maybe eight miles, the river and the swamp parallel to
the road only a couple of miles to the west, until the road crossed the
Little Withlacoochee. If Gardiner made it through there, crossed that last
river safely, chances were he'd make it all the way.

The strength of the Seminoles? According to the best official data,
their strength was estimated at three thousand, including men, women,
children, and blacks. Of these it was thought that there were sixteen
hundred females, leaving the male population at fourteen hundred, or up
to a thousand warriors. Assuming in this as in other cases every fifth
person to be a warrior, then the two companies might face anything up
to six hundred. Such a concentration was unlikely, but not impossible.[18]

On the other hand, there was an encampment of "friendly" Seminoles
just across the river waiting to board ship for the trip west. Zantzinger
had put them west of the river to keep them out of reach of the "Whisky
Gentry," white squatters whose only object was to sell them ardent spirits,
stir them up, and cheat them out of whatever they had. The Indians had
been coming in since September. As Belton was aware, another forty had
come in only a few hours ago, fleeing the hostiles, bringing their families—
even their horses. They could be seceders from the hostiles and indicate
a dissolution of the war party, or they might simply have been driven in.
At any rate, there must be four hundred or more over there by now.
Their leader was Holata Emathla. He was under deep concern to do
nothing that would excite further resentment or revenge from the hostiles.
His brother Chalo Emathla, or "Charley," as he was called by the whites,
had already been killed.[19]

It was rumored that the Seminoles had held a secret council in October
in the Great Swamp. The hostile faction had prevailed upon the leaders
of the Nation to adopt a policy of death to any Indian who would not
stand and fight for the land, who agreed to emigrate. Under the circumstances, Holata Emathla and his people could probably be trusted, but
that was as far as it went. They were allowed on this side of the river
only by Fraser's permission, generally to work, for which they received
rations, but as prudently as possible.[20]

So there it was. Whichever way you turned they had a real problem,
one that affected every man, woman, and child in the fort, military or
civilian. Send a relief column to Fort King and expose the column—as

well as the undermanned fort—to almost certain attack, or ignore a direct order and perhaps leave Fort King, Clinch, and his men at an unknown risk. The responsibility belonged only to "The Officer in Command." Starting today, that was Francis Belton.

A fellow officer had once written him: "Your case calls for the exercise of all your fortitude. Show yourself a man." The officer was Brig. Gen. Winfield Scott. The "case" was Belton's recent court-martial and suspension. Scott had asked, "How has it happened that you have so many enemies? This is a question for you to reflect upon. I will not believe there is anything wrong in your *heart*, but have been driven to the conviction that there is much which requires improvement in your *temper*. It would be idle to say that you could, otherwise, have made so many of your associates your personal enemies."[21]

Belton had come to Tampa Bay from Fort Morgan, Alabama, a vast, brick fortress standing like a single tooth in the mouth of Mobile Bay. Thousands of slaves had worked for fifteen years to transform some eight million bricks into a fort. Completed the previous year, it was probably as secure a structure as a man could find. If Belton had been in virtual exile for nearly two years where nothing threatened except the weather, in command of men who fought only among themselves, the vulnerability of this small, wooden fort was as shocking as a mortal wound.[22]

Belton was in his early forties, had entered the army in 1812, had served in the dragoons, as assistant adjutant general, assistant inspector-general, in the Fourth Infantry, First and Second Artillery. He had perhaps taken seriously Scott's advice of a decade before—to "show yourself a man"— for only a month earlier another friend, another officer, had referred to him as "one of the most intelligent and accomplished officers of the U. States army." The friend, Col. James W. Fannin, Jr., had offered Belton a high position in the service of Texan independence, and Belton had confessed "a great inclination . . . to join you . . . in your noble enterprise." It was in all the papers. The Mexican province was on the verge of secession. Distant drums. Americans were headed for Texas on foot and on horseback, by boat and railroad, to take part in the big adventure, make a fresh start. Fannin himself was headed for San Antonio along with men like William Barret Travis, James Bowie, and David Crockett. General Martin Perfecto de Cos had been asked by his brother-in-law,

Gen. Antonio López de Santa Anna, president of the Republic of Mexico, to take charge of the Mexican troops in Texas. Cos had fortified San Antonio, then established his headquarters in an abandoned mission east of town, a place called the Alamo.[23]

At Fort Morgan, as lonely a spot as the military service offered, the idea of adventure and military advancement had a lot of appeal, but for Belton it would be "a step of great importance." What of Harriet, his wife? And their only son, whom they were preparing for West Point? If Belton resigned his commission in the U.S. Army (as he must if he were to accept Fannin's offer) for the sake of the Texas adventure, "to discard as nothing domestic . . . duties . . . and military responsibilities," there would be no turning back. It would be a gamble of all against nothing, twenty-three years of slow progress rank by rank, years spent trying to overcome the stain of suspension, all gone for the hope of rank and glory under a foreign flag. He had pondered these questions at Fort Morgan, weighed Fannin's cry for help against the risk, waited for a sign, a portent. Then September was gone, October became November. On the twenty-second he had received an unmistakable sign—an order to take his company to Florida. The need for decision passed; the Texas adventure would have to wait.[24]

He had hardly gotten his foot on the Fort Brooke dock before he was in command of a naked wooden fort that held too few soldiers and too many civilians. Again he had to weigh a possible cry for help against the risk. Yet to a discerning officer, an order from the commanding general to move meant to *move*. Fraser had admitted he had no way of knowing what conditions were at Fort King, but Clinch was there (at least he had been when he issued the order), and he clearly had felt a need for reinforcement or he would never have sent such a message. Help depended on Belton's decision. Yet so did these people, soldiers as well as civilians. Not to mention the troops that must be dispatched. What of them? If half the stories he had heard were true, it would take not a hundred but a thousand troops to force a passage through to Fort King. And according to Fraser he didn't even have the hundred. Not in condition for the field. And if he could round up a hundred men that could stand formation it would leave the fort and its civilians to be defended only by the sick. Yet the orders were clear. He and Gardiner were both here. The order to move was already a month old. He needed more time. He couldn't make decisions based on a single briefing, a hundred rumors. But how long dare he wait?

Two days, three, four. No reinforcements, but no attack either. On the sixteenth he made his decision. Orders were given, and Gardiner and Fraser readied their companies for departure the next day. At the last minute, scouts brought intelligence that "indicated a determination to attack [the detachment] or the Work." To divide his force in the light of this threat would be against all reason. He suspended the order.[25]

Again they waited—for attack, for reinforcement. Supplies were running out. On Monday, the twenty-first, Belton ordered the forage allowance for the horses of the civilian rangers reduced. Then, a cry from the lookout posted on a platform high in an oak tree—a sail was in sight, the *Motto*, coming in from Key West!

The *Motto*, a transport capable of carrying a hundred men, considered "by all who know her to be one of the best vessels of her class afloat," had been only six months off the stocks when the government had bought her three years earlier at Key West. She was a schooner, a small, two-masted ship, a type designed for coastal sailing by a Massachusetts shipbuilder more than one hundred years before. The prototype had skimmed so lightly over the water at its launching that a bystander had cried out in admiration, "Oh, how she scoons!" "Scoon" was New England dialect for the Scotch "scon," meaning to skip a flat stone across water. "Scoon" became "schooner," a ship with a small foresail and with mainmast set nearly amidships, allowing the vessel to sail close to the wind.[26]

On that day the wind was out of the southeast. Captain Armstrong was catching all of it he could, the *Motto* skimming up the bay, Fort Brooke in clear view off the starboard bow, "this place *never fortified*, 2 block houses built at the end of a street of 4 or 5 barracks, and quarters on each side. The Secretary [of War] ordered 'Cantonments' to be called 'Forts' and, to that rule this post conformed. . . . All that is fort about the position has proceeded from the muscles of the garrison since 1st December." "To the south of the cantonment the land stretches round to a point which juts into the bay. This promontory is covered with . . . mangrove, Pine and Cabbage Trees. . . . Toward the north lies the river. The opposite bank slopes to the water, and is generally covered with wild flowers." It

was a familiar sight to Bvt. Maj. Francis Langhorne Dade. The sky was
clear, the sun shining like a brass button on a blue coat, the temperature
seventy-six degrees. Francis Dade was coming to the rescue.[27]

"He was a tall man," wrote a nephew, "but so well built that he did
not appear so. He wore a black beard that reached below his waist, and
hip boots, so that when he sat down I could scarcely tell where his beard
stopped and his boots began. On his shoulders he wore large epaulets and
on his hat the entire tail of a game rooster. He also had a large crooked
sword which he insisted on wearing all the time he was in the house, and
I can remember its clank yet as he walked about and it dragged on the
floor and struck against the furniture." The nephew wrote of an earlier
time—a time when he was a child and a visit by his Uncle Francis (veteran
of the War of 1812, Indian fighter, far-traveler) was a time to remember.
Perhaps the beard seemed a little longer than it really was, the boots a
little taller, and perhaps the hat carried only one rooster feather rather
than the entire tail, but the image carried by the boy may have been more
accurate than statistics alone could convey. Descended from the Francis
Dade who had come from England two hundred years before to settle in
Virginia on the hills overlooking the Potomac, Major Dade had carried
on the cavalier tradition of gallantry—drinking, wenching, fighting. He
was versed in the social graces; his courage was perfect.[28]

"Major Dade," a female admirer had written several years before, ". . .
for his known prudence and gallantry, had been placed by Gen. Clinch
in charge of the middle district [of the Florida Territory] and the protection
of its inhabitants." One evening a dinner party near Tallahassee was
interrupted, she continued, "by the rolling of wheels and gallop of horses;
it was an arrival, turning pleasing conviviality into a state of nervous
trepidation. Major Dade . . . appeared on the porch, as the dinner party
went out to see who had come. He was covered with dirt from head to
foot, and his beard had not been shaven for several days, though he was
accompanied by two young ladies. . . . News had reached [him], that the
Indians had murdered a . . . family. . . . Major Dade [had] followed in
hot pursuit, and captured the Indians. . . . 'I found the ladies very much
alarmed and though I think all danger is over for the present, I persuaded
them to let me escort them to the capital,' said Major Dade."[29]

Drawing only six feet of water, the *Motto* swung at anchor close in, the ship's boat lowered. Standing on the deck, Major Dade could sense the excitement, see soldiers and civilians strung out from fort to dock, hear their voices raised in excited welcome. It had been the same sort of excitement a week ago when he had returned to Key West aboard the *Motto* from leave in Pensacola. He had just come ashore when his adjutant, young 2nd Lt. Benjamin Alvord, in an agony of relief, had handed him an order received the last day of November. Alvord had been sitting on it for two weeks, expecting him every day, uncertain whether he should make a move without the major. The letter was dated October 17, signed D. L. Clinch. Clinch had written from his headquarters at Fort Marion in St. Augustine: "Sir. You will as soon after the first of December next as may be practicable, . . . place the remainder of your command on board the public Schooner Motto and proceed with them to Fort Brooke, and on your arrival there, should you be the Senior Officer, you will assume the Command, and govern yourself by the orders and instructions you may find there."[30]

"Assume the Command." Those were the kind of words a man liked to see. The letter went on with instructions to examine the coast on the way north and order any Seminoles he might find to get back to their reservation. Fortunately, that part was qualified with the phrase "as far as practicable." Alvord had said that he had received word from Fort Brooke just a day or two before that they were anticipating an attack anytime. The order to reinforce them was already two months old. There were women and children in the fort. Stray Seminoles could wait. They'd sail as soon as they could get the men aboard. And they'd sail direct.[31]

Alvord, a twenty-three-year-old West Pointer, had graduated in July 1833 with a brevet rank and had made second lieutenant only five months ago. Dade's first sergeant, Peter Thomas, was ten years older, a carpenter in Philadelphia before he had joined up. He had completed his second three-year hitch a year ago and signed on for another under Dade right here in Key West. Alvord and Thomas could ready the company. As commandant of the post, Dade had other responsibilities. He wrote to Clinch first, explaining his delay; the *Motto* had badly needed recoppering in her bottom, and the fine facilities at the Pensacola Navy Yard made it the time and place to have it done. Some accident had delayed the work, and so on. As to taking time to visit New River and Charlotte Harbor on the way, he explained that he had letters on hand from both places reporting

Brigadier General Benjamin Alvord about 1865. Library of Congress.

that the Indians had left. It was clear that Clinch was out of touch. Events were moving much faster than the mail.[32]

In response to a letter from Asst. Adj. Gen. Roger Jones in Washington, Dade pointed out that recent news from Fort Brooke made the situation there even more serious than Clinch knew. "I understand some Indian depredations have been lately committed calculated to create considerable alarm. . . . I am now much engaged in preparing to obey the Order [of General Clinch], and can only say that your plan for an increase of the pay of the Field Officers of the Army meets my entire approbation." His permanent rank as captain did not entitle him to field officer's pay, but as brevet major he was only a half-step away—which prompted another thought: "P.S. I am the senior Captain now on duty in the Regiment. Genl. Clinch, Col. of the Regt. on higher duty, makes the vacancy of a Major. Am I not entitled to the Command?" He was forty-three years old and had spent half his life in the army. A major's half-inch gold lace on his epaulets didn't count for much after seven years without a major's pay and command. But perhaps he was closer to promotion than he had thought.[33]

It had taken an day and a half to make arrangements, get men and equipment on board. They had set sail on the sixteenth, heading north across the Gulf, then north and west up the coast toward Tampa. He had left eleven sick men behind, had brought Acting Asst. Surgeon Benjamin Nourse along. Nourse had some report to make to the surgeon general and insisted that he was bound by regulations to consult with the major before replying. Dade had told him in Key West that he had no time to consider the matter, and once on board he didn't have much inclination for paperwork. He had asked Nourse to postpone the report until their arrival at Fort Brooke. Paperwork![34]

Belton introduced Dade, Alvord, and Nourse to the other officers present, some seventeen in all and mostly West Pointers. Richard Zantzinger, major since 1824, ranked them all. So much for taking command of the fort. At Key West Dade had at least had that satisfaction. Here he was just another junior officer. And the excitement generated by his arrival was not so much for the relief of a beleaguered fort as it was for the support that would allow two other companies to make a daring march to Fort King, companies commanded by officers junior to him.

An assignment like that could change everything for the man who led
it. It was evident that most of the officers looked on the pending move
as folly, Gardiner's command as virtually doomed. But promotion and
command might come along with rescue. As ranking officer after Zantzinger, and with more experience in Florida and with Seminoles than any
other officer in the fort—not to mention his knowledge of the route (ten
years ago he had taken two companies through to the relief of Fort King
under circumstances worse than these)—he might have insisted on the
right to command the detachment, but the order from Clinch specified
Gardiner's and Fraser's companies. Clinch had known he would be on
hand—he had been ordered here a month before the order was written
for troops to relieve Fort King. A dozen of his men would go (to bring
the other companies up to strength), but not Major Dade. And it was not
difficult to sense disappointment that his company numbered only thirty-
eight men and that the only supplies he had brought were a small quantity
of musket ball cartridges. As for the two companies daily expected from
New Orleans, all he knew (or cared) was what he had heard in Pensacola—
they were to ship in the schooner *Elizabeth* under Captain Forsyth. He
could make no accounting for the delay.[35]

Discussion and argument over Clinch's order filled the afternoon. Everyone was involved, everyone had an opinion. First Lieutenant John C.
Casey, born in England and a graduate of the academy, expressed the
view of many: "The General Commanding has not been to the Fort since
we have been here—and in opposition to our opinions, formed on the
spot, orders come for a handful of men to march through the heart of the
nation." Others pointed out that Clinch had specified the sending of two
additional companies to follow Gardiner as soon as they arrived—why
not wait for them, send all four at once? Or wiser still, Belton should
suspend the order indefinitely—don't send Gardiner *or* the other companies against probably superior numbers. Wait for *real* reinforcement. And
there were those with perhaps "an excess of that delusory valor which
contemns its enemy," who argued that discipline and training were more
valuable than numbers, who spoke of white men versus red and smiled
and nodded.[36]

Yet just this afternoon scouts had reported seeing a mounted, *naked* spy
in the vicinity of the spring. They were being watched, there was no

doubt of that. Indians might not have the organization and discipline of soldiers, but such incidents were not random acts. Some saw them as evidence of rigid subordination, proof of power and resolution somewhere in the Nation. In the course of ten days Belton had heard or been told the opinion of virtually every soldier and civilian, man and woman within the fort. Why not talk to Holata Emathla? *His* people were the enemy. Perhaps he could give them intelligence about the hostiles.[37]

The clear day had given way to rain-swept evening when a group of solemn-faced officers, accompanied by armed guards, were rowed across the river. In the Seminole camp, a collection of huddled shanties, in full council with Holata Emathla, Foke-luste Hadjo (called "Black Dirt"), Otulke Ohala (called "Big Warrior"), and their men, Belton tried to gauge, in the view of these "friendly" Seminoles, the mood of the hostiles, which would pretty much mean the mood of the Seminole Nation. Nervous, impatient, trying not to breathe too deeply the odor of anxious, unclean humanity, Belton waited through the halting translations, looking for reassurance from the impassive, dark-skinned, ragged-robed men facing him across the fire. The mood was not good. Yet destitute as they were, the chiefs made no attempt to curry favor by giving soft answers to his questions.[38]

He may have been stretching things a little when he referred to these stolid people as "friendly." Foke-luste Hadjo, for instance, had for years been an inveterate enemy of whites, had once fought hand to hand with General Jackson and been left for dead. He had "come in" with his wife and daughter from Chicuchatty, or Red House, a settlement fifty miles northeast of Fort Brooke. He wore a turban made of five handkerchiefs and claimed that each handkerchief would cost Osceola, called "Powell" (after his white father, William Powell), a leader of the hostile faction, one hundred dollars. Men like Foke-luste Hadjo had been forced by the militants of their own race to one extreme or the other—resist the whites or join them—but it did not necessarily follow that they were friendly to whites or their civilization. They would doubtless have preferred to live out their lives without making decisions forced upon them by others, without uprooting their families and going among strange people in strange places. But neither did they wish to die.[39]

Suddenly shouting and commotion outside, in the night, made the officers look quickly to one another, to their weapons. Then three strangers were brought in: Indians—Tallassees—their wet, tawny bodies glistening in the firelight. Belton waited for an explanation. The men were messengers from Micanopy, principal chief of the Seminoles, hereditary ruler of his people. The message could be good news or bad. Micanopy was acknowledged chief, but his words were generally those of his top advisers, who rarely had good words for white men. Abraham was one, a black man who had come to the Seminoles as an escaped slave more than a decade before, had risen from interpreter to adviser to the chief and was said by many to dominate him. Of even more influence was Ote Emathla, called "Jumper," married to a sister of Micanopy and determined not to give up the land. So these men might be merely the messengers they claimed to be, but on the other hand they could be spies, or worse, assassins.[40]

Belton put questions, waited through translation, discussion, answer, and retranslation. The messengers' manner was bold, arrogant. They claimed that the Micasuki were gathering at the forks of the Withlacoochee, were already 250 strong, including 40 mounted. If the "Big Knives" marched out—tried to force their way through the Seminole Nation—they would be killed. As their words stumbled through translation, tumbled out one by one, Belton tried to cover his dismay. All around talk was spreading, growing louder, the messengers' words creating great excitement throughout the camp. Without waiting for more, Belton gave an order, and soldiers moved in, disarmed the three, and put them under arrest.[41]

Their manner changed. Their messages were passive, neutral, they protested. Major Dade interceded, "express[ing] every confidence in Indian character, and particularly upon the salutary influence of Abraham upon Micanopy." Dade was by far the most experienced among them in dealing with Seminoles; he had known Micanopy and most of the others in his years here at Fort Brooke. Clinch himself had referred to Dade's "knowledge of the Indian character." Still, Belton considered it imperative to hold the three newcomers prisoner, "if they were spies and as much so, if they were charged with any propositions likely to detach the Chiefs from the treaty, or indeed . . . to take the scalps of" Holata Emathla, Foke-luste Hadjo, and Otulke Ohala. He would take them to the fort, let them rue their impertinence in the guardhouse.[42]

The meeting over, the officers returned to the fort, Belton in as tight a bind as a man could be. Sending 100 men out against 250 might look like suicide to him, but Clinch obviously thought otherwise. The order had not said "if" or "maybe." Coming up from the river, the little knot of officers paused by the surgeon's quarters and stood under the overhang, out of the rain. Anxious settlers hovered about the doorway. Grim, tight lipped, Belton, Dade, and other senior officers argued. Belton made no effort to conceal his misgivings from the others, telling them solemnly that "before *he* would go and face what he considered certain death for himself and his men he would resign his commission." At Fort Morgan he had considered resigning simply to join Fannin in Texas and improve his lot. After all, a career in the army was basically a means of earning a living, not committing suicide. Other officers agreed. If only Gardiner would decline the order, they would all be off the hook.[43]

Major Dade disagreed strongly, "repeatedly and earnestly insist[ing] that unless the clearest evidence was adduced as to the difficulty of the operation it was imperatively necessary to obey the order of the commanding general." That talk of 250 Seminoles lying in wait was likely just that—talk. Dade's words, his appearance, his bearing declared that honor and courage were the only appropriate concerns. They were soldiers, trained (and paid) by their country to fight its battles. Others might quibble over risk and talk of danger, but such considerations had no place here, in the face of the enemy. He stated flatly that "he could go through Florida with a Sergt's guard" and that in any case, for himself, rather than "be called a coward, he would 'die first.'" From someone else that might have sounded like barracks-room boasting, but no one doubted that Francis Dade meant what he said. Of course Dade wasn't under orders. Belton wasn't either, and neither of them was West Point. Gardiner's position was a little different. Fully conscious of the danger, he *was* under the order of General Clinch and he *was* West Point. "Duty, Honor, Country" were not just words bruited about at the academy—they were his life. He would march when Belton gave the word.[44]

Belton listened, pondered, struggled for a decision. On the one hand, the order to send one hundred men through the Nation struck most of them as astonishing, particularly in the light of the information just gathered in Holata Emathla's camp, but no one *knew* what the Seminole reaction would be. On the other hand, if Gardiner made it through it would be

pretty clear the threats were all sound and fury, signifying nothing—
"Indian talk." And even in the event of an attack by the hostiles, he had
every confidence that the detachment would give good account of them.
And if there was trouble, then again the Seminoles would clearly be seen
as the troublemakers. After all, two companies were hardly an invading
army; on the contrary, they were merely a relief column marching to the
aid of a sister fort, itself perhaps besieged.[45]

Perhaps he had waited as long as prudence and hope would allow. It
had never been a question of *whether* to obey Clinch's order, only a matter
of *when*. He had waited for further orders, for reinforcement. Dade was
here with the men to bring Gardiner's and Fraser's companies up to
strength. There was nowhere else to turn, no excuses left. Gardiner knew
the risk, was willing to go. Silence. The officers waited. All right, Gardiner's command would complete their preparations tomorrow. The day
after next, the twenty-third, he would put them in motion for Fort King.[46]

The twenty-second dawned cloudy, rain leaking from a heavy sky, the
temperature in the high sixties, weather to match the mood of the fort as
preparations got under way. Clinch had specified that each man be issued
thirty rounds of cartridges, "should there be a good supply . . . on hand."
Belton reviewed the inventory; there wasn't a good supply of anything
on hand. He could supply Gardiner with his thirty rounds per man, but
doing so would leave Belton seriously short for defense of the fort itself.
And only the men transferred from Dade's company were infantry—the
rest were artillery—and artillerymen as a rule weren't issued cartridge
boxes. Their cartridges could be carried on the supply wagon, but that
wouldn't be of much use to a man in a hurry—if he was going to need
them at all, he'd need them fast. Belton sent for Levi Collar, a respected
settler whose cabin six miles out had been burned by the hostiles, Collar
and his family barely escaping to the fort. Could the women put their
needles and thread to work? Soon Nancy Collar, Levi's twenty-year-old
daughter, with her sister Cordelia and the wives and daughters of other
settlers, were sewing powder sacks.[47]

Gardiner would take one of the six-pounders, a wheeled cannon that
fired six-pound iron balls the size of a grapefruit. Belton could spare fifty
rounds of ammunition for that—solid shot as well as canister and grape.

They would need four oxen to pull the cannon, a single horse to draw the supply wagon; he sent an officer to purchase the best he could find among the scrubby stock of the settlers. A young fellow named Stafford, son of another settler, had volunteered to go along as interpreter—through the years of peace he had picked up enough Seminole to make himself understood. Belton signed him on at three dollars a day. Holata Emathla had volunteered to have his son accompany Gardiner as both interpreter and as representative of the peaceful Seminole faction—for what that might be worth. Belton had accepted, grateful for any volunteers, but it would hardly be prudent to rely solely on a Seminole, even a friendly one, as Gardiner's only means of communicating with hostiles they might meet. Holata Emathla had also agreed to send some of his men on ahead to reconnoiter along the Fort King Road as far as the bridge over the Little Hillsborough.[48]

Belton wrote two letters, one to General Clinch and a second to the Seminoles' agent, Wiley Thompson. Belton was relieved to report that he was finally in a position to carry out the order for reinforcements, that Gardiner and Fraser "will move tomorrow morning upon Fort King." He covered events at the fort, Dade's arrival, went on to list his ordnance stores and the number of men standing for duty, and pointed out that with the departure of the detachment he would have on hand only "107 bayonets including 11 sick; some very badly." He closed with the hope that he would soon receive "commands and instructions."[49]

No messages had come overland from headquarters for months. Belton had no way of knowing if Fraser's and his own messengers were getting through. On reflection he determined to send the letters by runner, using the oldest of the three men taken into custody the night before, and directed him to deliver the letters to Abraham at Pelacklakaha, Micanopy's town, some sixty miles north by the Fort King Road, a couple of miles east. There was little likelihood that even an Indian runner could get through direct to Fort King; he could only hope that Abraham—former slave, "sense-keeper" to Micanopy, enemy—would honor his request to forward the letters. A forlorn hope, perhaps, but he could do no better. "These letters of course involved many details, but numbers and other facts, to guard against Treachery were stated in French." The man seemed to be an uncle of the other two—he would detain them as hostages to assure the good conduct of the older man. The runner left the fort at noon. Far into the night the women were still stitching up powder bags.[50]

On Wednesday morning, "as usual, reveille was beat 1/2 past 6 o'clock." Moments later the sound of "Assembly" brought men from the big, wooden barracks, across the wide porch, and down the steps to the parade ground and company formation. First sergeants John Hood and Benjamin Chapman, superintended by company officers, made roll call by lantern light. "Clark." "Here." "DeCourcy." "Here." "Jewell." "Here." "Thomas." "Here." "Wilson." "Here." One hundred men, half awake, a coat unbuttoned here, a shirttail out there, a boot untied, a runny nose, muttered words, a curse, a joke. Overcast and rain had given way to a starlit sky. The mercury stood at fifty-four degrees.

Roll call done, squad leaders directed the cleanup of quarters before "Peas-upon-a-trencher" sounded for breakfast. In the mess, before eating, roll was called again. Then back to barracks for canteens, knapsacks and haversacks, cartridge boxes (or bags), swords or bayonets, and muskets. "Assembly" sounded again. From a crowd of men and women, soldiers and civilians, two companies materialized. Sound faded. Silence spread.[51]

Captain Gardiner took the black leather reins in one white-gloved hand, put his foot in the gilt stirrup, and swung up into the worn saddle. The dark blue saddlecloth extended just beyond the saddle, gold lace stitched to the scarlet edging. He wore a dark blue, single-breasted frock coat, the standing collar secured with hooks and eyes over his black silk stock. His shoulder straps were bordered with an eighth of an inch of gold embroidery, his rank shown by two bars of the same material parallel with the ends of the straps. The coat was closed with ten large regimental buttons, belted around the captain's stocky figure with white leather two inches wide secured with a sliding frog, buckled with a round, metal clasp. A crimson silk net sash was wound twice around his waist and tied on his left hip, the silk bullion fringe ends hanging twelve inches below the knot. A short, straight artillery sword with a yellow grip hung in its scabbard below his left hip, a model 1819 .54 caliber smooth-bore flintlock pistol in a black leather holster on the right. His trousers were woven of a mixture of white and light blue thread that combined to produce a sky blue effect. A red stripe an inch and a half wide ran down the outer seam from hip to ankle. He wore black leather ankle-high boots with brass spurs. The grey in his hair hardly showed beneath the lacquered black beaver hat, seven and a half inches high with a patent leather peak. On the front of the cap was a gilt eagle, crossed cannons, and the numeral 2 for his regiment.[52]

Soldiers in the front ranks saw the little captain turn time and again in the saddle, look toward the hospital. It stood two hundred yards north of the parade ground, ninety yards back from the Hillsborough River just above its entrance to the bay, a big-frame, log building surrounded by a ten-foot-wide gallery and shaded by giant live oaks. Lieutenant Alvord had known the Gardiners since they had been stationed in Key West. "Mrs. Gardiner was exceedingly ill," he wrote, "and it was supposed that if her husband left, she would not live." A family friend had once written that George Gardiner was "a young man of promise . . . and very attentive to his duties." Where was his duty now? With his wife or with his men?[53]

Frances had sailed up from Key West with him. They had made their stark quarters in the fort more comfortable with their own furnishings: two bureaus, some chairs, a washstand, trunks and boxes of their possessions. With the Seminole trouble there was no telling how long he might be garrisoned here. The children had stayed on in Key West with Frances's father, but Frances was here, and sick.[54]

And if the Seminole threat and his wife's illness weren't enough, Gardiner had found little ground for comfort in her doctor, Asst. Surgeon Henry Lee Heiskell. "I never saw [Dr. Heiskell] have any lengthened transaction or a little extra trouble with a patient but he fell in a passion," wrote an orderly who made his rounds with him. The orderly, Pvt. John Bemrose, thought the doctor a "fine southerner with prepossessing features, but alas! A continual dark hour seemed to be upon him." Unaccountably ill tempered, his poorly smothered ill nature frequently "blaze[d] forth in passion." Even more serious, the orderly observed that Heiskell "had a great liking for the lancet; he seemed to feel he got rid of his patients the more readily." The Seminole threat might come to nothing; Frances's illness was a fact. Medicine and treatment, like everything else in a place like this, were meager. And perhaps leaving her in the care of a doctor who often threatened to beat his patients with a stick was worse than leaving her alone.[55]

Dr. Heiskell had worries of his own. Married only two years, he had brought his wife and children down with him from Fort Pickens, leaving the greater part of their furniture and belongings behind in the expectation of an early return. Month by month, a year had passed. They had made the best of bleak conditions while they hoped for reassignment, only to be crowded now within the fort by unkempt settlers while outside there were Indians, wilderness, and stark danger. Of the fifty or so other women in the fort, only three were the wives of officers and fit company for his wife. Many of the enlisted men had wives with them, but most were ignorant, many foreign. As for the others—settlers' women as well as the slatterns with shacks along the river—they were not the sort of people his wife could associate with. Medically speaking, Fort Brooke had always been considered a "delightful station," but there was not much delight here for a well-bred young woman of fragile health.[56]

A friend and fellow doctor described Heiskell as "a gentleman of correct deportment and urbanity of manners"; another referred to him as "an amiable young gentleman." That was six years ago, when he had first gone to Washington to apply for an appointment as an assistant surgeon with the army, confident in his qualifications and his connections. He had already completed four years of study with a physician in his hometown of Winchester, Virginia, had subsequently attended two full courses of lectures at the University of Pennsylvania, and graduated as a doctor of medicine in 1828. He was practicing in Nashville when presidential candidate Andrew Jackson had engaged his services, arranging for him to visit the Hermitage several times a week to treat the Jacksons' slaves. In November Jackson, now president-elect, asked him to attend the rotund and melancholy Rachel Jackson. A month later he was suddenly called again. He had found Rachel suffering from "a spasmodic affection of the muscles of the chest and left shoulder, attended with an irregular action of the heart." In spite of his efforts and those of other attending physicians, she died two days before Christmas. "How shall I describe," he had written, "the heart-rending agony of the venerable partner of her bosom!"[57]

In applying for a position with the army, Heiskell carried a letter of introduction to John Eaton, secretary of war and a close friend of the president. "As to his skill in his profession," the letter stated with confidence, "this is better known to the President of the U.S. than to myself.

. . . To him I beg leave therefore . . . to refer you." With this kind of reference his subsequent failure to obtain the appointment had been as surprising as it was discouraging. He had continued in private practice until 1832, when he learned that the medical staff of the army was to be increased. He reapplied in June, was accepted in July, and in August had finally taken up the duties of assistant surgeon at Bellona Arsenal in Virginia. For the past two years and more he had served throughout the South while maintaining a private practice whenever it did not conflict with his public duties. After fourteen months of military service at five different posts, he thought himself settled enough to marry his fiancée, a young woman from Staunton, Virginia. Seventeen days later he was reassigned again. He wrote from Fort Mitchell, Alabama, that he hoped for "a post presenting somewhat better prospects in regard to permanency," as "there is not the smallest possibility of getting my wife to my post." Before the end of 1834 his assignments had included Fort Coffee, Alabama, then forts Clinch and Pickens in Florida and, finally, Fort Brooke.[58]

Few married men—and fewer wives—would have chosen to serve at Fort Brooke. It was one thing for young, single officers who had no greater concerns than hunting and fishing, but for married men and their wives the isolated post had little to offer. For Henry Heiskell it was particularly disappointing that his desire for permanency had been fulfilled at one of the most remote posts the army had to offer. Discouraged with his military career, Dr. Heiskell, a man of "eminently social habits," was also becoming a man of "quick and ardent temperament . . . prompt to resent an injury or an insult." To prevent aggressive acts on his own part against those whom he was beginning to refer to as "stupid mortals," he had often to call upon his "sense of honor, and gentlemanly feeling." For instance, the surgeon general had recently requested a special report on the hospital. With twenty-five men on sick report already, some of them serious, and responsible for the health of several hundred other soldiers and civilians— every one of them a potential patient with every affliction from birth to death—facing a hostile Seminole Nation, his back to the sea, he was required to spend his time filling out reports, and that "with as little delay as possible."[59]

"If the required report should not reach you as speedily as desirable," he had replied testily, "it will be attributable to the irregularity of the mail from this post to fort [sic] King, as we are dependent upon armed expresses between the two places for the transmission and receipt of our communications." In fact there had been no direct communication from Fort King for two months. Dispatches had been held for the next ship to sail for St. Marks, Pensacola, or New Orleans. Delay indeed![60]

But there was more to the request than routine questions about the location of the hospital, number and size of rooms, uses to which they were applied, and so on. Was there not the suggestion, perhaps even the warning, of trouble to come? Puzzled, Heiskell replied, "To venture an opinion whether a new hospital is, or will shortly be necessary, I must confess that I am quite at a loss. My means of information furnish me with no correct data upon which I can form anything like a positive opinion." In minutes Gardiner and his command would march north for Fort King. Sometime tomorrow they would cross an invisible line and enter the Seminole reservation. Were one hundred muskets and a cannon enough to overawe the Seminoles, to keep the lion at bay? Did the surgeon general expect them to be clawed?[61]

Heiskell's long service at southern stations had accustomed him to diseases of the respiratory and digestive organs, brain and nervous systems, to rheumatic and venereal affections, ulcers and abscesses, injuries, ebriety, and the prevailing disease, intermitting fever. His standard treatments were bleeding, blistering, bandages, and bed rest—with quinine for fever. But sick men were one thing, wounded another. "In estimating the capacity of the Wards for the accommodation of the sick I take it for granted that I shall not be understood as basing my calculations on the presumption of there being *wounded* patients, but merely such as are to be ordinarily met with in camp or garrison." In reply to the question of "the full number [the rooms] can contain in cases of emergency," he had replied, "I know of no other means . . . than by putting two patients in a bunk."[62]

If the surgeon general's questions implied a coming emergency, Heiskell's only assistants would be Dr. Reynolds and an orderly or two; Acting Asst. Surgeon Nourse was returning to Key West, Dr. Suter was expecting orders any day, and Dr. Gatlin had been assigned to Gardiner's command. As to supplies, he would have to send a requisition to New Orleans for a few articles of immediate necessity. Under normal circumstances, these and the surplus medicines and stores turned over to him by Suter and Gatlin should be sufficient for the coming year, but these were not normal circumstances. Something was in the air, and if that something was trouble Fort Brooke might be the place it would start.[63]

Gardiner's Company C made up half the detachment. The other half was Company B, Third Artillery, commanded by Upton Fraser, the only one of the six line officers with the command who was not a West Pointer. Enlisting in 1814 as an ensign in the Fifteenth Infantry, he had been transferred to the artillery a year later and made captain in 1828, thus outranking Gardiner by four years. By military custom he should have commanded the detachment, but for an assignment like this Gardiner's field experience and West Point background made him the reasonable choice. Fraser, forty-one years old, was from New York City; his narrow face, sharp nose, small mouth, and pointed chin were kept from looking like the blade of an ax by his large, dark, kind eyes. In the bosom of his shirt he wore a miniature of himself done by a fellow officer. Another officer referred to him as "the soldier's friend, the gay and gallant." As a measure of their respect, the men referred to one of the newly constructed blockhouses built under his direction as the "Fraser Redoubt."[64]

Behind Gardiner stood his command, two by two, the column in close order stretching across the parade ground nearly two hundred feet to the supply wagon and cannon at the rear. The men's forage caps were black leather, seven inches high in front and back with a valley between, black leather bill below. Most carried a brass A for artillery in place of eagle and cannons; eleven carried a silver I for infantry. Their grey-blue great-coats were double breasted with stand-up collars, a cape. There were two rows of nine buttons each (gilt for artillery, silver for Dade's infantrymen) running from collar to hem, three inches above the knee. Their sky blue trousers bore no stripe. White leather belts were secured with a round, brass clasp surmounted by a spread eagle. Two more leather belts crossed each soldier's chest, one to carry a black leather cartridge box (if he had one) on his right hip, the other to support the sixteen-inch triangular blade bayonet in its black leather scabbard usually carried only by the infantry.

And only the gun crew were armed with the artillerymen's model 1833 Roman pattern short swords. The leather belts were about as white as an officer could expect, considering that cleaning them with white lead was

Likeness believed to be that of Capt. Upton S. Fraser. Oil on canvas.
Courtesy of Dr. Joseph D. Cushman.

forbidden now, "it being found to possess qualities injurious to health," according to regulations. Also across each man's chest was a white canvas strap supporting a haversack on his left hip. In the sack, along with his eighteen-ounce issue of stale bread (believed to be healthier than fresh), he carried three-quarters of a pound of raw pork or one and a quarter pounds of beef (fresh or salted), wrapped in cloth, paper, or even leaves in order not to stain the haversack. Here and there, added to his ration issue, a haversack bulged with sweet oranges, a rare treat for the men enterprising enough to have hustled them from a load just brought in from Cuba. High on their shoulders they wore black painted knapsacks with a four-pound blue woolen blanket, five feet by six and a half feet, rolled and tied across the top. On the knapsack cover in yellow paint were crossed cannons for artillery, a bugle in white for infantry. The one-and-a-half-inch number above indicated regiment, the letter below, company. With the exception of the gun crew, each man was armed with a model 1816 .69 caliber smooth-bore flintlock musket. The weapon was five feet long, weighed eight pounds, and had a leather carrying strap.[65]

The officers who would remain stood apart from the column. Suddenly one, talking with Belton, nodded, turned, crossed to Gardiner, saluted, spoke. Only the blind were not watching. Brevet Major Dade, tall, straight, spoke at length, gestured toward the hospital. Few could hear but all knew what he said. Gardiner listened, shook his head. Dade spoke again, earnestly. Silence, the two men staring at one another. Finally Gardiner nodded, spoke briefly, handed over his orders, then straightened in his saddle, raised his hand in salute, and with a flip of the reins moved toward the hospital. He would stay with his wife. Francis Dade would take command.[66]

Within minutes Dade's horse was brought, his gear put on the wagon, his double-barreled shotgun handed up to him. He directed Lieutenant Alvord to join the detachment temporarily, no time now to instruct him in the affairs of Company B while Dade was on detached duty. Only minutes ago had Belton finally granted his request to offer himself as substitute for Gardiner. On their arrival in the *Motto* Belton had ordered Alvord to turn the ship over to Casey for the return trip to Key West, so there was nothing to hold him here. At Dade's signal the officers with the detachment joined him in bidding the crowd of settlers goodbye. He spoke to them on behalf of the command, reassuring them as to its safety, thanking them for their concern. He sat his horse casually, elegantly, white-gloved hands holding the reins. From the white plume attached to the fur crown above the patent leather visor of the hat resting on his large head, to the gold leaf on his silver-bound shoulder straps, to his tall, black leather boots, he looked every inch a soldier. His black beard lay against the dark blue of his coat, a great curved saber hung below his left hip, the silver wire that bound the grip matching the white kerseymere stripe of his trousers. Beneath his coat he wore a blue vest that, like the boots and saber, was no part of regulation military dress. Nancy Collar thought "his words at parting were very brave, and tears were in many eyes." Several of the friendly chiefs, swathed in blankets, unsmiling, came silently to the front, moved from one officer to another, bidding each a solemn farewell, assuring them that "they would never see them again alive."[67]

The officers turned away and rejoined the column. "March" sounded, the heavy gates swung open, the advance guard moved out. Frances Kyle Basinger stood by the window of the block house where she and her husband had been quartered since their arrival from Fort Pickens nearly a month ago. She watched 2nd Lt. William Elon Basinger, suddenly in command of Gardiner's company, proudly follow. He, Dade, and Fraser were the only officers for whom Belton had been able to provide horses. Perhaps to make himself look older than his twenty-nine years, Basinger wore large whiskers. Under his regulation shirt he wore a fine white net undershirt, around his waist a red leather money belt, in one pocket a silk handkerchief, in another pocket letters. "He was all that an ingenious mind could imagine for a youthful soldier," wrote a friend. "Frank, brave, proud, warm-hearted, thoughtful, and yet gay—with the lurkings about him yet of boyhood."[68]

Basinger, a native of Savannah, had been raised by his mother, Elizabeth, "a woman of prudence, energy, and high character," after the death of his father when William was ten years old. He had entered West Point in 1826 and graduated in 1830 without a single demerit. He had served as cadet adjutant during his last year, succeeding to that honor upon the graduation of the cadet who had held the position before him, a Virginian and classmate for three years, Robert E. Lee. Basinger's high standing in class had been so nearly even with another cadet during the entire four-year course and through final examinations that it was decided to resort to a drill in the manual of arms to determine who would graduate in first place. Basinger had lost through having one finger a half-inch out of place in some position on his piece, and again, like Lee before him, had graduated second in his class. He had served in garrisons in South Carolina and Georgia before being assigned as assistant instructor of infantry tactics at West Point in 1831.[69]

During the two years he served at the academy he had met Frances Kyle, "an extremely beautiful girl," daughter of the bandmaster. They were married in New York City in December 1833 when his service at West Point came to an end, a marriage that his family in Savannah thought "injudicious." Fanny had accompanied him through two more years of garrison duty at Fort Jackson and Covington, Louisiana, at Fort Pickens, Florida, and now for a month at Fort Brooke. He had not taken her to Savannah, and she had met none of his family. Here he had been appointed acting commissary of subsistence as well as acting assistant quartermaster. Along with other officers, he had supervised the construction of defenses against the Seminoles. The work finished, he felt that they were "perfectly secure" within the pickets. He had written to his mother a week ago that "we are every day expecting an attack," had assured her that "all the Indians in Florida could not do us the slightest injury."[70]

But he was leaving behind whatever security the fort provided. His wife wrote, "Our dear William cheered me so with repeated assurances that there was no danger [to the command] that I thought there was none. . . . [H]e said he would be back to me in a couple of weeks at the farthest— he felt so fearless and appeared in such good spirits that I could not but try and banish my fears of danger." Basinger's second in command was Bvt. 2nd Lt. Richard Henderson, six months out of West Point, nineteen years old, on foot with the men.[71]

Fraser rode at the head of Company B. Marching were 2nd Lt. Robert Rich Mudge and Bvt. 2nd Lt. John Low Keais. Following the two companies were the horse-drawn wagon and driver, then the four oxen hitched to the limber, the limber supporting the cannon by its double trail. The wooden carriages of both gun and limber were painted light blue (a mixture of Prussian blue and white lead), the iron gun tube and the hardware of the carriages black. A driver with whip and goad kept place beside the

Likeness believed to be that of 2nd Lt. William Elon Basinger. Oil on glass.
Courtesy of Lt. Gen. Sterling Wright.

lead ox, the gun crew behind, and last was the rear guard. Dr. Gatlin, Stafford, and Holata Emathla's son walked where they would. Flankers would be sent out when they were clear of the fort.[72]

Belton watched them pass, took the salute, told himself they were in fine order for the service, that he had done his best, that the detachment would give good account of the Seminoles if attacked. Should he have sent them sooner? Should he be sending them at all? One hundred men against the Nation? Well, it was done. They were on their way. He could take comfort only in Dade's confidence, try not to think of the odds he might have to face.[73]

Orderly Sergeant Benjamin Chapman of Fraser's Company B, a thirty-six-year-old professional soldier from Rhode Island, caught a last look at his wife as he passed. Near the head of the right-hand column marched a black-haired, swarthy-skinned, hazel-eyed young man from Greigsville, New York. He was twenty-three years old, at five foot ten a little taller than most, a man who looked out for himself and didn't count much on luck, unless it was bad. His name was Ransom Clark. Another forty to fifty wives and children of other enlisted men watched as the soldiers tramped by, the men's small, tin kettles or stew pans buckled to their knapsacks, rattling like tiny bells. Ellen Kenny, thirty-four years old, who did washing for soldiers and officers, sought the dark eyes of her husband, Pvt. Michael Kenny. Married in 1820 in the parish of Armagh, Ireland, they had fled the famine and come to America, where Michael, a blacksmith, had joined the army a year before. Together they had gone to Fort Morgan, where he had served under Captain Belton until his transfer to Gardiner's Company C. Did Michael give a furtive wave? Then he had passed through the gate and was gone.[74]

The Fort King Road led northeast, rising gently toward a low ridge. Except for the great grey oaks, the land close by was barren; the original stand of pines had gone to build the fort, palmettos cleared to guard against the stealthy approach of Indians. On the right, swamps and marshland filled the interval between land and sea. At left, along the shore of the river, stood log shelters of assorted settlers. Once huddled in shacks directly under the protective walls of the fort, these men and women had edged out over the years, planting one store and then another until more than a dozen lined the riverbank. Quartered now within the fort, their buildings boarded, most of them stood around the gate and watched with mixed feelings as the soldiers passed.

Augustus Steel, a Connecticut entrepreneur, had been in the Territory for ten years doing one thing and another. Now he was the first county judge, having authority over five million acres of wilderness that had recently been set aside as Hillsborough County. This collection of log buildings they had begun calling "Tampa" was the county seat. As postmaster he knew most of the soldiers and sometimes read their letters to them—and knew, too, those who received no letters.[75]

William G. Saunders, from Alabama, had been living near the fort for seven years and had established the first general store on Florida's west coast. Less than a year before, Wiley Thompson, agent for the Seminoles, had licensed him to locate a trading house at the Big Hillsborough bridge, twenty-two miles north on the Fort King Road. And Levi Collar, the first white settler in the vicinity, made a good living by supplying the garrison with vegetables, pork, beef, and milk and cheese. Young Stafford's father was another who supplied the fort with meat. Now he stood and watched his boy pass.[76]

Men like these were always in places like this, on the frontiers that Americans had to have. They represented something basic in the makeup of the nation: a need for elbow room, a freedom from rules. Back home (wherever that had been), society would begin to settle its restrictive coils about them, and then one day they'd be gone. And if you watched, sooner or later they'd show up at a place like Fort Brooke—anywhere a man could simply move in, start scratching the ground for a garden, keep a couple of chickens, and trade whatever he could raise or make to others driven there by the same instinct. They weren't too constrained by the fine points of law, and yet in a pinch, without any speeches, they'd be pretty likely to risk what little they had—including life—to help a neighbor or even a stranger. They lived hard and worked hard and generally wore out and died early. They were here against every rule, including that of common sense, allowed to stay only by the sufferance of the military. Racial supremacy was their heritage, and they didn't wonder much about the possible rights of red men or black. They were too busy clearing and planting and building to concern themselves with the opinions of the Indians who lived in the forests, perfectly willing to ignore them while putting the earth to what they considered its proper use. It was a fact of frontier life that Indians would finally resist the steady encroachment, and then there was bound to be trouble—but that was the soldiers' job, and they'd better be about it.

Soldiers stared from side to side as they marched to the rattle of the drum, catching last glimpses of familiar sights, of safety. They crossed the path of beaten sand where in less anxious times then-captain Dade had raced his favorite mare, Richard the Third, in a three-mile heat, the first derby held in Florida. Perhaps no one but he remembered that he had lost. They passed the orderly grove of one hundred orange trees set out when the fort was new—dead now, killed in February's bitter freeze. It was said that an iceberg had floated down from the northern seas and lodged off the coast. At any rate there were no oranges, no leaves, no sign of life. Beyond the clearing the Fort King Road was a twenty-foot-wide path through palmetto scrub, cleared of all growth ten years before by two companies of pioneers under Capt. Isaac Clark. The sand was soft and loose, yesterday's rain already drained down and away, the marching hard. Dust rose in the air and settled on yellow palmetto blossoms. On either flank guards were moving out, pushing through the heavy growth, muskets in their hands, bayonets fixed. Hounds dashed back and forth like couriers, baying and barking their messages. There was a jingle of harness, the creak of leather, a screech of axles, and the muffled footfalls of an army. Long after the soldiers had crossed the ridge and gone from sight, the sound of their passage could still be heard by the watchers at the gate.[77]

A mile from the fort the column passed a worn trail leading away to the right and down to a flowing spring. Wells had been dug at the fort ten years before in an attempt to find potable water, but with no success. Since then water from the spring had been carried to the fort in barrels on a mule-drawn wagon. Now it sloshed in the men's wooden canteens as the long column trudged past. When the road to Fort King had been established it had simply continued the spring road north and east.[78]

From the start the oxen had been a problem. With no government stock of castrated bulls available, Belton had been forced to take what he could get—gaunt, rangy beasts to begin with, their strength and stamina further sapped by reduced forage. Trained to the plow, not artillery, they were simply not up to the task of hauling cannon and carriage, chest and limber, over three thousand pounds in all, the narrow, iron-shod wheels of carriage and limber cutting deep tracks in the sand. The driver walking by the lead ox could use his goad, crack his long whip, and curse, but his silent, lurching charges, heads bowed under the heavy, wooden yokes linking them two by two, were already doing their best. They struggled on— two miles, three, four in as many hours, an anchor on the end of the column that was gradually dragging it to a halt. The morning was nearly gone. Dade wheeled toward the rear, galloped back. The oxen stood dumbly in their yokes, sides heaving. Unlike horses, oxen would simply quit when they'd had enough. They were played out, and knew it.[79]

With the exception of Alvord, Dade was the only infantry officer with the command. The use of artillery, much less its care and problems, was not his first concern. His responsibility was to get this command through hostile territory to the relief of Fort King, with or without a cannon. At the rate they were traveling and with four rivers to cross, they'd be lucky if they got there before the emergency was over. There was only one thing to do: leave the gun and put the oxen to the wagon in place of the horse. Alvord would be going back soon—he could take a message to Belton, ask him to make up a team of horses if he could and bring the gun into camp.[80]

Orders were shouted up the line. Men stopped, stood at ease. The driver led the oxen, limber, and gun off the road. Willing hands unhitched the iron chain that connected the limber to the ring in the yoke and led the oxen to the wagon. The single horse was taken out of harness, the harness stored in the wagon, and the oxen chain attached to the wagon. The gun squatted in the palmettos, sullen, abandoned, breech elevated and muzzle down, vent covered with its lead apron, tampion in the barrel to keep out wind and weather. Artillerymen leaned on unfamiliar muskets and shook their heads; only four miles out and their gun was gone.

At Fort Brooke, Belton, still unable to rid himself of the feeling that the fort was under constant observation by the hostiles and in danger of imminent attack, had directed Captain Armstrong to prepare the *Motto* for an immediate return to Key West "for the purpose of enabling Lt. Duncan 2nd Arty to ship on board her 2 12pdr [cannon] field carriages

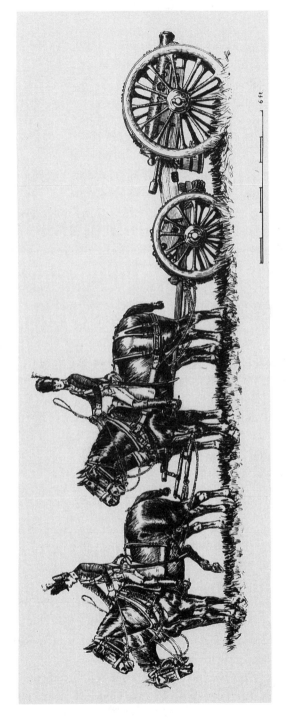

Four-horse team, limber, and six-pounder cannon of the type used by Dade's command.
Courtesy of the Fort Sill Museum, Fort Sill, Oklahoma.

complete with Implements and equipments and such Ordinance Stores
as may . . . be useful to the public service at this post." At 9:00 A.M.,
with an uneasy calm settling over the fort, he began a letter to Clinch
explaining his actions: "For transcending my authority, if it so presents
itself to you, I trust a suitable reason may be found in my desire to meet
all emergencies of the Service at this post."[81]

Then word was brought of a man just arrived by sloop who spoke fluent
Seminole as well as English, Spanish, and French. He was a slave who
belonged to Quintana Pacheco, widow of Don Antonio. He had come in
from his owner's trading post at Sarasota Bay, thirty miles down the coast.
Belton sent Lieutenant Casey, acting assistant quartermaster, to look into
the report; if it proved accurate he had authority to hire the man and bring
him to headquarters.[82]

Casey was directed to William Bunce, executor of Antonio Pacheco.
Bunce himself was just in this morning from his rancho at the mouth of
the Manatee River. He was considered "one of the most intelligent men
on the coast . . . and highly respectable." Hastily Casey explained the
circumstances, made his arrangements, and took the slave to Belton. The
man was in his mid-thirties, "able-bodied, good looking, intelligent, in
the prime of life." Bunce had assured Casey that he was honest and reliable.
Mrs. Pacheco had entrusted him with the management of her trading post.
His given name was Louis, and he had taken the name of Pacheco. Mrs.
Pacheco valued him at one thousand dollars, and would hire him out at
twenty-five dollars a month. Casey had made a verbal agreement with
Bunce, and had even come to an understanding about compensation for
the slave in the event of his death or capture.[83]

Pacheco was questioned in English, French, and Spanish, and his flu-
ency was obvious. He claimed to have learned Seminole from his older
brother, who had been taken by the Seminoles as a child and had lived
with them for twenty years before returning. The daughter of his first
master had taught him to read and write. He was far more qualified than
Stafford. Belton told him he was being employed as interpreter for Major
Dade's command and to make whatever preparations he needed to get on
the road and overtake the detachment.[84]

A better interpreter was no substitute for reinforcements, but Belton
couldn't help that. Completing his letter to Clinch, he explained that there

Louis Pacheco at the age of ninety-two. *Jacksonville Times-Union*, 1896.

was "no appearance yet of the Companies from the vicinity of N Orleans."
And, "I have just employed and sent an Interpreter to the Detachment."
At any rate, the use of the slave instead of the Stafford boy would save
the government some sixty-five dollars a month, if he should be gone that
long. He had the letter copied for Dade, gave it to Pacheco for delivery,
and sent him on his way.[85]

There was a shout from the rear guard a hundred yards and more behind
the stalled column—a black man was coming up from the direction of
the fort. Men straightened, gripped their weapons. The man was alone,
carrying a musket. He was passed through the guard, taken to the major.
The other officers waited, silent, while Dade read the message.

The letter was datelined "Fort Morgan." Belton had left there a month
ago. Must be a little edgy. Dade scanned the page for word of reinforcements, the only news that mattered. "No appearance yet of the Companies." Where the devil were they? If they didn't come in soon they might
as well not come at all. Docking, unloading, and fitting out the men would
all take time. Two separate groups of one hundred men each would be
no better off than one. Finally, the letter confirmed what the slave had
said as to being employed by Belton as "Interpreter to the Detachment."
Now Dade had two interpreters. What he'd like to have were more men
to shoot Seminoles, not talk to them. Well, the Stafford boy could go
back, they had no need of him now.[86]

While the transfer of the oxen was being completed Dade talked with
his officers, revised his plans. They would push on another three miles
to the Little Hillsborough and make camp. Without the gun they should
reach the river by early afternoon. Alvord would be returning to the fort.
If all went well he could take word of their location and circumstances,
and if Belton could find some horses and spare the men there would be time
for a crew to bring the gun on into camp tonight. Even more important, an
early halt would give reinforcements extra hours to catch up. Men and
muskets were what they needed. The failure of the team might be the
least of their problems before this trip was over.

The pace picked up, but not by much. Four oxen pulling one light
supply wagon were pulling nothing at all, but even an unburdened ox

would move only so fast. Driven with whip and goad, they could hardly
be counted on for more than a mile and a half an hour. Simply shooting
them because they were no longer useful, were in fact a liability, might
make sense here in the field but not to the quartermaster. And turning
them loose to be taken by Seminoles made no sense to anyone. Men and
oxen plodded on.[87]

The road proceeded over level, sandy, pine barren country, passing
several hammocks and ponds. Two companies of men had taken ten days
to cut their way through from the fort to the Little Hillsborough in 1825.
Timber, brushwood, and rubbish had been removed, the larger trees cut
as low to the ground as possible, the stumps hollowed in the center to
hold moisture and hasten decay.[88]

Thick palmetto had begun to fill the space between the trees on either
side, walling in the road, pressing close, blocking the view. Hidden Seminoles might see through, but moving soldiers couldn't see out. The pace
quickened, the column lengthened, and then the bridge was in sight, a
"good, strong, substantial" structure built less than a year earlier to replace
the old bridge. It was a relief to see it still standing, confirming the report
of Holata Emathla's scouts.[89]

Low banks sloped gently to the edge of the dark water that muttered
quietly as it crowded past the pilings. It was a narrow stream, low at this
time of year. Tall, virgin cypresses crowded the shore, winter-stripped
of their small, compressed needles, fine, grey bark silvery in the winter
sunlight. Back from the shore, on high ground, evergreen pines blanketed
the ground with fallen needles. Putting aside arms and accoutrements,
placing them so they could be found on the instant, experienced and
willing hands took axes from the wagon. With a rush of wind, a smashing
of limbs, and a shower of cones and needles, hundred-foot trees thundered
down. Trimmed and notched down one upon another, they would form
a three-log-high wall around the camp, a barrier to slow any Seminoles
that might think of attacking. Other logs, limbs, and pine straw were
gathered for fires to hold back the chill and dark of night that was yet to
come. "A few 'lightwood knots,' as the half burned forks of pine-tree
branches are called, were soon ignited by the flash of powder in the pan
of one of our guns, whose vent or touch-hole had previously been stopped

by a little wooden plug, in order to save the load of powder and ball or shot." Picket lines for the horses, another for the oxen, were strung from tree to tree, sinks dug.[90]

Dade wrote a hurried note to Belton explaining the predicament of the cannon, urging him to send a crew to bring it on. The gun would be an asset, if for no other reason than to frighten the Seminoles with its sound and fury if a contest came. And considering that 90 percent of his men and all his officers were artillerymen, the presence of the cannon would boost morale. His officers, two of them as new to the service as their uniforms, may have felt secure in their West Point training, but away from the fort, every step in the silent forest taking them further into Seminole territory, there was hardly a man—officer or enlisted—that had not begun to realize clearly the risk inherent in their mission. He had said that he could march through the Seminole Nation with a sergeant's guard, and by God he'd got the chance, but it didn't mean he wouldn't take all the odds he could get.[91]

Benjamin Alvord had gone to West Point from Vermont, graduated in July 1833, and was assigned to the Fourth Infantry Regiment. He'd had two years of garrison duty with his regiment in Baton Rouge before making second lieutenant last July. He had come to Florida and field duty four months ago, but there was no place for him here; the table of command allowed two lieutenants to a company, and these two companies were fully staffed. While camp was making he moved among the other officers, talking, shaking hands, saying his goodbyes. One of the men had been a classmate at West Point—Lieutenant Mudge of Massachusetts. Another, like Dade, had volunteered, Bvt. 2nd Lt. Richard Henderson. A graduate of West Point in July, Henderson had sent in his resignation four months later. The president's acceptance had come only two days ago—the same day that Belton had put his company on orders. He had "instantly con- cluded to march with the command." He'd have a story to tell when he got back to Jackson, Tennessee.[92]

Men labored to raise the meager barricade around the camp. Cooks were setting up, officers waiting for their batmen to prepare supper, men bringing out their rations. One officer, then another drew Alvord aside, gave him directions "to settle up their affairs in case they did not survive." Then Dade's letter was ready—it was time to go. In Alvord's pocket were forlorn messages. From the look in the eyes of men who stared and turned away, from the wave of a hand, a final salute, he judged them "fully aware of the danger of the march, and expecting a severe conflict, though with the hope that a portion of the command would get through."[93]

When word had gotten around that the *Motto* was returning to Key West, Captain Gardiner, already half out of uniform, wearing a citizen's plain frock coat, had gone to Belton and asked permission for his wife to be taken aboard in the company and under the care of Acting Asst. Surgeon Nourse. Key West had as good medical facilities as Fort Brooke, and equally important, was not under threat of attack. Her father was there, the children, his own brother. As for himself, he was no doctor—he was an artillery officer. With Frances in good hands his place was with his men—on the road to Fort King. Mounted, he could catch them in an hour. Belton had no objection. It had been Gardiner's command, he had yielded to Dade only because of his wife's condition. If he thought she would be in better hands with Nourse, safer in Key West, there was no reason to refuse her passage or his return to the detachment. By mid-afternoon Gardiner had seen Frances safely on board and was making preparations to rejoin the command when Alvord was sighted, passed through the pickets, and entered the fort.[94]

Alvord was taken to Belton. Responding to Dade's message, Belton ordered the purchase of three horses and harness, the best the settlers had left. Two men would go with Gardiner, take them out, hitch up the gun, and carry it on to the column. The captain was ready and waiting. As quickly as horses and harness were gathered, Gardiner, still wearing his civilian coat, again belted sword and pistol around his stubby figure, signaled his men to mount and move out, and they were gone at a gallop, the sun caught in the trees behind them, the wind in their teeth.[95]

Their horses' hooves were a muffled drumbeat on the sand, shadows of the pines lying diagonally across the road like cannon barrels. In a quarter of an hour they reached the abandoned gun, high wheels silhouetted above the palmetto. They reined in and jumped down, the sound of their snorting, foot-stamping horses suddenly too loud. Harness was buckled on, pole and whippletrees adjusted, traces fastened and hitched to the limber. Men and beasts working together, the wheels of limber and cannon began to turn. Three thousand pounds to pull, three miles to go, darkness coming fast.

Francis Dade waited at the river. Waited for what? So far he'd lost a gun and two white men and gained one slave. Around him the camp was quiet, the night as black as firelight could make it. The quarter moon wouldn't rise for a couple of hours. The clear sky had begun to cloud, blotting out the stars. The temperature had dropped to fifty-four degrees. Men lay on the ground, under blankets, muskets close. Sentries paced. Some men slept. Here and there a man took out his watch, tilted it toward the fire. Seven o'clock. Eight. Alvord would have reached the fort hours ago, the six-pounder should be on the way. Had he gotten through? Just seven miles back, but still. . . . And the reinforcements. Where in hell were the reinforcements? After tonight there would be no time to sit around and wait. Half the reason for planning an early camp was to give them time to land, time to catch up. If there was any justification for the risk they were taking it was in reinforcing Clinch, lifting the possible siege on Fort King, and they couldn't do that here. Back at the fort it had been easy to believe that reinforcements would be coming up the bay any moment with another hundred men, another hundred muskets. A man didn't mind starting out ahead when he knew there'd be plenty of help right behind him, but they had left the fort more than twelve hours ago.[96]

Nine o'clock. A shout from a sentry: someone on the road, someone coming! The long roll brought men up to sitting, clutching their muskets, then scrambling to their feet, mouths open to listen, blankets falling away. Reinforcements? The gun? Seminoles? Officers gave orders, noncoms cursed, pushed men into defensive position along the wall. This was no goddamned party. Could be anybody out there—Seminoles more than likely. Then they could hear them, see horses in the firelight, plunging and snorting, straining against their harness. White men! Gardiner! Captain Gardiner with the gun! Sweet Jesus, what a sight![97]

Cannon placed and ready, horses rubbed down, watered, picketed, men stood around, avoiding the glare of the fire, chewing, spitting, questioning the new men, building confidence with loud talk. Apart from the men, Dade, Gardiner, and Fraser talked quietly, soberly, junior officers a respectful audience. At West Point Gardiner had been considered "every inch a soldier, and one that few men would have cared to encounter," called by the cadets "the God of War." He stood before them now, short as a child, tired, dumpy in his citizen's coat without the brass-gilt buttons, the piping, the lace, the turnbacks of the military, looking more like a storekeeper than a captain of artillery. A man who could have stayed behind in perfect safety for the best of reasons. He explained the arrangements made for his wife to return to Key West for treatment so he could "thus gratify his earnest desire to be with his men." Dade offered to relinquish command; Gardiner declined. Dade ranked him as brevet major and even as captain (by fourteen years). Perhaps more telling was the fact that the major himself had volunteered for this mission out of concern for the health of Gardiner's wife. No, "the relation in which he stood to Maj. Dade of course induced him not to demur to his continuing in command." Fraser here had charge of the company of Third Artillery; he'd be content with command of the Second and to relieve young Basinger.[98]

Well then, what about reinforcements? Had they come in during the day? The night was half done. When would they join? There wasn't a man there who wouldn't feel a lot better with their numbers doubled.

Leaving his wife had not been easy. Riding out through hostile country, bringing the gun, had been a risk. This was worse—the fact was they had seen and heard nothing of the additional companies. As far as Gardiner could see, this was all the reinforcement there was going to be—himself, a couple of men, the cannon. Even if a ship *was* sighted down the bay in the morning, it would take at least a day to disembark the command, another day to catch up. And that only if they sat here for two days and waited. And that was it. No reinforcements. At least not here, not now. As far as he could see, they were on their own.

Silence, fire against the night, hushed movement of a camp in enemy country, whinny of a horse. The officers stood back from the fire, staring, thinking. Beyond the barricade there was an occasional glint of firelight on musket barrel or bayonet of sentries standing guard. Well. Tomorrow would be a long march. Better get what rest they could. One by one they said goodnight.

At Fort Drane, General Clinch was having second thoughts about two companies trying to force their way "a distance of one hundred miles, through the disaffected & hostile part of the Seminole Nation." He had decided to amend his previous order for Gardiner and Fraser to start out first, writing to "The Commanding Officer of U.S. Troops, Ft. Brooke" that, instead of two companies setting out alone, "the *four* designated in a previous order will proceed to Ft. King. The Commg. Officer will use much caution on the march, and avoid any possible chance of a surprise."[99]

Chapter Two

The Second Day

Thursday, December 24, 1835

Coffee was boiled and drunk, bacon fried and eaten with hard bread, before the sun was fairly up. Men did what they had to do and didn't move too far outside the barricade to do it. Through the night they had all heard more than owls and whippoorwills.

Dade sent for Pacheco. The man's literacy and education were not what the major considered assets. In Virginia it was against the law to teach a slave to read or write in *any* language, and Dade was a Virginian, a slave owner. He told Pacheco to get something to eat, then scout the road as far as the Big Hillsborough, some fifteen miles ahead, and look for Seminoles, or sign of them. If they didn't run into problems the command would make camp tonight at the river.[1]

Captain Fraser was apprehensive. A slave, alone, miles from help? Under other circumstances Seminoles might have welcomed him, but not when it was clear he was working for the soldiers, carrying a gun. With Pacheco standing there it wasn't the best time to question the commander's orders, but there was no other time, in minutes he'd be gone. Fraser spoke up, asked Dade if such an assignment might not seriously endanger the man's life. Dade dismissed his concern. He had not asked Belton to send the man out, interpreter or not. If they met no Seminoles that wanted to talk he was just another mouth to feed. If he was going to eat army rations he could do army work. He was a chattel, nothing more, and expendable at that. Fraser was silent. Dade was in charge. Pacheco ate, was given food and water, and took up his musket and equipment. He left the encampment, was passed through the guard, crossed the bridge, and in a moment was lost to sight.[2]

Louis Pacheco had been born a slave in 1800. "His parents were direct descendants of pure-blooded negroes, born in Africa." His father, Adam, was a carpenter, boatbuilder, and driver. Adam and his wife were owned by Francis Philip Fatio, who lived thirty miles south of Jacksonville along the St. Johns River, an area called New Switzerland. Susan Fatio, six years younger than Louis, taught him to read and write, oblivious of the laws that forbade it. "He was ambitious to learn, and of quick perception, acquiring a good deal more of book learning than was usually found among negroes in those early days when the laws prohibited the education of slaves."[3]

When Louis was a child, settlers were few and Seminoles roamed the land. These swarthy men and women of the forest occasionally visited the settlements, and the whites found them strangely impressive in their gaudy clothing, their beads and feathers. They came and went like gypsies and, like gypsies, had little sense of private ownership. On one occasion and then another they had carried away—as infants—an older brother and then a sister of Louis. After twenty-odd years the brother had returned. He spoke only Seminole, was for all practical purposes an Indian. He taught Louis his language, and in the teaching told him of the wild life, the free life.[4]

Susan Fatio thought that Louis, even as a boy, "was of a roving disposition that hated restraint." Not surprisingly, he had frequently run away, but each time he had been apprehended. At twenty-four he made another break, and this time he got as far as the Spanish Fisheries on Tampa Bay. Apprehended again, he had been taken north forty miles to the new military camp at the mouth of the Hillsborough River. Colonel George Mercer Brooke knew a bargain when he met one, particularly a bargain that spoke Seminole, and negotiated with the distant Fatio for the runaway's purchase.[5]

As unofficial interpreter for the military post, Pacheco had been passed from one commanding officer to another until 1830, when Bvt. Maj. James S. McIntosh sold him to Don Antonio Pacheco, a wealthy Spanish plantation owner. He was taken from the military camp (now Fort Brooke) to Pacheco's plantation and trading post at the Fisheries. Recently Antonio Pacheco had died, and his widow had returned to the small civilian settlement around the fort.[6]

While gathering his few possessions in preparation for joining Dade's command, Pacheco had "made inquiries as to what mission Major Dade and his hundred odd men were bent on." At the Fisheries he had heard "rumors of Indian depredations but the rumors were vague and not credited, as peace between them [the Seminoles] and the whites had reigned unbroken for a long period." The people around the fort, while fearful of an attack on the fort itself, seemed to him "almost unanimously of the opinion that the red men were not generally hostile," but the mood of Dade's camp had told a different story. The white soldiers had been moody, nervous, and jumpy, talking loudly when they talked at all. Here in the woods, far from civilization (and white men) and temporarily free, it was hard to imagine trouble.[7]

Even if he had been unfamiliar with the road, he could hardly lose his way. The route, built in 1825, had been cleared of all growth to allow the passage of wagons, an army. It unrolled easily across the vast pine barrens interspersed with blackjack oak, through palmetto and straw grass silvered by the cloudy sky, looping around an occasional pond with its huddle of cypresses, always taking the highest ground, affording dry feet (at least in this season) and the best visibility. It was obvious the soldiers had not been traveling this way recently—the sand, churned and rutted from ten years' use, was nearly covered with a green and healing growth.

By mid-morning he had come to the tilled fields of Thlonoto-sasa, or Flint-abundant, a Seminole town of some two hundred. He approached cautiously, staring, listening. The shelters, made of roofed platforms built of palmetto trunks and fronds, were silent, apparently deserted, the people gone. He passed by, saw between the trees ahead and on his right the large, oval lake that took the same name as the village. Down the long, sloping hill, across the wide, sandy beach the water shone like polished lead under the cloudy sky, a mile wide, two miles long. The road followed the high land west of the lake, turned due east above the north shore, dipped to cross a little creek that trickled toward the lake, and then held to its eastern course for three more miles past swampland visible to the north. Beyond the swamp the road turned north.[8]

During the afternoon showers came and went and came again, fogging the air, washing away any tracks that might have been left. Once or twice

Pacheco passed a settler's cabin, a tiny plot of untended field. There was
no sign of man or woman, pig or chicken. Then he caught the smell of
smoke in the heavy air. There had been no lightning—the smoke meant
man, and man here likely meant Seminole. Ahead he could make out an
army of cypresses marching across the horizon, a sure sign of water. It
had to be the river. White men called it the Big Hillsborough. The Seminole name was "Lokcha-popka-chiska, Acorn-eating-river; in other words,
the river to which we come to eat acorns." He approached slowly, watching, listening. No sound from the wet forest on either side except for the
quiet drip of rain. Then the forest ended, a clearing opened. The smell
of smoke was stronger now, a recent fire. There was a charred ruin to
one side, but it was wet, dead—probably what remained of the trading post
belonging to the white man Saunders. Then he was aware of something in
the road, something that had been alive. He stared, looked right and left,
behind, stared again. It was a cow, slaughtered, split open. It had not
been butchered for food. It was all there, no cuts taken. The major had
wanted a sign, and here it was. A threat, a warning? However you read
it, it was an evil omen. He moved past. The road rose in an earthen
mound as it approached the river, ending abruptly on a bluff ten feet
above the water. Planked beams reached up to the first trestle, across the
second and third and back down to the north bank. Planking, beams, and
trestles were black and charred from bank to waterline. Smoke still rose
from the near ruin, flames still danced here and there along the protected
floorbeams. Only rain had saved it from complete destruction. Anxious,
fearful, he turned away, headed back.[9]

The command had been on the march since sunup, advance guard
several hundred yards ahead of the main column, flankers out on either
side, rear guard following well behind the wagon. Five miles on the way
they too had reached Thlonoto-sasa, established between 1812 and 1820.
It was the nearest Seminole town to the fort, the first with which Colonel
Brooke had established contact ten years ago when Cantonment Brooke
was being built. The column passed, the lake visible now through the
forest that drank from it. The order to halt was given, sentinels posted,
and men immediately fell out to relieve their kidneys, sprawl on the damp
ground. Old soldiers were able to achieve instant sleep of a sort; others

pulled from their haversacks hard bread or oranges, and their stubbled chins were soon wet with the sweet juice, seeds spat on the fertile ground. Some men shrugged out of their equipment, pulled off their coats to roll or fold them, stuff them in their knapsacks, sweat-soaked shirts covered now only by short, blue jackets. Frequent short halts, no more than five or six minutes, were just enough for readjustment of equipment, a moment's rest. Then "Assembly" rattled from the drums and men scrambled up, corporals organized their squads, sergeants their companies, the distance between companies reestablished and the order given to march.[10]

Dade drifted up and down the column from rear guard to advance and back, sometimes reining in to stare down at the men of the main body as they tramped by, two by two, water dripping from the bills of their leather hats, bootsteps almost silent on the wet sand. Their voices were a muffled medley, a babel of dialects and languages. "Yankees with their 'I reckon so,' [Southern] crackers with their nasal twang in answer to queries. Germans spluttering in high and low Dutch. Irish were predominant, swearing by the Holy Spoon and all the patron saints, Scotch who praised the land o' cakes with here and there a John Bull minus the letter 'h' in all his aspirations."[11]

Only half of the men were native-born Americans. They represented ten of the twenty-four states, most of them along the Atlantic seaboard from Maine to North Carolina, with a dozen men from Pennsylvania and four from Vermont. Although a good many of the slave hunters—and even settlers—pushing into Florida and clashing with the Seminoles were from Georgia and Alabama, no man from either state was in the ranks. In fact, the only Floridian with this army was Louis Pacheco. The rest—forty-five men—had come from Canada, England, Ireland, Scotland, Prussia, and Germany. Short and tall, young and old, domestic and foreign, more than half had come to the army as common laborers with no claim to any special skill, trade, or profession, typical of the "rag-tag-and-bobtail herd drafted into the ranks of the regular army . . . either the scum of the population of the older states, or of the worthless German, English, or Irish emigrants." Most were illiterate, ignorant of their own ignorance, boys who had left the farm or small town and joined up in a confusion of boredom and patriotism.[12]

Dade had done his first recruiting back in 1817, as a second lieutenant,

when he was twenty-five years old. Since then he'd signed them up in
New Orleans, Albany, Baltimore, right down to Key West as recently as
last January. Aside from his officers, Sergeant Thomas and half a dozen
others in the ranks were the only professional soldiers he had.[13]

Among the rest, their service records showed he had a dozen one-time
deserters in the ranks—kids, most of them. "Desertion, which is stated
to prevail to the extent of one half of the whole army annually . . . keeps
up the call for new recruits." Dade had done enough recruiting to know
the type: young fellows with no job, no family, no prospects, ready to
pitch it all and join the army. Six dollars a month, clothing, three squares
a day, and a bed could look mighty good when you were broke, cold, and
hungry. Then a couple of months down the road, when the girls and
glory the recruiting officers had talked about failed to appear, when the
novelty was over and the army looked like just another job, a boy here
or there would figure he could walk out like he'd walked in, free and easy.
Two years ago in Albany he had enlisted only eleven men in two months,
and by the time he'd signed up the last man two of the others had already
deserted.[14]

Most volunteers were disabused of the notion that they could simply
walk off when someone—civilian or soldier looking for the thirty-dollar
reward—caught them and delivered them to an officer of the nearest post
or recruiting station. Chances were that when the man or boy was brought
in, when he understood that the army was serious about the contract he
had made and the oath he had taken, he'd settle in and make a good soldier.
Take Joseph Wilson there. A musician. Enlisted a little more than two
years ago at Sackett's Harbor, New York. After six months he had walked
off, only to be brought back the next day. He had brown hair and eyes,
a dark complexion; at almost five feet ten inches he was taller than most,
at thirty-four a little older than the average, but for a year and a half now
he had served his turn with no problems. Boys or men, civilians in uniform
or real soldiers—he'd know soon enough if trouble came. There was
nothing like battle for sorting men out.[15]

Close up, watching the column pass, it was easy to think of these two
companies as an army, a weapon, trained and ready, more than sufficient
to cow any mob of undisciplined Indians. Maybe there weren't many
professionals in the ranks, but they were a long way from being raw

recruits. Regulations called for only two months of training, but there wasn't a man here who hadn't served at least a year already—most had two or three years and a few even four and five—and most of that on frontier service dealing with one tribe or another. Then, a glance away— the waving winter grass, the seemingly endless pine barren—and his little army faded to an absurdity. North of Thlonoto-sasa they had entered the Seminole reservation. Ahead, north and east and west, stretched four million acres of wilderness, and somewhere within that four million acres were three thousand Seminoles—men, women, and children. Would they stand back and let him through? Generals in Washington might refer to Seminoles as "miserable Indians," but soldiers in Florida thought other-wise. Any man who had seen combat duty in the last twenty years, since the war with England, had to have fought against, or alongside, Seminoles. Dade had done both. No one needed to tell him of their courage—or their respect for courage in others.[16]

In July 1825, before Fort King was built, Dade and Lt. George McCall had been on temporary duty at the Indian Agency. The agent, Gad Humphreys, had set up near the agency a large pen where government cattle were killed and butchered for Seminole consumption. Humphreys had invited the officers to join him and the Indians in trying their marks-manship. A steer had been selected for Capt. Jeremiah Yancy, but his shot only staggered the beast. It stood enraged, blood streaming from a wound below one eye. McCall had been asked to try his luck with the agent's reloaded rifle. He went over the eight-foot fence crowded with Seminoles and soldiers and advanced halfway across the pen before he could get the attention of the wounded animal and a fair chance for a forehead shot. Immediately the beast lowered its head and charged while McCall coolly raised his rifle and sighted in on the juggernaut. Almost at the sound of the shot the beast was falling dead at his feet, and McCall had not moved. Then a shout from the crowd gave warning that another animal had broken away from the herd across the pen and was charging down on him. There was no time to reload and little time to reach the safety of the wall. He got to the fence and had his foot on the lower rail with the infuriated beast only yards away when a big Seminole who had sprung to the top reached down, grabbed his arm, and snatched him up just as the onrushing steer crashed into the fence. For a moment the Indian held him, his arms around his body, one hand on his chest. He put him down and turned to Humphreys: "His heart is quiet: he was not afraid."[17]

Then in early 1827, while Dade was stationed in Waukeenah, east of Tallahassee, a party of Seminoles had been attached to his command. Under his leadership they had rendered excellent service, had earned five government medals "for their zeal and Activity in Scouring the Country . . . and taking from their lurking places, fifteen or twenty Indians, supposed to have been Connected with the murderers of the Carr family." Many Seminoles were six feet tall and more, in excellent health. "Miserable Indians," indeed. Yet on their own, without leadership, they amounted to nothing more than any disorganized mob. Dade had given it as his opinion then that "he could march through the Indian Nation with a Corporal's guard," and nothing since then had caused him to change his mind. If their warriors were now lying in wait they would likely be well armed with Spanish rifles made in Cuba, but they would still be nothing more than a dangerous mob.[18]

The end of the column was coming up, horses' hooves digging into the damp sand, straining against the weight of limber, carriage, and gun, the creak of the slowly turning wheels on the iron axles silenced by the lubricant of rain, then the lumbering oxen and the wagon. Dade touched silver spurs to his horse and moved up the line. Clinch and Belton had seen fit to put one hundred men in the middle of Seminole country. His job was to make the best he could of whatever came.

Pacheco met the advance guard a few miles south of the river, was passed through them and back to the major. He gave his report, asked if the slaughtered cow and the burnt bridge were not a warning, a sign of hostility. The major laughed. "Hostile? No. . . . That's old Bowlegs did that, Louis. He's been in the guard house at Tampa. He got away a few days ago, and he did that out of spite." Old Bowlegs? Bowlegs was the name the white men had given King Payne's brother Boleck, or Holata Micco, chief of the Alachua Seminoles twenty years ago. The old man had been dead near fifteen years. If the major meant *young* Bowleck, and the destruction at the river was *his*, then the warning was even more serious than he had thought. Pacheco had seen the cow, the bridge. He didn't need to know Seminole to read messages of death and destruction, no matter who left them. As alarmed by the major's light treatment of the matter as he had been by the carnage, he risked a cautious protest that "more than old Bowlegs did that," but he was talking to himself. Major Dade had ridden on.[19]

Indians! That damn fool slave acted scared to death by a few sign. What had he expected to find along this road? They were ten miles into Seminole country and going deeper every hour. Chances were they'd find worse than a dead cow and a burnt bridge before they made Fort King. They were making good time today, a dozen miles already, maybe a little more. Bleak land, somber winter grey of Spanish moss in barren trees, with the vivid green of palmetto and the evergreen pine here and there. The road wound between cypress swamps, crossed shallow, sluggish creeks, tannic acid staining the water a dark red. According to Lieutenant Duncan's account, it was along here that the body of the mail carrier, Pvt. Kinsley Dalton, had been found back in August, two days after he had left Fort Brooke on a mule, bound for Fort King. A young white man had found his mutilated remains in a pond near the road. Duncan had immediately brought a detachment up from the fort and visited a couple of Seminole towns, but all they knew—or would tell—was that Dalton had been stopped by six Mikasuki who had shot and scalped him and disemboweled the body. Duncan had buried Dalton close by, the grave unmarked and obscured to protect it from wolves.[20]

The savagery of the killing and the fact that the murderers had also shot Dalton's mule gave credence to the rumor that the Seminoles were settling a grudge. During the past summer eight warriors in search of game had slipped past the troops who patrolled the boundary of the reservation. Their luck was poor, and they had separated to cover more ground. The larger party found and butchered a cow belonging to a settler, dressed it out, and moved on. A few days later, at a place called Hickory Sink, near Kanapaha Pond, they met a party of Alachua settlers, members of the Spring Cove Guards, who had discovered the slain animal. The white men accused them of stealing and demanded that they surrender their weapons; the Seminoles offered no resistance. The guards had begun flogging the unarmed men with cattlewhips when shots had suddenly rung out from the forest. Three of the whites were staggered by the fire of the smaller party. In the confusion one Seminole was killed and another wounded. It was believed that the relatives of the slain Indian had killed Dalton.[21]

Even the general commanding U.S. troops in Florida had taken note of the death of this soldier. Duncan Clinch, meeting with militia Brig. Gen. Richard Keith Call and his brigade of five hundred volunteers at Fort Defiance on December 21, had accepted the tender of their services "to enable him to protect the frontier . . . & to cooperate in arresting the murderers of Private Dalton." Grateful for reinforcements of any kind, Clinch was profuse in his praise: "The utmost confidence is placed in the long experience, skill & firmness of Brigd. Genl. Call & in the patriotism & bravery of the Officers & Soldiers under his Command." That was three days ago. Now, the twenty-fourth, Call and his men had joined the regulars at Fort Drane.[22]

Clinch had promised the adjutant general only a week before that "as soon . . . as the Volunteers . . . arrive, I will not delay a moment, but strike at once at [the Seminole] Stronghold." He had been able to accumulate only three companies of U.S. troops, 150 men at best, hardly enough for serious work. On paper the accession of five hundred men had looked like a godsend, but as they trooped past here at Fort Drane on horses taken from the plow, hungry, armed with small shotguns entirely unfit for the field, poorly equipped and with only one week remaining of their four-week enlistment, he had sudden doubts. With enough regulars he might make something of this enthusiastic mob, but without Fanning and his three companies from Fort King, and Gardiner and four companies from Fort Brooke, the militia would outnumber his U.S. troops by better than three to one. And that wasn't all. Besides this "army" of planters and farmers he had already become host to 150 settlers—men, women, and children had begun to take refuge in the fort, and more were coming in every day. If he didn't make his move soon he would have neither the men nor the provisions left with which to make it.[23]

Fort Drane had been put up less than a month earlier on a three-thousand-acre tract of land in Alachua County that Clinch had accumulated by 1825. He had called the place Auld Lang Syne, literally "old long since" in Scottish, a phrase made popular in song by Robert Burns, referring to "times long past," the "good old times." Clinch had been thirty-eight then, a colonel in the U.S. Army, married to Eliza McIntosh, with four children. He also had some money and a few slaves. His troubles had been few, his duties mostly routine and safe. Through the years the fertile land of Auld Lang Syne had been cleared and set in sugarcane. He had built a sugar mill, a treacle warehouse, furnaces and vats for the production of sugar, and a rum distillery.[24]

By 1835 he had earned the honorary rank of brevet brigadier general and was referred to by his fellow officers as "the Spartan General" because he drank only water and preferred plain food. Plain maybe, but plenty of it—he weighed 250 pounds. He had eight children, more money, more slaves. He still drew only a colonel's pay, had even tried to resign his commission. Instead of accepting his resignation, the government had given him central command of all the troops in Florida and told him to get the Seminoles out—peaceably if possible, at the point of a bayonet if necessary.[25]

In January he had left his family in Mobile and, grumbling that the force assigned him was too small for an officer of his rank to command, set up temporary headquarters at Fort King in central Florida. On April 24, having secured agreement from eight of thirteen Seminole chiefs that they would begin moving toward Tampa Bay in December and board ship for the West in January, he wrote confidently: "[I shall] leave here to morrow for Mobile & remove my family with the least possible delay to St. Augustine." As he wrote, his wife was nine days dead of scarlet fever. Upon arrival in Mobile he could only attend her memorial service and arrange for the children to join Eliza's parents on their plantation in Georgia before setting off to take up lonely quarters in St. Augustine. The summer had brought more Indian trouble, not less. In August they killed Private Dalton, in November Chalo Emathla, a Seminole leader who supported relocation. By December Clinch had returned to Auld Lang Syne to wait for reinforcements in order to take the field against the Seminoles. The "good old times" were gone.[26]

Adjutant General Alexander Macomb, from Washington, had expressed in March the War Department's opinion that "two or three officers assisting the Indian agent for three weeks could accomplish the removal of the Indians." Clinch, in Florida, held a decidedly different opinion even then, based on "some small knowledge of the Indian character. . . . [T]hey have

not the least intention of [leaving Florida], unless compelled to do so by
a stronger force than *mere words*." While he had a low opinion of the
Seminoles' fighting ability and was frequently heard speaking of them to
his officers in a voice of "pity or disdain," even referring to them as
"children of the forest," he had no illusions about their ability to defend
themselves. "If a sufficient military force, to overawe them, is not sent
into the Nation, they will not be removed, and the whole frontier may
be laid waste." He had asked that four companies—"completely equipped
for active field service (& not with [only] 13 rounds of cartridges p[e]r
man)"—be sent to Fort King and two to Fort Brooke, each company to
be equipped with two six-pounders. Compared to the three officers suggested by Macomb, six companies had seemed like plenty.[27]

The soldiers had come, but not the cannon. In March, Clinch had
convened a council at Fort King. It had taken nearly a month to get down
to business. Meanwhile, he had made his few soldiers as conspicuous as
possible before fifteen hundred Seminoles. "On driving up to the fort . . .
we saw them in all directions; young and old, big and little; men, women
and children. Their *shantees* [sic] were to be seen in almost every quarter,
at irregular distances—as if dropped by chance—as far as the eye could
reach. They looked like men who had came [sic] there on business of
moment to them and theirs." When it finally came time for talking, the
only subject that mattered to either side was removal.[28]

The meetings were held on the open grounds, two hundred yards from
the fort. General Clinch, Agent Wiley Thompson, and all the junior
officers not needed elsewhere were in full military dress, seated in the
front rank. Behind them sat unarmed soldiers and a few civilians drawn
by business or curiosity. A young officer with pen, ink, and paper sat on
Clinch's right, prepared to report the proceedings. On the general's left
sat a black interpreter named Cudjo. "Near him stood a tall, square-
shouldered, weather-beaten looking man about 50 years of age, who had
been long amalgamated with the Indians, having married a squaw—and
who was present for the dual purpose of aiding Cudjoe [sic] when at
fault; and of seeing that he faithfully transfused from the English into the
Indian."[29]

Cudjo, a runaway, had first come to the notice of the whites during the
meetings at Payne's Landing in 1832, had been referred to—along with

Abraham—in the treaty as the Seminoles' "faithful interpreter." At the same time, he was considered a partisan of the whites and had been given quarters and rations in garrison as well as a monthly salary. He moved with a seeming stateliness of gait that had earned him the nickname "King Cudjo," though his carriage was involuntary, an apparent consequence of partial paralysis. It was assumed that his growing preference for white service rather than Seminole was the availability of better medical care. A small figure, with "cunning, squinting eyes," he sat, "hands folded across his lap, in seemingly meek attention to the scene around him."[30]

"The day was fine; and quite a sensation had been produced. Presently it was announced that the Indians were coming. There is something in the sound—Indian!—that seems to startle, always, the white man. . . . And even here—in a talk with the then pacific Seminole—the announcement of his approach to the Council, caused all present (even the cool Clinch) to give that sort of heed which seemed to say—'Look out!'[31]

"Up they came along the narrow path, and in the wonted 'file'—a long array!—silent, grave, and self-possest [sic]; and with all the dignity so peculiar to the Indians as a people. The first one who walked into the council, was a short, thick set, battered-looking old warrior, who had borne the brunt of many a fight; and brayed the soldiers of General Jackson. Oceola [sic], Jumper, and the rest (all but Micanopy), succeeded, one by one; and went through the ceremony of shaking hands.[32]

"We had all of us to give our hands of course; and a trying ordeal it was, not only from the number of palms we had to take, but from the quite too energetic *gripe* [sic] which each was sure to give us. The Indian, in shaking hands, raises up his arm, bringing it down with a *vim!* that is exceedingly expressive—for it not unfrequently forces the blood down into the very ends of your fingers. Before we had gone through with this preliminary, our hands had become all of the same charming colour—that is, black as the soot from the pine fires![33]

"General Thompson, a man of tall, powerful, frame rose, and commenced a speech. . . . Cudjoe, with his eyes rivited [sic] upon the speaker, appeared to drink in every word that he uttered." When Thompson paused after each sentence or two Cudjo addressed the waiting Seminoles, struggling to translate the agent's meaning. Observers, both military and civilian, were amused by his "wrapt [sic] attention" to the speaker, "satisfied that . . . he was not comprehending perhaps a syllable that was said," until assured by the white interpreter that "Cudjoe [had] reported faithfully—almost word for word—the language of the Agent."[34]

Most of the chiefs and warriors of the Seminole Nation sat facing the white men. One, evidently appointed speaker for the Nation, rose to his feet. There was whispering among the white visitors as those who knew him identified him to the others—Ote Emathla, or Jumper. A Creek, he had been a leader of the Fort Mims massacre in Alabama in 1813. When Andrew Jackson had defeated the Creeks, Ote Emathla had escaped to Florida, joined the Seminoles, and become adviser to Micanopy and "one of the most important men in councils and consultations." He was married to Micanopy's sister. He began speaking in a peculiar, musical voice.[35]

Impatient with the speed of translation, Thompson prompted, " 'What's he say, Cudjoe?' " The interpreter "sufficiently understood the Indian tongue to have easy converse with them, but to change a nation's language into our own, with his paucity of ideas, must have required a greater amount of skill than poor Cudjoe possessed." His English was not elegant. A former slave, he spoke "in the common negro jargon of the plantation, generally ending his translations with 'He sess so' or 'He say he sess so.'[36]

" 'He say he no go, he like this country very well, he born here, he not like to leave in his old age. He say Micanopi sent him to say so, and he also say he thought when last war hatchet was buried, you promised him no more trouble to his children. He say he did sign at Payne's Landing, but now dey had anoder governor and he must obey him. If he say "Dig up de hatchet" he is ready, he fear not death, it is his duty to die for his people.' " When Ote Emathla finished speaking, men who drew out their thick, gold watches noted that he had spoken for two hours. When pressed to explain his talk more fully, Cudjo could only grunt " 'he say he no go, dat all he say.' "[37]

" 'Tell him, Cudjoe,' said the agent, 'if he breaks his word with us,' at the same time pointing to Gen. Clinch, and the soldiers collected at the back, 'I shall be obliged to call upon the White warriors to force him.' "[38]

Ote Emathla watched and listened to Thompson, then Cudjo. He rose quickly, his arms spread, his expression scornful. He spoke again, interrupted by his own derisive laugh.[39]

" 'What's he say, Cudjoe?' "

" 'He say talk not to him of war! Is he a child that he fear it? No! He say when he bury the hatchet, he placed it deep in the earth with a heavy stone over it, but he say he can soon unearth it for the protection of his people. When he look upon the White man's warriors, he sorry to injure them, but he cannot fear them, he had fought them before, he will do so again, if his people say fight.' "[40]

Clinch, impatient with "unmeaning talk or idle objections," in a voice described as something "between a croak and a whisper," reminded the Seminoles that "their great father, the President, had told them that they must comply with their treaty & go to their new homes; that it was his wish that they should go quietly and peaceably; that he had caused every arrangement to be made for their comfort & convenience on the journey; but that he had also given [Clinch] the means, if they would not comply with their solemn treaty, to *compel them; and that [he] would do it*."[41]

But, another of the chiefs protested, I did not *sign* the treaty at Payne's Landing. Thompson, furious, turned to the interpreter. " 'Tell him from me, Cudjoe, that he lies!' The Indian plied his pipe, the while; and seemed coolly to puff away the insult with the smoke." With that, eight chiefs, with "a sullen, dogged air," had reluctantly signed a paper acknowledging the validity of the treaty. Ote Emathla, Halpatter Tustenuggee, Sam Jones, and Foke-luste Hadjo refused and stated that they spoke also for Micanopy. Furious with their audacity, Clinch concurred with Thompson in striking the names of all five from the list of chiefs.[42]

Still, not even the eight would agree to immediate removal. With the majority agreeing at least in principle, Clinch reported that he thought it best to give them an extension (approved beforehand by the War Department) until January 1836, particularly in the light of the fact that "the appropriation for their removal was made so late, that the agent . . . could not have made the necessary arrangements . . . before the hot season set in," even if the Seminoles *had* been willing. And he still thought that punctuating the talks with an occasional practice round from the six-pounders "would have had much weight in our deliberations." All things considered, he thought "the arrangement made with them, was . . . the best that could have been made."[43]

Perhaps the arrangement was the best in the logic of diplomacy, but many among the white observers, soldier and civilian alike, were troubled about the position of the United States in this whole affair. James Simmons, a white visitor from St. Augustine who had been at the fort for several days and had attended the meetings, pointed out that regardless of whether the Seminole leaders had signed the Payne's Landing and Fort Gibson documents or had been coerced, "Our Government has yet to answer the question, 'Were you not aware that the delegation had no authority to do what they did? that the Seminole . . . [people] had never agreed to be absolutely bound by what might be the views, or mere will, of that delegation? that they had instructed the chiefs to go and look at the land, and then to lay before them an account of all that they had seen? that, under these circumstances, the treaty, signed as it was, was something more than a mockery, was an attempted fraud upon the Seminole nation? that, being thus null and void, as wanting the high sanction of the people, with what show of justice, of fair dealing, of honor or humanity, did you hold up this faithless deed to that people, and because they indignantly disavowed it, call to your aid the sharp but unworthy argument of the sword?"[44]

Such musings had no place on the military agenda. Rather, Clinch had hopes that if the show of troops and cannon could be continued, "the whole Nation may yet be induced to move together by the 1st December." But it was his decided opinion that "not a soldier should be ordered from Florida, until after the removal of the Indians, as the least move toward diminishing the present force would ruin every thing." To keep up the pressure in the face of discharges and desertions, he urged that recruits be sent to fill up every company in Florida by the first of November. Equally important, any reinforcements for Fort King should come down the St. Johns River to Picolata, then march south, entering reservation land only a few miles from the fort. If troops were sent down the Gulf and landed at Fort Brooke, their entire march to Fort King would be through hostile territory.[45]

This matter of logistics was becoming crucial. Back in January when Clinch had first asked for more support, the threat of war had been only a cloud on the distant horizon. Then troops could march in relative security wherever they chose throughout the territory, the Seminole reservation notwithstanding. This great oval, lying like an undigested pill in the belly of the land, was veined with military roads, a right of the government stipulated in the Treaty of Moultrie Creek. It was true that in surrendering all their land but this at Moultrie the Seminoles had been guaranteed "peaceable possession" as well as "protection against all persons whatsoever," but the United States reserved "the right of opening through [the reservation] such roads . . . as may . . . be deemed necessary." The Seminoles had further accepted the provision that "any citizen of the United States . . . shall be permitted to pass and repass through the [reservation] and to navigate the waters thereof without any hindrance, toll, or exactions from said tribes."[46]

Slave hunters were citizens. They had every right to pursue their quarry, wherever the trail might lead. Clinch, like everyone who owned slaves, had a just regard for the monetary value of such property. He was still attempting to recover the cost of two slaves recently killed by Indians at his Auld Lang Syne plantation. He believed that slaves were inferior beings who had an obligation of servitude and obedience to their masters; like a horse or dog, if a slave ran away the owner had every right to reclaim him. Naturally, if a slave hunter found a runaway within the Nation it followed that he would apprehend the fugitive. Proof? What proof of ownership would make sense to a Seminole, who in all likelihood could not even *speak* English, much less read a legal document?[47]

Of course, it was to be expected that "interested and designing men" among the Seminoles would make the most of every such little problem in an attempt to cause unrest. Ote Emathla had made much of them at countless dreary, inconclusive meetings. "We have submitted to one demand after another . . . in the hope that they would cease, but it seems that there will be no end to them, as long as we have anything left that the white people may want. . . . We were promised justice, and we want to see it!"[48]

Slave hunters and the "Whisky Gentry" on one hand, Ote Emathla and—more recently—Osceola on the other, had continued in relentless pursuit of their goals through the spring, summer, and fall, turning resentment into anger, anger into hatred, hatred into violence. The reservation had become a hornet's nest, Seminoles darting out to burn and kill, then returning, disappearing into the nest.

The once distant cloud of war was now directly overhead, hopes for peaceful removal all but gone. Surrounded, outnumbered, and "willfully deluded," the majority of the Seminoles seemed simply to ignore the fact that once again the date for emigration would soon arrive. By October 8 Clinch had come to the conclusion that "we shall have to strike a blow at the Mickasuki tribe, before they will . . . agree to comply with their Treaty." But to patrol the Seminole border, "enforce a compliance with their Treaty . . . give such protection to the frontier settlements, as their apprehensions from the Indians . . . induce them to expect from the Government," and mount an offensive required more men than he could put in the field. His total command of regulars in Florida was 536, only 26 of them officers. Since the frontier alone was over five hundred miles long, if he posted one man every mile there would be no one left to water the horses. "I strongly . . . recommend, the calling into the service of the U. States . . . one hundred and fifty mounted volunteers." "This specie of force would . . . be the most efficient & least expensive . . . that could be employed—Being well mounted & all of them good woodsmen & good riders, & well acquainted with every part of the country—& . . . deeply interested in its protection—would give them a decided advantage over any other species of Troops." Perhaps most important, they were near.[49]

Expresses continued to bring reports of depredations by the Seminoles. It was said they were collecting stores of war materials; Osceola was heard to boast that he had 150 kegs of powder. A letter from Bvt. Lt. Col. Alexander Fanning, in command at Fort King, pointed out the weakness of the garrison, while Asst. Surgeon Archer reported that nearly a hundred men had been on sick report and were still unfit for active fieldwork. Growing more anxious by the day, Clinch had written Macomb again on October 17: "I may have rather underestimated the means necessary to carry into effect the views and plans of the government." He admitted that in his previous letter he had given it as his opinion that "the force [of Regulars] already in Florida [is] sufficient to meet and control the whole of the Refractory Seminoles if they could be concentrated." However, he reminded the adjutant general that he had also pointed out that, "when Scattered over a large extent of Country, composed of marshes & swamps that are almost impenetrable to the white man, [my force] is entirely inadequate to give that protection and quiet to the frontier inhabitants which they Expect. I therefore . . . request that three additional Companies be ordered to Fort King with as little delay as practicable." Time and route were critical. "Should this request be complied with, and the Companies ordered from the North it would be economy of time and money to engage transports drawing not more than eight feet water to take the Troops direct to the St. Johns river and land them on the west side of that river opposite Picolata, where there is a good road leading to Fort King."[50]

On the same day, he wrote to the officer in command at Key West, Bvt. Maj. Francis Dade, directing him "as soon after the first of December next, as may be practicable, [to] . . . proceed with [your command] to Fort Brooke." Key West was about the only point in Florida *not* under threat of attack. The commanding officer at Fort Brooke could use all the men he could muster to defend the post, protect settlers in his vicinity, and guard those Seminoles agreeable to emigration who had fled to the adjacent encampment.[51]

Responding on October 22 to Clinch's letter of the eighth, Secretary of War Lewis Cass replied that there was no authority to grant his request for mounted volunteers, but "a few days since . . . two additional companies were placed at your disposal, and I have this day directed the Adjutant General to put two more companies under your orders. . . . This force, it appears to me, must be sufficient for all the purposes required."[52]

Enclosed was a copy of the order directing the commandants of forts Wood and Pike in Louisiana, Fort Morgan in Alabama, and Fort Pickens in Florida to hold their companies in readiness to join Clinch. Four companies, fifty more men than he had requested. Well and good—on paper. But Pickens and Morgan were four hundred and more coastal miles from Tampa Bay, Wood and Pike six hundred. The commanding officers wouldn't set sail until confirming orders were received, which would likely be two to three weeks. If they were ready to board immediately upon receipt of the order, the trip down the coast would take another two weeks at least. Which all added up, assuming they had good luck and good weather, to an arrival in mid-December at best, God knew when at worst. And where would they be on that distant day? Fort Brooke—another week away—one hundred miles, and every foot of it through hostile country. Mr. Cass's smug complacency and refusal to consider the logistics involved were infuriating. Perhaps Seminoles were not the only people "willfully deluded."[53]

Clinch sent the orders, four of them, while hourly he was "importuned for protection, arms &c from every quarter." Frustrated, he left St. Augustine for Fort King on November 4. Forbidden to enroll volunteers, he had only one source of reinforcement—the four companies from the west. It was much to be regretted that Washington had ignored his advice, that the companies had not been ordered from the Atlantic instead of the Gulf. As it was, it was impossible for him to form any idea of when they would arrive at Fort Brooke, much less when—and if—they could cross the Seminole Nation to join him. Yet until they joined, his forces would be equally divided, neither force strong enough to effect much in country like this. He had no choice except to take the risk. From Fort King on November 13 he sent a second order to "The Officer in Command" at Fort Brooke, directing him to order Fraser's and Gardiner's companies "to proceed to this post as soon as practicable," the other two companies to follow as soon as they arrived. Of the many officers due to converge on Fort Brooke it was difficult to determine who would be in command, but whoever he was Clinch would have to leave it to him to judge from the movements of the enemy in his own neighborhood as to just when "practicable" might be.[54]

When Clinch left Fort King a few days later, everything had appeared quiet within the Seminole boundary, but he had no sooner returned to St. Augustine than an express from Fanning brought word on the twenty-ninth of the assassination of Chalo Emathla. Fanning stated flatly that Osceola was at the bottom of "a deep laid plan of villany [sic]" and he "intended that Cohadjo & Hotatkee OMatler should share his [Chalo Emathla's] fate." The next day another express arrived from Fanning with the warning that "you are marked as a victim; therefore, be wary, come quickly, but come with force.—I need not tell you of the practice of the Indians to send out small skulking parties to way lay [sic] their victims."[55]

Exposure to frequent rains and the first breath of winter had laid the general low with an attack of chills and fever. From his sickbed on December 1 he reported to Macomb that he had been too unwell to travel but would start for Fort King the next morning and "will make an effort to collect on the way a sufficient number of volunteers to protect the Northern Section of our frontier, & if I can do so, will indeavour [sic] to give the hostile party sufficient amusement within their own limits."[56]

There seemed no shortage of volunteers in St. Augustine—the evening before "a volenteer [sic] Company Called the Florida rangers recently organised [sic] in this City, tendered to me their services in a very spirited and soldierlike manner and expressed a willingness to march at a moment's notice to any point they might be required, but I had no authority to accept them." Being urgently in need of men and yet unable to accept them when they offered was a galling and paradoxical position. As an officer of the regular army he had no authority over either volunteers or militia; only state or local authority could organize or officer them. If such an officer cared to *cooperate* with federal forces, well and good, but to reach that point took time that Clinch didn't have. He had to move *now* with whatever regulars he could muster. On the other hand, all indications were that the problem would be a long time in the solving, and such local assistance, however long in coming, would likely still be useful. He wrote to Florida's acting governor G. K. Walker, "I . . . suggest to your Excellency the importance of immediately calling Out, and placing on the Indian Frontier; one hundred & fifty mounted men.—This force if ordered to cooperate with the regular Troops under my command, will in my opinion be sufficient to give protection to the frontier settlements."[57]

With his staff and a single company under the command of Capt. Gustavus S. Drane, Clinch set out once again for Fort King, traveling west to the St. Johns River, a distance of eighteen miles by good road. Crossing the mile and a half of river, they entered Picolata, "a beautiful spot indeed," shaded by giant oaks, where "I found every one in a state of much allarm [sic] and excitement." He witnessed firsthand "the panic and suffering of the white . . . inhabitants." The urgency of settlers fleeing the frontier with their stories of death and destruction at the hands of "these incendiary and murderous wretches" decided him on a change in strategy. He had planned to march directly to Fort King, then strike south at the Seminole towns in the Great Swamp, where it was understood that the Seminoles living in the vicinity of Fort King had gathered after the killing of Chalo Emathla. But that course offered only the possibility of a battle—he wanted war. The fundamental problem in fighting Indians was to bring them to bay, make them stand and fight. Civilized men had brought art to war, using organized bodies of men, well trained and well armed, to fight other men similarly equipped, supported by ever larger wheeled guns, supplied by ever greater numbers of wagons; more and more powerful, more and more ponderous. Seminoles, on the other hand, "spread themselves through the Country, taking advantage of their knowledge of the swamps and hammocks to conceal their operations." It was like attempting a game of chess with an opponent who was ignorant of the game: without his making the proper moves he denied you the chance of winning. "The time has arrived when it becomes my duty, to act decidedly and efficiently, as far as my means will enable me to do so."[58]

Instead of turning south for Fort King, he would continue west fifty miles to Newnansville, encouraging volunteers from the white settlements along the way, then head south to Micanopy and on to his plantation, Auld Lang Syne. From there, as soon as he was in sufficient strength, he could continue south to strike a blow at the heart of the Seminole stronghold, the swamps and hammocks, the Cove of the Withlacoochee River where the *families* of the Seminoles were supposed to be concealed. When the Seminole warriors learned that he was a threat to their nest they would swarm to him, thereby "fulfilling his hope of bringing on a general engagement."[59]

The road to Newnansville looped south below Big Sante Fe Pond, passing some thirty miles north of Fort King. Along the way the need of the settlements for protection seemed so desperate that Clinch took the unprecedented step of appealing directly to the people for two hundred and fifty mounted volunteers to provide the protection that he could not. Reaching Newnansville on the fifth, he found the town overflowing with refugees and reported to Governor Walker that "I find the allarm [*sic*] still increasing and familys [*sic*] flying in every direction. . . . Information has this moment reached me that the houses are burnt in several directions on the immediate line of frontier."[60]

From Newnansville to Micanopy was a thirty-mile march, passing the San Felasco Hammock, crossing the Alachua Prairie, two days of tramping around the marshes, through the pine barrens, fallen needles smothering all growth except the tall winter grass. Only upon reaching Micanopy, when Captain Drane, scornful of the Seminole threat, ordered his men to load with powder and ball, did the staff learn that they had made the entire journey protected by men with unloaded muskets.[61]

Gustavus Drane was an old-timer, in years as well as service. Now in his forties, he had enlisted as a private in 1812, had come up through the ranks without missing a step; corporal, sergeant, third, second, and first lieutenant by 1817, brevet captain ten years later, and captain in 1832. His attitude reflected that of many officers—that Seminoles would strike a lonely cabin anytime but that an attack on armed men was another story. Men in the ranks might be fearful of attack, but if the captain and even General Clinch saw fit to march them through enemy country with empty muskets a man could only hope they were right. As for Clinch, his concern was to bring on a battle, not avoid it.[62]

Micanopy, established in 1821, was the oldest settlement in East Florida. From nearby Fort Defiance, Clinch reported to the adjutant general on the ninth: "It is truly distressing to witness the panic and sufferings of the white frontier inhabitants. Men, women, and children are seen flying in every direction, and leaving everything behind them save a few articles of clothing. Many families that were comfortable and independent in their circumstances, are now reduced to want; their houses and their all having been plundered and burned. . . . My first object is to throw a sufficient force on the Indian line to drive [the Seminoles] within their limits. . . . I will teach them, that altho' the Government has been heretofore mild and indulgent to them, that it knows when and how to punish them for their treachery and bad faith." As for raising volunteers, "it was in vain to urge them to organize and throw themselves in advance of the enemy to check their progress. Nothing could be done until their families were secured." Clinch sounded a second ominous note in concluding his report: "It appears also that [the Indians] are joined by the negroes, and if they are not promptly put down, this spirit may extend to the plantations." No man who owned another could put aside for long the fear of revolt.[63]

With his small but growing force, Clinch left Fort Defiance on December 14 on the final ten-mile march to his own plantation. Drane sent out no scouts or pickets, only a few woodchoppers two hours ahead of the command to clear the path of windfalls. One soldier in the column wrote, "Ours was a miraculous escape, for if we had met the foe none would have survived to tell this tale." Secure for the moment at Auld Lang Syne, they would await Fanning, Gardiner, Fraser, and their regulars, Call and his militia, then settle this Seminole problem.[64]

Afternoon was nearly gone. Even on the march, rain-soaked clothing would soon begin to chill. Dade planned to make camp at the river, cross in the morning one way or another. According to the slave there was nothing left of the bridge, but what would he know of bridges, engineering, construction? There might be a chance to fell trees, reach to the pilings, cross dry. Otherwise they'd ford. If they weren't delayed too long they should be able to reach the comparatively high land between the two major rivers by tomorrow night. Then it would be downhill to the Big Withlacoochee. That's where the real danger lay, at the Withlacoochee and beyond.

According to Holata Emathla, hostile Seminoles were lying in wait somewhere in the forks of the Withlacoochee, the six- to seven-mile stretch between the Big and Little Withlacoochees. Swampland, most of it. Should be dry now, but there had been plenty of years when the rainy season had put most of it underwater. Seminoles could slip and slide through it like the snakes and alligators they shared it with, but it was a tough place for white men—for men who moved and fought on their feet instead of on their bellies. If Belton's intelligence was accurate, the Seminoles lying in wait outnumbered him better than two to one, but it would also be regular army against Indians, disciplined men against a mob. Experience had shown that organization, training, and discipline could outweigh sheer numbers, particularly when fighting Indians. With guards on the flanks and advance and rear guards out he'd have plenty of warning if hostiles were sighted. With a few men on the gun and the rest deployed as infantry, taking cover as they could, it should discourage any mob from attack. And if they made it past the forks and reached the high land beyond, their difficulties and dangers should be over. No Seminole with any sense would let them pass through the swamps and then attack in high, open country. Finally, of course, the whole thing came down to a gamble, a bluff, but if a man wanted guarantees he shouldn't join the army.

The Dade family tradition held that the progenitor of the family name in America was Francis Dade I, born in England in 1600. Attached to the court of the Stuarts, he had been captured in battle, sold into slavery in Russia, had killed his master with a flail, fled to France, changed his name to John Smith, and come to America. As Capt. John Smith he became the first governor of the infant colony of Virginia. It was a fine tradition. It might even be true.[65]

Francis had been born to Townshend and Elizabeth Dade on February 22, 1792, in King George County, Virginia. It would not have been overlooked that it was the sixtieth birthday of President Washington. In 1808, when Francis was sixteen, his father's death had left his mother with two daughters and one son older than Francis, one daughter younger. At twenty-one he had taken a commission as a third lieutenant in the Twelfth Infantry. He had served with his regiment in the war against England. In 1814 he had been promoted to second lieutenant, transferred to the Fourth Infantry in 1815, and had made first lieutenant in 1816. He had served for the most part in southern stations: South Carolina, Louisiana, Alabama. He had chased Indians, cleared roads, built forts.[66]

As a newly appointed captain in 1818, Dade and his regiment were serving under Gen. Andrew Jackson when Jackson entered Spanish-held Florida and seized Pensacola, bringing negotiations for the purchase of Florida to a halt and the country to the edge of war. Dade thought Pensacola "delightfully situated, possessing in a great degree that most valuable of all blessings, health." In spite of the threat implied by the American soldiers, Dade found the inhabitants "polite and disposed to be friendly towards us; a few weeks ago the American officers gave them a ball, at which I had the pleasure of seeing many beautiful Spanish Damsels, who were very affable and enticeing. Could I have spoken their language I should have fallen in love."

Back in Pensacola in 1821, he had been officer of the day on August 22 when then-governor Jackson demanded that certain papers in the possession of Don Jose Callava, the former governor of West Florida, be turned over to him. Captain Dade had taken personal custody of Lt. Domingo Sousa, a clerk of Callava, who stated on examination that he had ordered the papers taken to Colonel Callava. Dade escorted Sousa to the residence of George M. Brooke, colonel of Dade's regiment, where Callava was a dinner guest. Sousa asked for the return of the papers in question. Brooke and his wife, along with Callava, expressed their outrage that their guest had been disturbed. Polite but undeterred, Dade took Callava's refusal back to Jackson. When the former governor returned to his home, Dade arrested him and brought him before Jackson. Upon his continued refusal to turn over the papers, Dade finally escorted the outraged diplomat to jail. Now Brooke was a brevet brigadier general in command of the Fifth Infantry in Michigan Territory, Jackson was president. Connections like those couldn't hurt a man's career.[67]

Since then he had returned to Florida again and again, serving at most of the posts, camps, and stations maintained by the army from Pensacola to Key West. The exertion and the hot, damp climate had combined to send him home to Virginia, sick, for months at a time. Aside from illness, his only time out of the Territory was generally on recruiting service in the north—it was this duty that had kept him from taking part in the establishment of Fort Brooke—but he had enjoyed a return to civilization as much as any man. The recruiting rendezvous in Albany, New York, for instance, could bring back many a memory. There was his favorite oyster and porter house where he sometimes had found it necessary to ask the innkeeper to help him up the stairs and into his bed; the group of females at his boardinghouse with whom he'd had a frolic and who then complained to the authorities that they had been insulted; the look on Captain Fay's face that last Saturday night when he had gone by to settle his accounts with him. Thomas Fay was a quartermaster captain, straitlaced and finicky, a man obsessed with his clothing accounts, invoices, and receipts—a bookkeeper, not a soldier. It was January, maybe February, 1827. Orders had come for Dade to close the rendezvous, return to duty in the South again. While celebrating the night before leaving he had drunk perhaps a little more than was wise, but he had remembered that he needed to see Fay before leaving. The difficulty he encountered in getting out of his carriage and into the house had brought the realization that he was not in any condition to do business. About all he remembered saying was "Well Fay, I'm going off—I want to do some business with you, but am too damned drunk." Never did see him again.[68]

But those were the last adventures of his bachelor days. Soon after returning to Pensacola he had met Amanda Malvina Middleton, daughter of Isaac Middleton, a carpenter in the shipyards. Pensacola was a city where you could meet a lot of women—Spanish, French, English, Creole. The air was soft, sultry, the ladies lovely, their "languid mode of utterance, accompanied by the luring sweetness of expression natural to their soft, dark eyes . . . well calculated to wake the tender passion," in the words of his friend and fellow officer, Lieutenant McCall. Amanda Middleton was sixteen, living with her younger sister, Mary, and their widowed father. On December 6 she and twenty-nine-year-old Francis Dade were married by Charles Hardy, a minister of the gospel. Amanda had been born in the District of Columbia, but she grew up in Pensacola. Francis was content to make the ancient city their home. They bought a comfortable frame house near the bay on the north side of West Gregory Street, between Baylen and Palafox. He was there on leave three years later when their daughter, Fannie Langhorne, was born.[69]

Since then he had been posted to New Orleans again, then Albany, Baltimore, and, since November 1833, Key West. The island had long been a naval depot and station where as many as three thousand American ships alone passed in one year. Commodore David Porter considered it the best harbor in the United States south of the Chesapeake. A temporary military camp had been established in 1831 on the northwest edge of the two-thousand-acre island, fronting the bay. By 1834 it had grown into a twenty-two-acre military post. Benjamin Nourse, ranking medical officer, believed that "if ardent spirits could be kept entirely from the men there would be but very little for the Doctor to do among them," but Dade considered Key West "the most sickly post of the South." In March he was granted a seven-month leave, his "constitution having been much impaired by severe attacks of disease brought on by exposure in the discharge of my duties" as commandant.[70]

By November he had recuperated and was able again to resume his duties at Key West, as well as continue his broad social acquaintance among the four hundred or so white civilians living on the island, by whom he was "highly esteemed." This time he took Amanda and Fannie with him, along with fifteen recruits, arriving on the twenty-second. Dade put the new recruits to work as carpenters and masons in an effort to complete the construction of the public buildings, never completed and falling into decay.[71]

Fortunately, Amanda and Fannie had returned to Pensacola when a hurricane struck the following September. The storm lasted three days and left the coast strewn with wrecks, blowing a dozen large ships onto

the reefs near Key West and terrifying the islanders. There was a theory
that Halley's Comet was responsible for the storm. According to the Key
West *Enquirer*, an English officer had predicted that the comet "would
cause the year 1835 to be remarkable for the frequency of gales and other
atmospheric phenomena." The *Army and Navy Chronicle* had reported that
the comet was visible to the naked eye in Washington the same month
the hurricane occurred in Florida, but it was generally considered no more
than a coincidence.[72]

Fannie would be five years old in a few days, about the time he ought
to be bringing this bunch into Fort King. With a safe trip, Colonel Fanning
reinforced, and Clinch on higher duty, was it too much to hope he might
make permanent major—with a permanent increase in salary? The year
after his marriage he had been promoted to major—by brevet—"for 10
years faithful service in one grade." Now he was forty-three years old and
had spent half his life as an officer in the U.S. Army. Brevet rank wasn't
much consolation after seven years; half-inch gold lace instead of quarter-
inch on his epaulets didn't count for much without a major's pay and
command. Except in his case, now. According to regulations he would
draw a major's pay as long as he commanded two companies, which looked
like maybe ten days. As a captain he drew forty dollars a month; as a
major, fifty. So as far as this little jaunt went he could expect an extra
$3.33 at the end of the month. Amanda would like that.[73]

The Table of Command called for 316 lieutenants and 136 captains,
but only 22 majors. In time of war the mortality rate among majors was
high enough that waiting captains could anticipate early promotion, but
there hadn't been a real war for nineteen years. It was a fact of military
life that the only hope for rapid advancement and higher pay was through
the death of one's superior officers, and it followed that an officer who
cared to advance in the world might look forward to the possible outbreak
of war in spite of the often-touted blessings of peace. Most peacetime
blessings were for civilians. A soldier's blessings were promotion and
higher pay, and a little war could do wonders for those—provided, of
course, that you didn't get yourself killed. Real promotion depended on
war, and these days war depended on Indians. Not much in that for a
man to stake his future on.[74]

Indians. Killing some poor devil like Dalton was their idea of war. Six to one. This command numbered over one hundred guns and a cannon, disciplined men, well-trained officers—five West Pointers, for what that was worth. To get the kind of odds that Indians liked they'd have to round up maybe a thousand warriors. And who would lead that kind of mob? They had no discipline, no chain of command, no real leader. Each man was independent, could fight or not as he chose. Chasing some poor slave hunter out of their camp or shooting down unarmed settlers was one thing, but going up against armed soldiers, trained and ready, and against a cannon to boot, was something else. Not many would be likely to choose battle. As Dade looked out across the grass, beneath the high-limbed pines, it was hard even to picture such an attack, waves of Seminoles coming on in line, taking orders from others, firing on command. Not likely. If the men all kept their heads up, eyes open, they had nothing to fear. After all, it was Fort King that was supposed to be in danger. Again.

Ten years ago last July a letter had come from then-agent Col. Gad Humphreys at the Seminole Agency, asking for as strong a military force as could be spared from Fort Brooke. Fort King had not yet been built and the agency stood alone. Serious trouble was expected from the Seminoles. As senior captain and commanding Company C, Fourth Infantry, Dade had been in charge of the detachment, with Lieutenant McCall in temporary command of Company D. Equipped with sixty rounds of ball cartridges, ten days' rations per man, and four pack mules carrying subsistence and extra ammunition, they had left Fort Brooke the morning after receiving Humphreys's request. The whole country seemed to be in alarm, troops at St. Augustine ordered into the field, Seminoles organizing war parties, settlers running for the towns and forts. There was no road then, no bridges, just an old Indian trail. "One day was a counterpart of the preceding one: a march through woods of the long-leaf pine, occasionally intersected with savannas of tall grass, either wet or dry, according to the season, and now decidedly wet; or obstructed by rivers. Three of the latter, besides small streams, we forded; the water being from two and a half to three and a half feet deep. At night we slept on our arms, having no tents." Yet Colonel Brooke had commended him "for the quickness and rapidity of the movement through a country . . . almost impossible to the Indians themselves [because of high water]." Of course they hadn't had to struggle with a cannon that time, but, in spite of Seminole threats, he'd brought his command through in only five days and without a scratch. No reason he couldn't do it again.[75]

It was late afternoon when they came through the last pine barren before the river. The grey sky had stopped its weeping. On the left the sun was a silver glare above the trees. From the saddle he could see a smudge of smoke hanging in the misty air, the cypresses beyond that marking the river's edge. The road divided short of the river, the left-hand branch wider, passing the remains of the sutler's store, beyond it rising gently to the bluff and the burned bridge. To the right was the old path that sloped to the river and the ford. If they had to use it, the water would be no more than waist deep this time of year.

Again he ordered a half-dozen guards to be posted no less than one hundred yards out around the camp perimeter, gave particular orders that no one be allowed to straggle off into the woods and that the men not race down to the river for water in a disorderly manner. Unseen Seminoles would be watching their every move, ready to cut off any man that got careless. Noncommissioned officers set the men to making camp, and axes began biting into pine.[76]

Seminole fire had done its work on the bridge. Nothing was left but the charred remains of the trestles and here and there a few main timbers and planks dangling by one end, flames still flickering along their edges. Looked like it might have been set on fire a day or two before, time enough to nearly consume the huge uprights, hewed and squared to fourteen by sixteen inches, some twenty feet tall from mud sill to cap sill. Bridges in this part of the country were commonly built of " 'light wood' or heart of pine," hard and durable "whether under water or exposed to the air," but the very pitch that preserved it made a ready and furious fire.[77]

Dade wrote a brief report to Belton. He assured him that there had been no trouble so far, though the bridge was no good to them and would necessitate making a ford and cause delay. If reinforcements were ready to move out and could make good time, if this detachment held up for a day or two, perhaps they might still effect a rendezvous. It was a slim hope, but not one to be ignored. He sealed the report and called for a volunteer. A soldier from Gardiner's company was brought to him, Pvt. Aaron Jewell, Company B, Second Regiment Artillery. He was twenty-four years old, stood five foot six and a half inches tall. He had brown hair, a light complexion. He stared at the major through grey eyes. He had been a farmer in Vermont, had gone down to Rochester and joined up a year ago last October. Like Joseph Wilson, the army hadn't been just what he'd thought it would be and he had left it after two months' service, just chucked it all and walked off. For its part, the army didn't care much for that and had brought him back after only four days. Since then he had been pretty steady, had served one year with two more to go. Maybe he thought volunteering for a job like this would do something to offset the desertion on his record. He might be right.[78]

Jewell had discarded his haversack, eaten and drunk his fill. He was ready to head back. With luck he could figure on averaging maybe three miles an hour, reach the fort around midnight. It would mean traveling the road—through the woods it could take twice as long—but one man, on foot and alone, would be a small target in the dark. Seminoles had been around the camp last night, would probably be just out of sight, out of range all the way to Fort King, but they couldn't cover the whole road the whole time. No reason for them to expect a courier to be traveling at night. If their plan was to pick them off one by one from ambush they could have started anytime. Everyone in the outfit had his own theory as to whether Jewell would or wouldn't make it. He had twenty-three miles to go, night was coming. No one had any doubts about his courage.

Other messengers prepared to travel north. As evening fell beyond the soldiers' fires, dark-skinned men rose from the ground here and there, men who wore turbans of trade cloth wrapped about straight, black hair, cotton hunting shirts with long sleeves that hung nearly to the knee, tanned buckskin leggings, and single-piece moccasins gathered and tied on top of the foot. They drifted through the woods like smoke, slipping into the water of Lokcha-papka-chiska as silently as wee-hatke, the water snake. Across the river the scouts began a tireless trot along the old Indian trail, widened by the soldiers in times past in order to bring their wagons and guns into the Seminoles' land. The night was half gone by the time the runners came to the high south bank of the Weewa-thlock-ko, flowing through a narrow gorge cut through a pine bluff. They waded through, followed the far shore west and north, mile after mile. When they reached the Wewachatkwa, low and barely flowing, it hardly slowed them, and

by the time a slice of nethle-hasse, the night sun, had begun to shine in
the dry, black sky they had reached the Great Swamp. From the combined
waters of the Weewa-thlock-ko and the Wewachatkwa on the west the
swamp was an hour's travel wide to the rising woodland on the east, a
half day's travel to the north. Jumping from one half-submerged log to
another, then walking backwards, crawling on hands and knees, twisting
their way through heavy timber and a matrix of vines across the dryer
stretches, crossing and recrossing their own tracks, they left no trail a
white man could follow. Finally, the gleam of fires on a hammock, warriors,
camp.[79]

A chief, a man of forty years, well made, his face long and narrow,
eyes small and keen, nose prominent, tall, as lean and hard as chuli, the
pine, listened to their reports. Ote Emathla was acknowledged above all
other Seminoles as an orator, a man of sense, and a brave warrior. He
was counselor and sense-bearer to old and indolent Micanopy.[80]

Iste-hay-chulkay-mastchay, the-men-who-had-gone-to-see, had been
out from the time the soldiers had left the fort. Last night and now again
they reported that the soldiers were coming closer. They had been coming
closer for as long as he could remember, they and the slave catchers. First
the white people of Carolina had tried to enslave Creek Indians, and later,
blacks. The Creeks had retreated into Georgia. When blacks escaping
slavery had followed them, even moving further south into virtually unin-
habited Florida, the Indians referred to them as runaways, or Seminoles.
Then a portion of the Creeks had broken with their fellows and, under
their chief, Seacoffee, had also come to Florida, become Seminoles, or
runaways, themselves. The soldiers and slave catchers were not far
behind.[81]

Against their own laws, the American, Jackson, had brought his soldiers
into Florida. It mattered nothing that many Seminoles, black and red,
had been born to this land, and their fathers and fathers and fathers before
them. They had taken the land from no one. The ancient Indians were
gone, the white men who called themselves Spanish lived in small towns
mostly far to the east and west near the great seas. Here Seminole birth-
blood had sunk into the land and made the country dear to them. They
had lived a free life, farming and hunting, with none to question their
bounds or dispute their range. Bark and palmetto dwellings had multiplied,

become villages, grown into towns surrounded by acres of cleared fields. Wild offspring of strayed Spanish cattle had been developed into herds.[82]

Jackson had killed and gone away. The Seminoles, red and black, had been driven down and down, to Tampa Bay and further, bands scattered throughout the land. For a moment there was peace, but then the soldiers and slave catchers were back again. This time settlers came with them. When asked by what right they had come the Americans talked of having "bought" the land from the Spanish. Could a man "buy" totika, the fire, hulallay, the wind, wewa, the water? No more could he buy ecunnraw, the earth. Totika, hulallay, and wewa were the gifts of the Great Spirit that gave humans life, ecunnraw the place where he could live that life and have his being. They belonged to a man only so long as he could feel the fire, breathe the air, drink the water, walk the earth. Then they were given back and given back forever. How then could it be that the Americans could *buy* Florida when no one could own it? Yet if the land belonged to anyone it belonged to the Seminoles.[83]

It made no difference. White men seemed to fill the land like okeepa, the mosquito, biting at the People. They came down from the land of the now-hated Creeks in the north, in from the great seas on east and west. They infested the land like fleas on an unclean blanket. And still no Seminole had been able to believe their numbers, their greed. They would kill a bird for a feather and never miss his song, a bear for his coat and leave the meat to rot. They respected the spirit in no living thing. Gain was all. They claimed that blacks who lived among the Seminoles were slaves who had escaped them, and demanded their return. Indifference among the Seminoles turned to hatred, and here and there meetings led to murder. Soldiers came, searching for guilty Indians. It was not known if they ever looked for guilty white men.

Neamathla, principal chief of the Mikasuki, had said to the white man who was called the governor, "Do you think . . . that I can see nothing of what is going on around me? Ever since I was a small boy I have seen the white people steadily encroaching upon the Indians and driving them from their homes and hunting grounds. When I was a boy, the Indians still roamed undisputed over the country lying between the Tennessee River and the great sea of the south, and now, there is nothing left them but the hunting grounds in Florida, the white men covet that. I will tell you plainly, if I had the power, I would cut the throat of every white man in Florida."[84]

Finally word had come that the Great Father in Washington, chief of all the Americans, had offered to make a treaty, an agreement that would separate the white men from the red and black, would let the People live in peace. No Indian wanted a treaty. No Indian wanted to touch his hand to the pen and make his mark on the white man's paper. What else could they do? Go to war? The wise men of every tribe in Florida knew that concession, retreat was the only way to life. The Americans had come like hutallay-cluccko-mast-chay, the great wind that sometimes howled across the land, destroying everything in its path. But a man knew the great wind would finally go away. The white men would never go away. They would never give up. Young braves might boast of courage and threaten war, but theirs was not the responsibility for the women, for the old and the very young, for the future. Personal glory, a settling of scores were their concerns, not the survival of the People. To refuse a treaty, to go to war, would be to lose what they still had. Everything else must be tried first.

Summer was gone when the People had done with talking. Neamathla had agreed to a meeting, Micanopy had agreed, and even he, Ote Emathla, had agreed. Representatives of many tribes had come in from all across Florida, more than four hundred Seminoles. They had gathered near the meeting place selected by the whites. Here the tribes thought it best to appoint one man as spokesman for them all. Neamathla was their choice. With drums and singing, carrying a white flag, they had come to the treaty ground. In a bark house on the north bank of the Hutchee, the creek the white men called Moultrie, they had talked. The governor was there, and soldiers, and a white man called Richards who spoke Seminole. There were many papers, much writing.[85]

The Great Spirit had not intended that the Seminoles should know how to read or write. Long ago, when there were only red men and white men on the earth, a blind man holding a book had told them both that the first to kill a deer would be given the book and taught to read and write. The white man soon came upon a sheep, which he easily killed. He took it to the blind man and told him it was a deer. By the time the red man had tracked and killed a deer and brought it to the blind man, he was too late.

The blind man had given the book to the white man and taught him to read. If this cheat had not been practiced, the red men now would be as the white men were. But if the Great Spirit had intended that the red men should read he would not have allowed the white man to have the advantage. Now it was better to remain as they were and live in their own way. The white man Richards would tell them what the Americans said, what the papers meant.[86]

Talk followed talk as day followed day. Neamathla had tried to understand all that the white men said, listening to Richards as he translated the incomprehensible language. Much of it was threatening, all of it confusing. The white men had insisted that the Indians did not "own" the land. No Indian had thought he did. Yet the white men wanted them to give up "all claim or title." How could they give up that which they did not own? Yet if the Seminoles agreed to do this thing the governor told them that they would be "allotted" certain lands and, if he and the others understood him correctly, the Great Father would "prevent all white persons from hunting, settling, or otherwise intruding upon it." They would be given cattle and hogs, corn, meat, and salt. They would be given "money" to compensate them for the loss of their homes, their crops. Other monies would be given them each year for twenty successive years to establish and maintain a school, to provide white men who would repair their rifles, who could work the black metal. Most important of all, it had been his understanding that if he and the others would sign the paper they and their people should "rest in peace upon the land . . . for twenty years." One by one they touched the pen, made their mark upon the paper. He thought "all difficulties were buried, and we were assured that if we died, it should not be by the violence of the white man, but in the course of nature." Only long after it was done did they learn that they had given up possession of the land. All of it. As their Great Father had reminded them: "You have not a piece as large as a blanket to sit down upon."[87]

More than thirty chiefs had signed the treaty. It pleased the white men to think that they now "owned" the land because marks had been made on a paper. Ote Emathla, Micanopy, and the other Seminole leaders had taken what satisfaction they could in the promise of peace and security upon land "allotted" to them and their people. They had returned to their towns, their families, their people, telling them what they had done, what they must do. Day by day the word had traveled, and in towns across the land the People had begun selling off their cattle, taking up what they could carry, walking away from their homes, their fields, putting all their faith in the promised land. It was in the center of Florida, three days travel wide and six from north to south. Nowhere did it come closer than a day's travel from the sea. Ote Emathla knew that his men no longer would bring him rum from Havana in the fishing boats belonging to the Spanalkay, the white men who came from the sea and called themselves Spanish. No more would there be a question of Indian bounds, dispute of Indian range. The Americans had settled both. White men with strange tools were already going through the woods marking trees, "running lines" they called it, as though to say "this far the Indian may go and no further." The old, free way of life must be given up forever, but within the land allotted them they would have peace. The same power that had enabled the white man to take the land would assure them of that at least. The Great Father had said so in the writing.[88]

That was the time of hope. But that time was long ago, ten winters and more. That time was gone. There was no time left for talk, or hope. The soldiers were very near. Now there was only time for killing. The fires were low, the warriors slept. Perhaps tomorrow Osceola would return from the agency where he had gone "to see to his friend," Thompson. Micanopy should be coming in. Then they would kill the soldiers.[89]

A ship's lights had been sighted on Tampa Bay. A messenger carried the word to Belton, assured him that this was not a rumor. It looked to be the transport so long and anxiously awaited. God willing, they would make all speed coming in, disembarking their men. Every minute counted.[90]

Chapter Three

The Third Day

Friday, December 25, 1835

Captain Francis Belton was sleepless, uneasy. He looked at his watch by lamplight—one o'clock Christmas morning. Suddenly there was a shout, the challenge of a sentry. Within minutes the officer of the guard was at the door with a soldier—a courier from Dade! Private Aaron Jewell was dirty, unshaven, red-eyed. He fumbled papers from a pocket, handed them across with a grimy hand. Belton read eagerly, feeling better with every word. Delayed at the Hillsborough! The best news he could have hoped for. If Dade was held up long enough at the river, if Mountfort and Taylor made their landing without delay, there was still a real possibility they could unite forces.[1]

Belton praised the soldier, sent him off for food and rest. He gave orders for one of Holata Emathla's men to be brought immediately, then scribbled a message to Brevet Major Mountfort, urging him on:

> Sir,
> I am induced to reinforce him [Dade] by all means in my power and therefore expect you to move your transport as soon as circumstances permit and be ready to disembark the commands without delay with your ammunition, F [field] pieces & musket ball Cartridges—Your heavy baggage will be the last concern. [T]o obviate delay you will issue 42 rounds each for the Mens boxes and Send me a list of Your Ordinance & Stores & Numbers. Your transportation is very limited indeed being 1 Waggon and 2 Yoke Oxen and those of doubtful draft to go light is highly important.[2]

He wasted no time with closing sentiments or even signature, handed the letter to the waiting Indian, and told him to get the message to the transport any way he could.

It was a long night. Overcast dawn grudgingly revealed Mountfort's ship far from shore. It was mid-morning before he docked, noon and raining when he landed his company. They were well equipped with a string of packhorses, extra ammunition and rations. In response to Belton's anxious questions, Mountfort explained that the express had only reached him at dawn. It was the first news he had that Dade had gone on ahead with only two companies. As to the second company (commanded just now by 1st Lt. John Breckinridge Greyson), it had shipped on another transport, which had somehow become separated from his own, though it must be near at hand. Regardless, he would have his company organized, rested, and ready to march first thing in the morning. If Greyson was landed and ready so much the better. By a forced march they could reach the Big Hillsborough by tomorrow night with one hundred men and ammunition to spare.[3]

The warm rain felt like an April shower. From the slight eminence of the fort, Belton could make out Mountfort's ship against the grey sky, rocking gently on grey water. Elation had faded, doubt taking its place. Even without Greyson, Mountfort was determined to pull out tomorrow morning. But by morning Dade might have crossed the river and be on his way. And if Dade and his command were at risk, what would Mountfort's chances be with half the men? Mountfort was willing, there was no doubt of that. He was a fighter, had been breveted captain during the war with England for gallant conduct in the attack on Plattsburg, New York, had insisted that he was "very anxious to proceed forthwith" after Dade. But the lookout high in the oak had given no signal. Where was Greyson?[4]

Well, Dade must be informed of Mountfort's landing. Belton wrote quickly, reassuring him that Mountfort would be leaving at dawn, that Greyson's transport was expected anytime. With Mountfort's packhorses he could bring thirteen hundred rations and what ammunition they could spare. He gave Dade all the facts he had, urged him to regulate his movements so as to allow the reinforcement to join him. Dade would have to ford the Hillsborough or repair the bridge, one or the other. Either way it meant delay and possibly camping on the north shore or not far beyond it tonight. A messenger could still reach him during the night, Dade could hold up wherever he was, and Mountfort, with a forced march, could join him by tomorrow night.[5]

A soldier was waiting, a volunteer. Aaron Jewell had eaten his fill, had slept for twelve hours. It was his company up there on the river, and he insisted that he was the man to carry the captain's message back. Belton gave him the letter, considering him "a Most Gallant Volunteer," and wished him godspeed.[6]

On the south bank of the Hillsborough River, Dade and his men had been up before dawn, cooking fires kicked into flame, coffee put on to boil, blankets rolled and secured across their knapsacks. Another night behind them, another day ahead. Men stood in groups around the fires, stamping their feet, stretching, yawning, cursing, gnawing biscuits hard as bone. Every man knew the Seminoles were growing bolder, had heard them calling out in the night, a few wild shots fired. What would the day bring? A wet crossing, probably. And then what? A hard march, battle? Here and there men stood apart, silent. Only fools were not afraid.

Every man, officer and enlisted, had the privilege of an opinion; Dade had the responsibility of decision. As far as he was concerned, speed was more important than safety. Safety had been left at Fort Brooke along with wives and children. He'd heard the complaints about fording the river, talk that they could repair the bridge and walk across dry. But repairs took time, and he had no time to spare. The men at Fort King needed help, and help that came too late was no help at all. As for reinforcement, how was help going to overtake them when time and speed were of the essence? Would the croakers have him sit down and wait? As far as he was concerned this command *was* the reinforcement—reinforcement for Fort King.[7]

Dade called up the slave, told him he was sending him on ahead. Across the river, two miles or so up the road, there was a branch turning off northwest, the road leading by Toadchodka, a Seminole village, and continuing on to the larger town of Chocochattee. Pacheco was to reconnoiter the Toadchodka area, then beyond the village take the branch off the Chocochattee road that angled back to the east to rejoin the military road some fifteen miles ahead. Camp would likely be made tonight at

Hagerman's Hole, a spring where travelers were wont to camp, just below
the intersection of the roads. "If you see a black man in the road named
Sam, tell him I'll see him—to wait."[8]

The advance guard crossed first, muskets and ammunition boxes or
bags above their heads, knapsacks high on their shoulders, cold, swift
water filling their boots, soaking trousers, then above their waists, tugging
them to the left, toward the ruined bridge a hundred yards downstream.
An officer on horseback went ahead, probing with a pole for the shallowest
path. Men stood on the south bank with weapons loaded, cocked, covering
the advance. The six-pounder, unlimbered, crouched between its high
wheels, muzzle leveled at the far bank, Lieutenant Basinger and his crew
were in position, silent, ready. Then the first man was across, stumbling,
scrambling up the gentle slope, streaming water that turned the clay to
grease. He moved up the bank, crouching low for support and safety,
musket in one hand, the other clutching at roots, brush. The rest of the
advance made the shore, lips blue, teeth clenched to keep them still,
scrambled up left and right, fanned out. Then the main body, two by
two, down the south bank, pale blue trousers turning dark, sinking deeper,
deeper into the black water. The river reached loin height with the ache
of a wound, then waist deep, and still the bottom angled down. Men
grumbled, cursed, a sharp intake of breath here and there from those less
stoic than others. Regulations called for a man to bathe once a week
whether he needed it or not, but this was a hell of a way to do it. For
Pvt. Ransom Clark a few minutes in belly-deep water wasn't much to
notice compared to twelve hours in Mobile Bay last February, men around
him freezing, slipping down in the dark water. But little George Herlyhigh,
only five foot two, was chest deep before his numb, booted feet felt the
bottom flatten, level out, finally rise.[9]

The rear guard was spread like a screen across the night's bivouac,
facing south, backing step by step toward the crossing at their rear. The
long, blue files behind them moved through the river like sand through
an hourglass, half on one bank, half on the other. Dade, on horseback,
tense but ready, watched and waited. The river crossings were the time
of greatest danger, his force split in half, only a handful of men at any
given time to hold off whatever might come. If the Seminoles didn't strike
here now, or at the rivers ahead, they'd likely not strike at all.

Gardiner and Fraser directed their companies, junior officers leading, sergeants shouting. The supply wagon, still loaded, secured with prolonge ropes at the rear, was rolled down to the water, pulled in with drag ropes held by men on the north bank, bed barely above water, hauled across. Horses were ridden, oxen led, paddling like great dogs, heavy, horned heads thrusting above the water, drivers goading, cursing. Basinger ordered the gun wheeled about, drag lines across the river attached to the trail, prolonge lines to the carriage. Working together, the men on the far side began the pull, those on the near bank restraining, keeping the tension steady. Trail high, barrel low, the iron gun backed reluctantly down the slope. Rear ropes fell slack as the gun entered the water, wheels going deeper, deeper until only their tops still showed, men on the south bank paying out the line.[10]

On the far side men were lined up along the ropes, feet braced, bodies leaning, pulling against the dead weight of gun and carriage. The high wheels turned slowly, bumping, lurching over the uneven bottom. The rope crew groaned, strained together. The gun reached the north bank, its weight seeming to double as it began to climb the slope. Suddenly a cry—a man was down, body twisted, fingers clutching at the sand. Men near him cried out, stared down. Officers shouted, soldiers along the road ahead, wet, shivering, confused, fumbled with their weapons, stared fearfully toward the forest. Along the drag ropes men drew the fallen soldier from the line, slack was taken up, and with the strength of sudden danger the gun was drawn up the bank.

Dr. John Slade Gatlin knelt by the man. The soldier was taller than most, maybe five foot ten. His tousled hair was yellowish-red, sandy. His complexion was fair, pale now with pain. He appeared to be in his midthirties—older than the average. His rigid position, grunts of distress, and stentorian breathing were evidence of exquisite pain. Gatlin made his examination, checking for injury. There was no blood, no wound. He got the man's name: Thomas, John Thomas, private. There was no need even to open his bag here. No call for medicine or surgery—even bloodletting would be of no use. The man had injured his back while assisting in lifting the six-pounder from the river. Crushed a disk in his spine, most likely. A casualty just as surely as if he'd been struck down by a Seminole bullet. And his injury was as simple to prescribe for as it had been to diagnose:

bed rest, a little laudanum for the pain. The nearest bed was at Fort Brooke.[11]

When it came to a choice, Dade's first responsibility was to his command, not one individual. Already the sun was above the cypresses. Thomas was from Dorchester, Massachusetts, had joined up just over a year ago. This detachment was made up of everything from barbers to bakers, hatters to hairdressers, teachers to tailors, but Thomas was the only wheel-wright they had, a man whose trade was the building and repairing of wheels. If gun carriage, limber, or wagon wheel broke down they could be in real trouble without him, but as an invalid he'd be no help at all, even if he could stand a journey of seventy-five miles stretched out in the wagon, jolting over every rock and root from here to Fort King. They had no horse to spare even if he could ride. He'd have to go back, on foot, alone. The man would have his musket, canteen, a little food. A couple of men could help him across the river. It was tough luck, but Dade had more serious concerns than one man with a bad back.[12]

Thomas stood awkwardly on the south bank and watched them go. The rear guard had crossed as the main body passed from view, relimbered gun and wagon trundling along behind. Then the guard followed, a last man turning, a wave. Thomas was soaking wet, cold. The pain in his back was excruciating. The road back was more than twenty miles. To take a step, to move at all, seemed impossible. In his pocket were six dollars, more than a month's pay. Right now it didn't look like he'd have much chance to spend it.[13]

Dr. Gatlin, along with the other junior officers, marched with the men. As an assistant surgeon with fewer than five years' service he ranked the four lieutenants, but that gave him neither military command nor a horse. About all that set him apart from others were his cocked hat, black velvet collar, and dark blue trousers with a black stripe. Back at Fort Brooke Dr. Nourse had offered to trade places with him if Belton would supply him with a horse, but there had been no government horse available. Gatlin thought of himself as "constitutionally melancholy" and had "always found horse exercise necessary to cheerfullness [sic] of mind, and health of body." Now, soaking wet and chilled to the bone, the prospect of a seventy-five-mile march did nothing to lift his spirits. Not to mention the smell. A man instinctively breathed through his mouth to keep out the stench of mud, the sour smell of rotting vegetation near the river. It was common knowledge that the foul miasma created by decaying vegetable matter was the essential ingredient for the yellow fever, an even more deadly killer than Seminoles.[14]

Perhaps Gatlin had made a mistake in joining the military in the first place. Ten years ago his family had been affluent, his father a well-to-do farmer and merchant in Kinston, Lenoir County, North Carolina. Their family line extended back to the fifteenth century and included soldiers, statesmen, and high public servants among its members. His mother, Susannah, was the daughter of Richard Caswell, the first governor when Carolina became a state. Caswell had been regarded as a wealthy man during his lifetime, but at his death in 1789 his family was left honored but penniless. Susannah and her husband, John Slade Gatlin, Sr., had struggled to raise two sons and two daughters, only to suffer crippling financial losses with the depression of property and produce in 1828. Their younger son, Richard, had been forced to withdraw from college in his sophomore year but had been fortunate enough to get an appointment to West Point. He had graduated in 1832 as brevet second lieutenant, was now twenty-six years old, a full second lieutenant and serving with the Seventh Infantry at Fort Gibson, Indian Territory.[15]

Kinston, which lay on the east bank of the Neuse River, was a town of some one hundred whites served by an equal number of slaves. When established in 1762 as the twentieth town in the province (and destined for fifty years to be the only town in Lenoir County) the name had been Kingston, but revolution had changed respect for the king to scorn and the name of the town to Kinston. In 1833 the name had been changed again, that time to Caswell in memory of the governor, John Gatlin's grandfather. The name soon slid back to Kinston, but the pride remained.

Perhaps it had been a preoccupation with his own health that led John to serve an apprenticeship with a local doctor and, on August 3, 1834, accept a commission in the army as assistant surgeon. Three weeks later he had written to the surgeon general in Washington that "my health is much improved. I wait with impatience for orders, but I hope not to go north-wards." By October he was a thousand miles west at Fort Gibson, attached to the Seventh Infantry. The only good thing to be said for the assignment was that it reunited him with his brother.

Fort Gibson was less than two years old, a bleak outpost at the far edge of the United States. It might as well have been the edge of the world. It wasn't the North, but it wasn't home either. His complaint to the surgeon general resulted in an immediate transfer—farther west to Camp Arbuckle, possibly the only post with less to offer than Fort Gibson. His only consolation was that Arbuckle was soon to be abandoned. Again he asked for a return to the East and civilization. His next assignment was Des Moines, in the dreaded North.[16]

The surgeon general, Dr. Joseph Lovell, couldn't seem to get it through his head that a gentleman did not enter the military service in order to tend fever-ridden soldiers at bleak outposts far from the comforts of civilization, places where a doctor spent as much time suffering from fever and dysentery as he did treating the same disorders in others. Gatlin felt that he would be "grosely [sic] negligent of my duty to myself if I should fail to inform you of my preference of stations—Anywhere south rather than west—but should prefer Florida for its climate." If his services should be needed in the southwest, then Baton Rouge, New Orleans, or Fort Jesup in Louisiana would be "very acceptible [sic]." On the eastern seaboard he would like "any post South of New York." He went on to explain that he was "one who does not wish to stand still in the world as he most certainly will if he remains on the frontier." In the view of one traveler/ writer, "the post of an officer on the frontiers is by no means either an enviable, or in the idea of many of his fellow-citizens, an honorable one," frequently spent in an "utter state of exile from good society." Unfortunately, the frontier was the principal reason for the existence of the army, and an army surgeon had little choice but to accompany it to those frontiers. Still, John explained that his constitution could not stand a cold climate, and the fact was that if he could not serve in more congenial circumstances he would be "compeled [sic] to resign."[17]

Instead of Iowa he received orders for Fort Jackson, Louisiana, seventy-three miles southeast of New Orleans and considered one of the most unhealthy posts in the country. He arrived on April 1, 1835, took one look around, and immediately renewed his application "for any Atlantic post south of New York—any post in Florida—or Jesup, New Orleans or Baton Rouge. . . . I am particularly anxious to get to Florida—next to N. Carolina or South Carolina, but anywhere in the region I have mentioned rather than a confined and unhealthy place like this." In a postscript he pointed out that "a clean exercise [such] as riding cannot be enjoyed here and I have always found it necessary to my health." As a matter of fact, "even our walks are confined to the levy."[18]

By the time he got home on leave in July he had pretty well decided that the best place for him would really be some station right there in North Carolina, with Florida as his second choice. The West hadn't worked out, neither had the South, and he had never wanted the North. There was nothing but the Atlantic Ocean to the east, so the possibilities were limited. But nearby was Fort Macon or even Beaufort; the latter place "has no chance for any man in the service but myself, being but seventy miles from my home." It was as though no one read his letters—or no one cared. It was small consolation that when his next assignment came it turned out to be his second choice.[19]

He had requested transfer to Florida so often and for so long that perhaps the reality could never have matched his hopes. He had found Fort Pickens on Santa Rosa Island, nine miles south of Pensacola, "little better than [a] place of Exile, where a man is almost as much confined, as if he were on a rock in the ocean—the abode of melancholy. It is nothing more than a brown sand island. Such places can not be otherwise, than unpleasant to any man." Isolated, lonely, and homesick, he had perhaps too much time for reflecting on his own misfortune. Although he had once written that he would "prefer Florida for its climate," he now complained that "in this warm region I find myself very liable to disentery [sic] which is here very prevelant [sic]. . . . I have also been much troubled with fevers. These diseases have made serious inroads upon my health. From a station of health I have been reduced to a state of great debility." It was galling to read in the *Army and Navy Chronicle* that medical vacancies had occurred in both Savannah and Charleston and had been filled by officers junior to himself. Just in case his previous applications had slipped the surgeon general's memory or perhaps been misunderstood he wrote once more, making no effort to conceal his disappointment. "My hopes of getting a N. Carolina station are crushed."[20]

Through September, October, and into November he had endured, often reminding the surgeon general of the places he would rather be. Then orders had come for Fort Brooke, Tampa Bay. As if that wasn't the last word in lonely outposts on godforsaken frontiers, he had no sooner landed there than he found "an order for this Co. to which I am attached to proceed to Ft. King." One hundred miles. On foot. He had turned over to Assistant Surgeon Heiskell most of the medical supplies he had brought from Fort Pickens, and in return he received Heiskell's invoices and receipts for delivery at Fort King. Now they rode in the wagon along with his assortment of saws, knives, and potions, as well as his two double-barreled shotguns for hunting. The only quarry that counted here would be on two legs. The dogs, heedless of danger, ran through the woods, jerking at his nerves with their baying as they crossed the trail of rabbit or deer. And if illness and melancholy had not been sufficient burdens, he had come to realize that on this journey he might be in mortal danger.[21]

Coming up from the river the road was almost a tunnel, boring through a thicket of oak and hickory. Frequent use and maintenance had held the growth at bay, but for the past several months only solitary runners had passed this way. The matrix of restless limbs, branches, and vines on either side was reaching out, trying to close the wound. Only on the path could a soldier move, load, and fire, while a Seminole could hide behind the living screen to slash, cut, and disappear. The men marched close and fast, the files almost brushing one another, bunched and anxious.[22]

Suddenly the tunnel ended, the land opened out. Men slowed, straightened, confidence coming with a rush. The advance guard increased its distance from the main body, flankers fanned out through the pine barren, the rear guard dropped back. Even under unrelenting grey skies a man could see across the high grass, beneath the straight pines still interspersed with oak and hickory. Mile after mile of forest could grow monotonous, but better monotony than the drear and gloomy cypress swamp, or worse, the impenetrable, clutching thickets of the low riverland.

This far from the coast the land was higher, rolling, good land for farming, stock, white men. The soil was strong, able to raise a good crop of cotton. Of course Indians would never raise it—never even try. They liked the dyed cotton cloth the white men would trade and were eager to sew it up into shirts or frocks, but they had no interest in the planning, the relentless labor, of farming. Their idea of harvesting was to take an ax to a wild orange tree. "Nature has been so bountiful in the bestowal of her gift of miles upon miles of groves of this prolific tree, that the improvident children of the wilderness hesitate not to lay the axe to the root of the tree as the most convenient mode of gathering the fruit. . . . [A]n Indian who 'wants to eat oranges' encamps with his family somewhere on the edge of the grove, cuts down a tree, fills his blanket, and they all fall to and eat oranges for a week at a time."[23]

They passed a settler's cabin, and then, miles further, another. They were hardly more than huts really, silent, stone-and-mud chimneys smokeless in spite of the damp and chill. An officer with another outfit, at another time, could have been describing the scene for Dade or any of his men when he wrote: "The face of the country began to assume a more hilly or rolling appearance . . . and [we] discovered at the edge of a gentle dale, two settlements enclosed by fences made of whole trees cut into long huge logs, and piled up into a barrier impenetrable to everything but Indians. The settlements appeared to have been but recently located and recently deserted; not a soul was to be seen, nor a sign of any living thing, and I was struck with the unnatural stillness and cheerlessness of the scene. . . . [H]ere the very genius of silence and desolation seemed to reign; the curse of the Indian panic had passed over the domestic quiet of the simple abodes; the ploughshare had been turned into a weapon of war; the sorry team had been taken from their . . . drudgery to be made fierce chargers of; the master of the domain had left his rustic occupations to become a volunteer. . . . The grass was springing up in the fields. The corn crib shewed its skeleton frame stark and empty and the barn door gaped, and creaked upon its hinges in harsh dissonance with the death-like silence which reigned over the deserted settlement."[24]

Jacob R. Motte, an army surgeon, described settlers' dwellings, "alias shantees [sic]," that he had visited in Florida as being "built of slab-boards enclosing an area about twelve feet square." The settlers themselves, he concluded, were "mostly small farmers who had emigrated from different States . . . to plant corn, hoe potatoes, and beget ugly little white-headed responsibilities. Which occupations they pursued with praise-worthy industry and perseverance in the pipeing [sic] times of peace; but imagining it much easier to be fed by Uncle Sam, they provoked the Indians by various aggressions to a retaliation, and then complained to their venerable

Uncle of the mischievous disposition of his red nephews. [Uncle Sam] immediately issued his mandate to the [Indians], that as they could not live in brotherly affection with his white nephews and nieces, their health must be in a bad state, and a change of air would be very beneficial; whereupon he prescribed that west of the Mississippi as being very pure and wholesome. [The Seminoles] not coinciding with him on the subject of their health, and discovering the authors of their Uncle's displeasure, undertook to revenge themselves upon their white cousins who immediately congregated in spots, built pickets or stockades—which they called forts—drew rations—as they designated themselves 'suffering inhabitants'—and devoted their attention entirely to the last of their former occupations."[25]

Other travelers told their own stories of men and women encountered at these desolate outposts. "We approached [a] miserable log hut . . . where sat a wretched woman, with a snuff brush in her mouth, while her [husband] sprawled full length on the dilapidated porch. . . . Five or six emaciated children, rolling in the sand, and a sow with half starved pigs, were the only living objects in view.

" 'What do you live on here?'

" 'Wall, (yawning and stretching,) fish is plenty, and when the 'simmons is ripe, possums is fine; but it seems like thar was a spell on my fishing pole, lately like. To be sure the ground is rank poor, so no use of a digging it; but stranger, them thar pigs will make a right smart pasle of meat on to Christmas; they is good breed, for in this kentry it's root hog or die.'

". . . [W]hat an amount of endurance that woman must possess to live thus all her life, bearing children without even the prospect of food for them; and for a time her beamless eye and shadowed face haunted me."[26]

Another visitor to central Florida remembered "the welcome bark of a dog [that] told of a habitation which consisted of two log rooms on stilts, connected by an open passage, upon the floor of which reposed a white man. . . . Peeping from a door was a slouching white woman who wore a dirty sun-bonnet, who . . . called: 'Git up, Alik Smith! thar's folks a callin on you.'

"Mr. Smith was aroused, and . . . came out to greet us:

" 'Light gentlemen; hitch your creturs. . . . Hoculas [Hercules], see how you give feed to them horses.'

"As we got under the roof of the building, (for it could scarcely be called entering a house) he called aloud to the woman no longer seen, 'Ole Sweet, push up the pot, for the gentlemin will be agying haungry;' and . . . he offered us seats, which he called *cheers*, adding, 'Make on yourself at home, gentlemin.'

" 'Hoculas, you d——d lazy scoundrel!'

" 'Sah,' answered the black. . . .

" 'Fetch a pail of fresh water, you rascal,' which being brought, the master turned to us, . . . 'Gentlemin, won't you be after a wash? Thar's the tin, and thar's the wiper,'—which we found in a basin and a circular arrangement of toweling that turned on a roller. . . .

" 'Ole woman, if you don't be up with the cooking, we'll be after helping you. Whar's Vittals [Victuals] and Cloze [Clothes]?'

"From a sort of shed in the yard there came a cracked sound. 'I ain't afear'd on your a helpin on me, Alik Smith, and as fur "vittals and close" I dun sent her to Sister Betsy Hales, to see as how we couldn't borrow a small pasle of "short sweetning," an she ain't no turn'd up yit.' I ventured to inquire what this strange-named feminine could be.

" 'Waall, stranger, you must know as how niggers is mighty high, and they is gitting higher. It took my level best with five crops on this poor piney woods land, to git done paying for Hoculas—and sure and sartain I can't buy agin right off—so you seed'd, to sorter help the "ole woman," I gin vittals and cloze to a little nigger gal, and her mistress takes it for hire, cause she ain't got no use for her nohow, and she helps the ole woman right smartly.' "

When they had finished a meal that was "well cooked and clean," their host stood up. " 'Gentlemin, I ain't a doin of it to skear, but it's on the rise of two clock, jedging by the sun, and my advize is fur you to be gitting along—for you mought and you mough'nt run agin Ingins . . . fur they's bin a swarmin. . . .' And then in a semi-apologetic tone, as we opened purses, he said: 'Wall, gentlemen, fifty cents for feeding of the creturs, and that'll pay back the corn, but don't be of insultin my ole woman, fur she'll gin a dinner just to be seeing somebody.' "[27]

Dr. Nathan Jarvis gave it as his opinion that "the common term for the Floridian is 'Crackers,' probably from their living mostly on crack'd corn. [I] visited some of them who were sick and found them excessively rude and ignorant."[28]

Around the cabins stood stump-filled fields that had once been forest, crops burnt or gone to seed, the forlorn settlers gone to Fort Brooke if they were lucky, dead if they weren't. They had left the land to wilderness and Indians, but they'd be back sooner or later. Rude and ignorant they may have been, but no man or woman without courage had come to scratch this little patch of earth. They would leave when they must but return when they could as surely as the green shoots that would start up through the blackened stubble. The soldiers stared as they passed, called back the dogs who explored the sites, their noses to the ground, sniffing the charred, sour smell of desolation.

Each man in the party had his own reasons for being here. For some it was simple patriotism—fellow Americans were in danger, and it was part of a citizen's duty to help out. For others the army was three meals a day, clothes, and a place to sleep, even if the place was sometimes bare ground and the bed a handful of pine straw. For the officers it was a different story. They were professionals, every one. And perhaps George Gardiner was the most professional of all. The ninety-first graduate of West Point, ranked first in his class, he had been an artilleryman for twenty-one years.[29]

Gardiner had graduated from West Point in 1814 as a third lieutenant in the First Artillery and been promoted to second lieutenant six weeks later, in time to serve during the final months of the War of 1812. He had returned to West Point for further study in April 1816, and in October been appointed post adjutant, in spite of his diminutive size. Lieutenant Gardiner and John Taylor Pratt, a cadet, had been rivals for the favors of a young woman named Kingsley. Filled with one form or another of the spirit of his native Kentucky but a little short on good (not to mention military) sense, Pratt had gone to the little lieutenant's quarters one day to pick a fight, "when Gardiner seized a pair of tongs in the jaws of which he embraced Pratt's neck, and gave to the tongs such a twist as to render their removal no easy matter." Gardiner won the fight, Pratt won the girl.[30]

Brevet Major Sylvanus Thayer had been appointed superintendent of West Point in July 1817. Impressed with Lieutenant Gardiner's "zeal and ability," Thayer had recommended him for temporary instructor of infantry tactics in August. A month later Gardiner was appointed instructor of artillery and also singled out as the first man to fill the newly created

post of commandant of cadets. He handled the three positions well enough
to earn promotion to first lieutenant six months later. In 1820 he left West
Point for a series of garrison assignments, beginning in New York Harbor
and followed by three years at Fort Mifflin in Philadelphia. For a twenty-
four year old in an army where promotion was notoriously slow, for the
shortest man in probably every gathering of an organization that valued
size, he had done all right.[31]

George remembered his childhood years in Kingston, New York, as a
life of "comfort & happiness." His father, Barent Gardenier (either George
had changed the spelling or West Point had changed it for him), was a
lawyer and "an easy, fluent, graceful speaker" who had built a large practice
in spite of—or possibly because of—a reputation of being a "dashing,
humorous, thoughtless good fellow." These were the elements of a popular
politician, and he had been elected a representative in Congress from the
state of New York in 1807 and moved his family to Washington, D.C.
Gardenier was strongly Federalist, violently anti-Jeffersonian, and a witty,
reckless speaker, pronounced by John Randolph of Roanoke to be "the
most eloquent man he had ever heard in Congress." His eloquence brought
him reelection, his recklessness brought him to a near-fatal duel. Public
opinion in the North was not well disposed toward such encounters, and
by 1811 Gardenier's political life was played out. When George received
his appointment to West Point in 1812 his father had retired from politics
and returned to New York with his wife, two daughters, and George's
four-year-old brother, John Randolph. Gardenier resumed the practice of
law in Ulster and Columbia counties, serving two years as district attorney
for the first district. Ten years later, after a brief illness, he died on January
10, 1822.[32]

Barent Gardenier had known presidents Monroe and Van Buren, had
been a friend of John Calhoun (now secretary of war), and had been
considered by his friends "a man of genius and talent," but interred with
his body beneath the First Dutch Reformed Church in Kingston were
any plans for the financial security of his family. At once homeless and
destitute, they were dependent upon George for their means of survival.
Desperate, George wrote to Sylvanus Thayer for help in getting his
brother, John, now fourteen years old, appointed a member of the military
academy. In the words of a friend, the appointment would "retrieve a

promising young man from Poverty," providing him with food, clothing, and shelter. "If the application of his brother should succeed, [George] thinks he will be able to support his mother and family by his business." Business? A first lieutenant in the artillery? George wrote letters to everyone he knew, everyone his father had known. In March 1822, despite the fact that John was the youngest and smallest applicant, he passed the entrance examination with grades "far superior to the greater part of the class, who were generally about eighteen years of age."[33]

Perhaps it was a sign of his desperation, but whether driven by need or lured by hope, George applied "to be admitted to the bar of New York's Supreme Court." The sudden "business" with which he expected to support his family was the law. Meanwhile, Calhoun had had second thoughts, had withdrawn John's appointment on account of his age, wrote that "his admission next year would depend upon his physical abilities to discharge the duties of a cadet." Then George failed the bar. Now it was the military or nothing.[34]

Garrisoned at Fort Mifflin, George continued trying to fulfill what he considered to be his family responsibility, John's readmission to the military academy. Their mother, Sarah Gardenier, wrote from Albany that John had been pursuing his studies and, more important, "he is much stronger and nearly 3 inches taller." He was allowed to reenter in April 1823. Graduated in 1828, he was commissioned brevet second lieutenant in the First Infantry. Now he was a full second lieutenant and on leave in Key West.[35]

George had been transferred from Mifflin to Fort Delaware, then to the Augusta Arsenal in Georgia, the Cherokee Nation, Fort Marion in Florida, Fort Mitchell in Alabama, Fort Jackson in Louisiana, and back to Florida at Fort Pickens, then Key West, and finally Fort Brooke. Along the way he had married and had fathered two children. He had devoted his life to his two families—and to the corps of artillery. His duties now were several and clear. He had put Frances in the best possible hands. Fully conscious that this detachment was taking a fearful risk, he would do all that life allowed to help bring it—and the cannon—to the relief of Fort King and its commander, Lt. Col. Alexander Fanning. If for no other reason, he owed that much to Frances. Her sister Sarah was Fanning's wife.[36]

Colonel Fanning, like his brother-in-law, was a small man. He was forty-seven years old, had graduated from West Point two years before George, and had promptly lost an arm fighting the English in Canada. In 1815 the government had sent him from the northern border of the United States to the southern border, where he had crossed into Spanish Florida with Andrew Jackson, been in a few skirmishes with Seminoles, and served as provost marshal at the execution of British emissaries Arbuthnut and Ambrister. Since 1822 he had done garrison duty in Michigan, New York, Delaware, Virginia, and Georgia. This year he had returned to Florida, and he had been commanding officer at Fort King since April. His military command included four companies of U.S. Regulars, but his responsibility included the Indian agent, the sutler, a handful of civilian employees, and anyone else within fifty miles or so who called for help. During the past month there had been a lot of calls while "discharges, and the detachments sent to protect the citizens have much weakened our force. We are almost continually under arms and I have not put off my clothes for the last five days. Solicitude and want of sleep have much worn me down."[37]

Back in April he had felt a sense of harmony in the arrangements that Clinch and Thompson had made with a majority of the Seminole chiefs whereby they had agreed to leave Florida peaceably. He had even thought briefly that the discontented chiefs would soon "come into the measures of the executive and depart with their brethren." Unless, of course, "the cupidity of our own citizens" upset the balance. When the news got out that the Seminoles were leaving the country, it would be assumed that they would be disposing of their black "slaves" along with their other property preparatory to removal, and, "under an impression that the Indian negroes can be bought for little or nothing," speculators would be "flocking in the country." To try to prevent this he had "*particularly requested*" permission to turn back every white man who attempted to cross the Seminole boundary.[38]

Since then, through summer and fall, the disruptive work of slave hunters and whiskey peddlers on the one hand and the murderous work of the shrewd leader of the hostiles, Osceola, on the other had created what Fanning, by the end of November, had come to describe as the present "horrible state of things." When writing to General Clinch at his headquarters in St. Augustine he had felt compelled by the urgency of the situation to offer advice: "Permit me to give you my decided convictions of what should be done, and done immediately, raise fifty or one hundred mounted men with Rifles; pick up every man who is willing to join you on your march [to Fort King].—Bring Drane's Company. Order in Captain Graham's as you come along, and then without a moments [sic] delay or making further arrangements, take every man who can shoulder a Musket, and dash vigorously on the Big and the Long Swamps.—My word for it General—any other cause, any delay, will prove fatal to the lives of many settlers, and probably to ourselves. . . . Again I must say—lose no time— make every exertion to reach this post, where your presence is absolutely necessary."[39]

Fanning was convinced that "it is their [the Seminoles] determination with the mass of their force to attack this place." He had four companies— two hundred men—nominally on hand; that is, their names were on the roster, but half the command had been sick within the past several months, "and although many of them [are] fit for Garrison duty, and most of the others are convalescent, they cannot be relied on for active efficient service."[40]

Yet the anxiety that was wearing Fanning down "was as much for his friends [in] Tampa as for his own position." The reports of runners had left no room for doubt that the Seminoles had thrown themselves in full force upon the route between Tampa Bay and Fort King, resolute to prevent any reinforcement from reaching him. The safe return of Paymaster John S. Lytle from Fort Brooke on December 1 had only confirmed his fears.

In his anxiety to warn Lytle not to attempt the passage, Fanning had considered every expedient. A message could be sent overland northwest to St. Marks at the mouth of the Withlacoochee, then carried by ship down the Gulf to Tampa Bay, but the time required would make the effort pointless. To send a soldier down the Fort King Road would be folly. He had even offered five hundred dollars to any runner, Seminole or black, who would undertake the journey with a verbal message. All had known the impossibility of passing without discovery and the certainty that Osceola would catch them, kill them for attempting it. As a last resource, futile as it might prove, he had dispatched Indian Bill, a trusted

runner and interpreter, to Osceola himself with the message that Paymaster
Lytle and four mounted men were scheduled to leave Fort Brooke in a
few days—that his money would have been dispensed and consequently
he would be no object to the Seminoles. Putting by his pride, he *requested*
that Osceola permit Indian Bill to pass on and direct Lytle to remain at
Tampa. "Tell Colonel Fanning," Osceola had replied, "that Major Lytle
shall not be molested—but that no one shall live to pass *from* Fort King
to Tampa."[41]

Lytle and his companions had passed the Great Swamp unmolested,
had ridden into the fort on Tuesday evening, December 1, unaware that
the eyes of eight hundred armed Seminoles had watched their every step.
To Fanning it was clear that this rigid subordination of the Seminoles
was intended by Osceola as formidable proof of his power and resolution.
The safe passage of a black from Fort Brooke on the fifth was a further
display of his tactics and influence. *To* Fort King messengers might go
freely, but not *from* it—and Osceola evidently felt equally secure of his
prey on each side. "Colonel Fanning had now only the hope that such
information as the Commanding Officer at Tampa Bay had of the movements of the enemy in his own neighborhood, would be a sufficient clue
to the dangerous state of the whole region for deciding him upon retaining
the two companies, and even *all four* when they . . . arrived."[42]

In mid-December, expecting attack on Fort King at any moment, yet
fearful that Gardiner would attempt to force a passage through from
Tampa, Fanning received orders from Clinch to bring the remaining three
companies to Auld Lang Syne as soon as Gardiner arrived and leave Fort
King manned by a single company. The general had moved quickly, but
evidently he had determined to use Auld Lang Syne—his plantation some
twenty-five miles northwest of Fort King—as his headquarters rather than
Fort King, and was gathering his forces there "preparatory to . . . striking
a blow against the families of the Seminoles supposed to be concealed in
the swamps and hammocks of the Withlacoochee River." Fort King, the
agency, and perhaps the fifty or so men left to defend them would likely
be a sacrifice to the Seminoles. Fanning considered it a fact that they were
determined to destroy the fort, "having come to the conclusion that nothing
effective can be done, whilst we hold it." Still, whether he marched to
join Clinch or directly into battle, fort and agency must be left behind.[43]

But Gardiner was long overdue. It could mean that the officer commanding at Fort Brooke had exercised common sense, had not sent *anyone* on
so hazardous a mission. Or it could mean that Gardiner and his command
had already attempted to reach him and failed. Regardless, Clinch obviously was in no position to wait any longer. Several hundred militia should
have joined him by now, and their enlistments were bound to be of short
duration. Meanwhile they would have little to do but eat. Rations, always
in short supply, would not long be able to sustain the onslaught. Time
and food would run out together, and soon.

Fanning understood Clinch's need and was bound to obey his order,
leave Fort King seriously undermanned, and take his own chances with
less than 150 men in Seminole country. Still, his chief care and fear was
that his brother-in-law—with only *two* companies—would attempt to cross
the country in the face of what he considered certain destruction. Writing
to his wife on December 16, he had tried to reassure her (and himself),
saying that he thought that "those two companies will not leave Tampa,"
and again on December 21, "they will await the arrival of the other two
companies and all four come on together, or what is still more probable,
all of them remain at Tampa." That was four days ago. Time had run
out. Tomorrow he must go, do his best to reach Clinch before his militia
dissolved and left him with only a handful of regulars. As he had told
Clinch a month ago, "We have fallen into the error committed at the
Commencement of every Indian War: The display of too little force—
The attempt to do too much with too little means." God help them all.[44]

He would leave one company to man the fort under the command of
Capt. Thomas W. Lendrum, a middle-aged West Pointer. The departure
of the detachment would, of course, make precaution all the more necessary. He had already ordered the sutler to bring his goods within the fort
and he and the agent and their people to move within the pickets. In spite
of a heavy rain, they had been working most of the day bringing in barrels
and boxes of supplies. Captain Lendrum's men would continue the work
of securing and strengthening the defenses.[45]

The fort, begun in 1827, had originally consisted only of officer's quarters, a two-story barracks for enlisted men, kitchens, mess halls, and
ammunition and weapons storage. Later a small hospital—made of hewn
logs, chinked and plastered, and surrounded by an eight-foot-wide pi-

azza—had been built forty yards from the barracks. Attached to the hospital was a small log kitchen. During the past summer, Assistant Surgeon Archer had had the north and south ends of the piazza boarded up and converted into two additional wards and a dispensary. He could accommodate twenty patients comfortably, but recently there had been as many as sixty on sick report. The fort was surrounded by a palisade of split pine logs planted deep in the sand, edge to edge, standing a dozen feet high. The walls formed a box 152 by 162 feet, with gates at front and rear and blockhouses at opposite corners to provide enfilade fire if the occasion demanded. During the eight years of its existence the fort had never heard a shot fired in anger.[46]

"The site on which the fort stood was somewhat elevated, gradually sloping off, however, on either side, and, at the distance of several hundred yards, again rising to considerable height, beyond which the vast interminable woods were seen to stretch far as the eye could follow them." The home and store of Erastus Rogers, the sutler, was six or eight hundred yards northwest of the fort on the border of a hammock. His household consisted of two clerks—a Mr. Kitzler and a boy, Robert Suggs—as well as an elderly black woman who did his cooking. His store was nearly empty, although the half basement was still stocked with several hundred bottles of spirits: beer, wine, liquor, even champagne. The bottles were crated, the wine bottoms up to keep the corks wet, crates in orderly stacks on the dirt floor against the low, brick walls to maintain as cool and even a temperature as possible. They would be left undisturbed. In the fort, without proper storage, they would have been subjected to pilferage as well as every fluctuation of the weather. In compliance with Colonel Fanning's recent order, Rogers and the others now slept within the fort, though they continued to take their meals at his home.[47]

Closer to the fort, only a hundred yards outside the walls, stood a second log building, this one with a high roof and surrounding porches, the office of Wiley Thompson, for the past two years agent for the Seminoles and more recently superintendent of emigration. On this Christmas Day he was fifty-four years, three months, and two days old, lean, tall, grey haired, and not in the best of health.[48]

Thompson had been born in Amelia County, Virginia, but Elberton, in the northeast hills of Georgia, had been his home since early childhood.

He had spent most of his life in public service, beginning as a commissioner of the Elbert County Academy in 1808, followed by service in the War of 1812 and an appointment as major general of the Fourth Division of the Georgia Militia in 1817—a position he held until 1824 even though he was elected to the state Senate in 1817. In 1819 he resigned from the Senate and served on a commission to determine the boundary between Georgia and the province of East Florida. He was elected a representative to the U.S. Congress in 1821 and was reelected for five terms, serving until March 1833. Six months later he had accepted appointment as agent for the Seminoles. On October 8 he had left his wife at their estate in Elberton to attend to agency business in north Florida, finally arriving at Fort King on December 1. The next day he reported to the secretary of war, "I arrived here last evening and found the Agency House untenanted except by a Single individual—a mechanic by the name of Dunlap. The Office door was secured by a latch only, the lock being entirely out of order."[49]

He found the records and files few and in disorder, the condition of the Seminoles within the reservation "deplorable": "A destructive drought which prevailed throughout the Southern Section of our Country was fatal to the Crops of these Indians. They are roaming without the limits of their reserve in quest of Game and other Sustainance; and especially in pursuit of Ardent Spirit. Many individuals (white men) like so many hungry Vultures hovering over the dieing [sic] Skeleton of some fallen Animal, have located little dirty Whiskey Shops around the Indian borders, who deaf to the cries of humanity . . . regardless of the principles of honor & common honesty . . . guided alone by avarice, sell spirit to the Indians, swindle them out of their horses, cattle, hoggs [sic], corn & Peltry [sic], and . . . turn them a drift with appetites & feelings vitiated & inflamed by intemperance want & hunger, to prey upon their neighbours."[50]

He had vowed to "do all in my power to suppress this disgracefull [sic] [liquor] trafic [sic]," but when he overhauled the records and studied the treaties and correspondence regarding the Seminoles it became apparent that the previous agents, Col. Gad Humphreys and Maj. John Phagan, had come to grief at least in part because they had spoken up too often in defense of the Seminoles. Closing down whiskey shops and protecting the Seminoles against slave hunters, swindlers, and thieves was not what he was being paid fifteen hundred dollars a year to do. It was evident that a man who wanted to keep his job would be well advised to keep his mouth shut about matters moral and philosophical.[51]

Thompson's instructions were to prepare the Seminole chiefs for removal beyond the Mississippi, yet it was difficult to read the Treaty of Moultrie Creek and not conclude that the Seminoles had been assured of possession of their reservation land for twenty years, only half of which had passed. Well then, how had arrangements in the treaty for a reservation within the Florida Territory come to a demand for removal? There were plenty of letters in the files detailing troubles: settlers complaining of starving Seminoles outside the reservation stealing cattle, Seminoles complaining about slave hunters inside the reservation carrying off black men, women, and children without any proof of ownership, and on and on. He knew enough from his dealings with the Creek Indians in Georgia to recognize the pattern of irreconcilable conflict created by daily contact between different cultures, different races, different languages. Even the sound of an Indian's name could hardly be made to fit a white man's tongue. Chalo Emathla could be made to sound like Charley, even Charles E. Martla by some officers, but for the most part they had to use a translation of the Seminole meaning: Jumper for Ote Emathla, Alligator for Halpatter Tustenuggee.[52] But troubles alone were not enough to abrogate a treaty. Unless changed or rescinded by a subsequent contract or convention, the Moultrie treaty was the law. However, quite apart from any concept of legality or justice, it was clear from the records that removal of the Seminoles was the only alternative to destruction. Ten years of trouble, as documented in the files, made it obvious that a Seminole reservation surrounded by whites simply would not work. No military force conceivable could stop harassment by the whites, but military force *could* remove the Seminoles. There was no doubt of that, nor that the government had come to the only rational, humane conclusion; the Seminoles *must* go. As early as 1829 one of the commissioners of the treaty, James Gadsden, had stated plainly to the president that the commissioners understood that the real purpose of the treaty had been to concentrate the Seminoles preparatory to later removal.[53]

And there was, in fact, a subsequent contract—the conditional Treaty of Payne's Landing. Colonel Humphreys, agent for eight years, considered

"a sincere and uncompromising friend of the red man," had been discharged, and James Phagan, who some thought to be "totally unqualified,
both by education and morals," for the job of Seminole agent, had taken his
place. James Gadsden had again been appointed special agent to negotiate a
new treaty. For three months he had traveled among the Seminoles,
explaining, cajoling, saying whatever had to be said to induce them to
come together again and listen to the *new* American plan. There was little
in Gadsden's records about his methods. All that seemed clear in the few
reports and letters, and in the treaty itself, was that commissioners and
Seminole chiefs had finally met in May 1832 at a place called Payne's
Landing, on the west bank of the Oklawaha River, seventeen miles northeast of Fort King. Eight days later Gadsden claimed that seven chiefs and
eight subchiefs had touched the pen, had made their marks on a new,
tentative treaty. They had presumably agreed to let the government take
a group of them west of the Mississippi to examine land that was offered
in trade for their reservation in Florida. If they were satisfied with the
land (among or adjacent to the previously deported Creeks), the new treaty
would go into effect—the Seminoles would relinquish all claim to Florida
and move to the western land.[54]

Charges of bribery, force, intimidation, and misrepresentation had been
voiced by Seminoles—and even by a few whites. The charges by whites
had faded, just as the charges relating to the Moultrie treaty had faded
when it was seen how beneficial the results had been. As for the Seminoles,
a little grumbling was to be expected, but they had known where the
power, the strength, lay. They had been paid—or were in the process of
being paid—for the land, after all, three quarters of a cent per acre at
Moultrie, more than doubled to two cents per acre at Payne's Landing.
And perhaps it was just as well that Gadsden had not kept notes. The
methods used to induce the Seminole leaders even to consider trading
their Florida land for a piece of the western desert, to rejoin the Creeks,
from whom they had fled one hundred years ago, might have been misunderstood.[55]

At any rate, in September 1832 the delegation had left Tampa Bay, led
by Phagan with white and Indian interpreters and an escort of soldiers,
had crossed the Gulf to New Orleans, gone by steamboat up the Mississippi
and Arkansas rivers, west by wagon, horseback, and foot to Indian Terri-

tory. By the end of the year they had come to the western edge of the United States. For three months, through the winter of 1833–34, they had been taken back and forth, up and down a prairie between two rivers, a rectangle of land that measured twenty miles by forty. Perhaps the land was stark by Seminole standards, and smaller than their Florida reservation—on the map it looked to be perhaps one-tenth the size—but there at least they would be free of slave hunters, whiskey peddlers, and white settlers. Certainly no white man wanted the barren, dreary land. And they would be surrounded only by other Indians.[56]

In March, after their tour, the Seminoles had been taken to Fort Gibson in Arkansas and given a paper to sign. Their marks were on the paper. By the Payne's Landing treaty, that was all that was needed to give force to the removal. Returned to Florida after seven months travel at government expense, the chiefs had protested that "the deputation . . . was *only authorized to examine* the country . . . and *report* to the nation. . . . [W]e considered we did no more than say we liked the land, and when we returned *the nation would decide.*" As if anyone cared what they thought of it. They said they wanted time to travel among their people, tell them of the new land, and let the people make their own decision. This in spite of the fact that the wording of the Fort Gibson document (with just a small change from that of Payne's Landing, which perhaps had not been explained to the Seminoles) clearly specified, "should *this delegation* be satisfied." Quibbling. Meanwhile, Phagan had been dismissed and Thompson appointed.[57]

In one of Thompson's first meetings with the chiefs (more than two years after the Treaty of Payne's Landing had been signed), Micanopy, the head chief, claimed that he had not even made his mark on the treaty, and Chalo Emathla said that he and others had been *forced* to sign. They would impugn the honor of the commissioner, Colonel Gadsden, the witnesses Vass, Phagan, Richards, and Erastus Rogers? All of them white men? Furious, Thompson had told them, "If you were so cowardly as to be forced by any body to do what you ought not to do, you are unfit to be chiefs."[58]

That was more than a year ago. And while the term "agent" might seem to imply that Thompson was simply an interlocutor between a naive, nonmaterialistic people and a strong, aggressive society—someone to oversee the distribution of allotments while holding the Seminoles to their promises—in a more literal sense he was an "agent" of government policy, and the policy was removal. He had continued, time after time, meeting after meeting, to coax, urge, even threaten the chiefs, had brought up and repeated every argument for removal that he could think of. The Seminoles, impressed by the number and availability of soldiers that frequently came and went, seeing the inevitability of removal, had gradually begun to come around. But working against a resolution of the problem were the slave hunters snatching black men and women away from their Seminole "owners" without right or title, and the "Whisky Gentry," who had no wish to lose their customers. They provided a constant agitant to the already volatile mixture of white settlers seeking a new life and red and black men struggling to maintain the old. And beneath and behind every move of red or white was the ceaseless anxiety connected with removal.

Thompson knew now that when he had come from Georgia two years ago he had been naive, even ignorant of Seminole character, of the things they held dear and those they scorned. But experience had made it clear that an insult was never forgotten by a Seminole, that revenge was a cherished virtue. Every intemperate word, every overt act of hostility, every broken promise made his job more difficult. A case in point was the problem last June created by the Alachua settlers that had disarmed and horsewhipped half a dozen Seminoles and killed another. Two months later a group of Seminoles had killed the mail carrier coming up from Fort Brooke, mutilated the body. An eye for an eye.[59]

Then, just last month, the Seminole chief Chalo Emathla had been murdered. A stipulation in the general plan of operations for removal was that the government would purchase the cattle of Seminoles willing to emigrate. Chalo Emathla was a farmer and rancher, his village situated in the Wetumka area, only ten miles or so northwest of Fort King. Thompson considered him the most intelligent and enterprising chief in the nation, a man who knew which way the wind was blowing—and when it changed. For years he had spoken eloquently against removal in every official meeting. Last April he had finally given in, signed a statement of capitulation along with fifteen other chiefs. Since then he had been as firm in his plans *for* removal as he had previously been against.[60]

A month ago Chalo Emathla had brought his cattle to the agency pens in preparation for departure, taken his payment in gold coin, and headed home. With him were his two daughters and a black man. Not far from the fort a dozen or so Seminoles hostile to emigration had waylaid him and shot him down. The killers had thrown away his gold, making it clear that robbery was not the motive, that they would kill anyone who attempted to surrender his cattle, give up the land. A few of Chalo Emathla's followers had come to the fort for protection, but most were assumed to have gone over to the hostiles. In short, the tide had turned, and two years of effort on Thompson's part might as well be written off. There had been a general defection among those Seminoles who had pledged to remove voluntarily, and he had reluctantly concluded that actual force, often threatened, was the only means left.[61]

Osceola was at the bottom of it. He was sure of that now. Osceola, a half-breed, was also known as Hasse Ola and Asi-Yahola, though the whites usually called him Powell. Last fall it had become obvious that he was vehemently opposed to removal and determined to prevent it if he could. Such a scheme would not have been surprising coming from a full-blooded Seminole, a native Floridian, a chief, but Osceola was not a full-blooded Seminole. His father was said to be a white man, an Englishman named William Powell, his mother a Creek, and Osceola was thought to have been born in Alabama or Georgia. As far as Thompson could discover, he had no inherent claim to leadership at all. He seemed to have gained a following among the more audacious Seminoles through his self-assurance, his sometimes reckless strength of will, his persuasive manner. Yet even now he was ranked as no more than a subchief at best.[62]

Osceola had begun coming to the agency not long after Thompson arrived. He had appeared to be about thirty years old at the time, of medium height, well built, though with a slight stoop or roundness in his shoulders unusual in an Indian. His complexion was lighter than that of other Seminoles, who were themselves generally lighter skinned than Indians of other tribes. His hair was black but not coarse, his hands and feet small, his voice high and shrill—never more shrill than on the day Thompson had finally had him put in irons.[63]

At the start Osceola had been affable, his smile easy, his handshake firm. His clothing was simple and neat: a long-sleeved hunting shirt of colored calico that came nearly to his knees, secured with a bead-decorated woolen belt tied in the back, the ends brought to the front and retied, the long fringe hanging loose; leggings of tanned buckskin or red woolen broadcloth, with a row of brass buttons down the outside; a length of patterned trade cloth wrapped turbanlike around his head, with three or four heavy plumes stuck in the back and hanging down.[64]

A visitor to the agency commented, "He would come frequently and familiarly to the General's [Clinch's] quarters, and "Well, Powel [sic]," was the accustomed salutation. It was neither idleness, nor idle curiosity, that brought him so often to the quarters of the officers. He profited [sic] by all he saw and heard—appeared to guage [sic] the capacities, and comprehend the qualities of those around him; and would always go away, if not a better, yet a wiser man than when he came. He was never to be seen vaguely and idle [sic] mixing with his people. We do not remember to have once observed him in any of the numerous groups that would be collected for miles around the fort. His presence was felt without being seen. He ruled the many through the agency of the few. *His* 'talks' were in the lowest key, and generally in private. He would take his auditor aside—but without appearing to do it—and would achieve more in few words than the majority of our Congressional orators in their vasty speeches."[65]

Through an interpreter, Osceola and Thompson had had many friendly talks, yet on several occasions, when the subject of removal had come up, Osceola had become abusive, making threats and insulting remarks. He had always calmed down and apologized, and Thompson had overlooked the offense. Then one day last June he had been sullen and moody, carrying the white man's gift of liquor in his belly. It did not create his words, it only released them. In a fit of passion he had told Thompson that Florida belonged to the Seminoles. "The country is ours. We do not want any agent. You should get out." With that he had turned and walked out. Behind him shouts, commands, footsteps of four men running. Osceola was no farther than two hundred yards from the fort when they put their hands on him. He struck out with fists, feet, knees, sending one man staggering back. Another man went down, but the first was back. The soldiers, too, were strong, determined, and they were four. His shrill

voice had shredded the air as he was half-dragged, half-carried back to
the fort, put in chains and irons, locked in a cell. His frenzied cries went
on and on. Thompson was told that the curses, the threats, were aimed
at him: "The sun is high. I will remember the hour. The Agent has had
his day. I will have mine."[66]

Indian talk. Nothing had come of it. When Osceola had realized that
his shouts and threats were getting him nowhere, he had finally calmed
down, even sent word the next day that he would sign the capitulation if
Thompson would release him. Where indulgence had failed, force had
succeeded. Thompson knew the idea of incarceration carried terror to an
Indian mind. But horses had to be broken before they could be trusted.
Only then were they given an apple. So be it. Thompson replied that the
prisoner would be released only if he would publicly acknowledge his
acceptance of removal and, in addition, arrange the intercession of other
leading Seminoles as a guarantee of his own good conduct. Provide hostages, in other words.[67]

Osceola had responded cheerfully and with friendly protestations that
he would do all that was asked and more—if he was freed he would convert
his own followers and bring them back to the fort. Gone now was his
proud and insolent manner. He had clearly learned his lesson. And sure
enough, it wasn't long before several influential chiefs, Chalo Emathla
among them, arrived at the fort. A free man, Osceola was polite, repentant.
He left the fort with a promise to return within five days, bringing his
people. On June 3, the appointed day, the cowbell in the cupola on the
barracks roof rang out the alarm. It was Osceola with seventy-nine men,
women, and children. Publicly, witnessed by the chiefs, he made his mark
on the capitulation.[68]

Emigration wasn't scheduled to begin at Tampa Bay until January 1,
1836. There were no facilities yet at Fort Brooke to take care of Osceola's
followers, and certainly there were none at Fort King. Relieved, confident,
Thompson had sent them home, returned to his office, and written to
Quartermaster George Gibson: "I now have no doubt of his [Osceola's]
sincerity, and as little that the greatest difficulty is surmounted." It was
time for the apple. He wrote to a gunsmith in Savannah, and at a cost of
one hundred dollars ordered a handsome silver-mounted rifle for Osceola.

Later he told his wife with some satisfaction what he had done. She replied: "General Thompson, Osceola will kill you with that gun."[69]

That was six months ago. Now it was Christmas Day, only a week before emigration was to begin. It was hard to say just when and why the "deep laid plan of villany [sic]"—as Colonel Fanning called it—had begun. When Osceola, who from the first had been the leader of those hostile to emigration, had made his elaborate concession in June it had looked like removal was as good as done. In spite of the unfortunate whipping incident and the killing of Dalton, the general plan of operations for removal had been completed by the end of August. Thompson would assemble the emigrants at forts King and Brooke and provide them with rations as well as pens for their cattle while they waited to take the long journey west. They had already begun coming into Fort Brooke to await removal. But it was apparent now that Osceola had never meant to leave.[70]

During a contentious meeting last year between Thompson and a number of chiefs and their followers, all the old arguments over removal had been repeated, back and forth, on and on. Finally Osceola had taken the floor, unasked and defiant. "If I *speak*, what I say, I *will do*. Speak or no speak, *what I resolve, that I execute*." Sure enough, his murder of Chalo Emathla had produced a general defection among those Seminoles who *had* pledged to emigrate. Thompson had given him friendship, had received treachery in return.[71]

Heavy rain pounded the agency roof, thunder boomed like cannon fire. Conflict was now inevitable. Thompson had tried reasoning, persuasion, had summoned patience and Christian forbearance, had done all he could to convince these refractory people to follow the path decreed by the American government. Instead they had willfully chosen to bring down upon themselves the power of that government. Though Fanning's departure tomorrow would leave him with only a handful of men to defend the fort, the necessary concentration of troops under General Clinch would force the Seminoles to yield or be crushed. Already there were twelve companies of regulars in Florida, three more on the way. Gardiner and two companies were expected hourly. More men would be needed, of course—hundreds, perhaps thousands. Too few at first, and late, but they would come, and, eventually, the Seminoles would go—what was left of them. Osceola might talk of resistance, but the course he was pursuing could hardly have been better calculated to bring ruin upon himself and his people.[72]

Fort Brooke stood barely fifteen feet above high tide on Tampa Bay. The elevation had increased by only ten feet when Dade's command had made camp at the Little Hillsborough. Sixteen miles east and north, their bivouac at the Big Hillsborough was still only sixty feet above sea level. Gardiner's map showed that the morning's road would continue flat, easy as marches go, due north no more than half a mile, swing east or west, skirting pond or swamp. In the afternoon they would enter the hills.[73]

Shallow pools of stagnant water spattered the land, waiting only for the spring rains to spread and join, cover the land in a thin flood. All marshy, miry, or swampy ground in the path of the road had originally been causewayed with poles or split timber fifteen feet long, five to eight inches in diameter at the small end, laid down compactly side by side across the direction of the road and secured at each end with heavy riders firmly staked down. Ditches four feet wide and three deep had been dug on both sides, the sand thrown onto the causeway and graded down from the center toward the sides. Poles and timbers had long ago decayed, but the grade remained.[74]

The sky was cloudy, leaking rain. A breeze from the southeast didn't do much to offset nearly seventy-degree heat. In woolen jackets and pants soaked with riverwater, rain, and sweat, the men hiked on, mile after weary mile through woods of long-leaf pine, frequent stretches of scrubland—low, sandy ground, barren except for tough, stunted thickets of scrub oak, dwarf pine, myrtle, prickly pear, and palmetto, savannas of tall grass. Advance, flankers, and rear guard saw no sign of Seminoles. By the noontime halt they had crossed the flatlands. Entering the hills, the road began to bend to one side, then the other, rising a little on a slope, swinging around instead of up and over, down across a shallow valley, then up and around again, bearing a little east, a little west, but like a compass needle always coming back to north. The road had been built as straight as possible, steep hills in the path cut down and so wound around as to reduce as much as practicable the steepness of the ascent and to render them passable for carriages and loaded wagons.[75]

The hills grew higher around them—100 feet, 150, 200—seeming mountains in this table-flat land. By mid-afternoon they had crossed the western slope of one and then, soon, another that must have reached a height of 250 feet. The road curved around the flanks at a level of 150 feet, then a hilltop towered above them on the right, a two-mile-long lake filling the hollows between lesser hills on the left. Here was the divide between the rivers, the rain of the morning flowing back toward the Hillsborough, and ahead the watershed for the Withlacoochee. Across the flatlands of morning and now from the hillsides a man could have seen for miles except for the endless forest, a composition of 180 varieties of trees adapted through a million years to every type of soil between the Atlantic and the Gulf, from Key West to Georgia. And behind every tree could lurk a Seminole.[76]

Hagerman's Hole lay a few miles ahead. Beyond the spring the hills would begin to fade, the land smooth out, beginning its fall north and east to the Big Withlacoochee. They would make camp at Hagerman's; tomorrow they would reach the river, enter the dread Cove of the Withlacoochee.

The advance guard came out of the hills, passed a pond on the right of the road, flankers pushing through tall grass and palmetto on either side as the main body came up, deployed. Pacheco was waiting. He stood alone, apart. The major would send for him when he was ready. The oxen lumbered in, the supply wagon was uncovered, axes passed out, and eager hands swung them with a will. The horse team brought the gun. It was unlimbered, readied for use. The night's barricade rose log by log, one notched down upon another to a height of two or three feet. Men were organized by company and squad, details read off for outpost or picket guard, water, fire, and latrine duty. In spite of time lost in crossing the Hillsborough they had made a good fifteen miles. Not a bad day's work. Now hungry bellies and tired bodies wanted only food and rest. They soon had both.[77]

Pacheco made his report. He told of seeing the grass flattened down in the woods along the road, a sign that the Seminoles had been hovering around the camp. He had passed the vacant cabins, the empty fields. He told of finding Istowatchotka. He reported that he had not seen the black man, Sam, but did not reveal that he had seen another black man on the road, a man who told him that Major Dade had been warned at Fort Brooke of the likelihood of an attack at the Withlacoochee. Yesterday the

major had assured him that the Seminoles were not hostile. To tell him
now that he was privy to the major's information would not be wise. In
any case, the major seemed to pay little attention to his report. His only
response was, "I guess Sam's gone to Wahoo Swamp to keep Christmas."[78]

"No, Major. It's worse than 'keep Christmas.' There wasn't a soul on
the place."[79]

Again Dade ignored the comment, merely telling the slave to be prepared
to go on to Wahoo Swamp in the morning, again scout out the land.
Officers nearby listened to the exchange. Captain Fraser knew the danger
as well as any man among them. As past commander at Fort Brooke,
perhaps he felt he knew it a little better than some.

"Major, it's dangerous to send this man on. You don't know what the
Indians will do." Dade turned on his heel in disdain. Fraser turned to the
scout. "What do you think about it, Louis?" Pacheco had no illusions
about what his treatment would be at the hands of Seminoles. They
accepted blacks (as they had once accepted whites) as equals, allowed them
all that they allowed an Indian—life, and opportunity. But he was no
Indian and had no wish to live in the wilds. He had lived all his life with
white people, was as much a product of their civilization as any white
man, in spite of the fact that he was a slave. He did their work, carried
their gun. The Seminoles would doubtless deal with him as they would
a white man. "If they catch me, Massa, they'll kill me sure."[80]

Eleven o'clock. A shout came from the darkness beyond the fires, south
on the Fort King Road. "Who comes there?" Men stumbled to their feet,
loading muskets as they rose. Again they could hear the challenge of the
outpost guard. Men stared, listened, waited. "Corporal of the guard!"[81]

Finally one man, a soldier, was brought through the barrier by the
officer of the guard and taken to the major. Those close by recognized
him in the firelight. Word passed swiftly through the camp—it's Jewell,
Aaron Jewell, back from the fort. Goddamn! Went back twenty-two miles
yesterday, came back today. Guess Seminoles ain't no worry to him. Just
walks right through 'em.[82]

Himself a volunteer, the major could appreciate this quality in another.
As a matter of fact, this little army had plenty of volunteers. Lieutenant
Henderson was technically a civilian, but there he stood. And Gardiner,
safe at the fort, had left safety behind so fast he still wore a civilian coat

over his uniform. What made them do it? He didn't know. Maybe nobody did.

He opened Belton's letter knowing there could be no news that would make a real difference now to him or to those who stood about, waiting. Jewell had already been asked by every man that saw him if reinforcement was on the way. It wasn't. Wouldn't even start until tomorrow morning. What could *it* do for them? Thirty-eight miles behind and not much chance of getting closer. He opened the letter. Well, Jewell was right, if there had been any doubt. Mountfort's company was still at Tampa Bay. What was this? With or without the second company? *One* company? *Fifty* men? Good God! If *this* command was in peril, what chance did a single company trailing two days in the rear have? They wouldn't be at risk— they'd be doomed. Seminoles could pick them like a ripe orange. At Fort Brooke, Belton had debated the advisability of sending *two* companies, had said he'd resign before *he* would accept the command, yet now he thought it proper to send out *half* that number? He read on. Mountfort would bring thirteen hundred rations on packhorses . . . and what ammunition Belton could spare. Belton was going to risk fifty men on a forced march, burden them with a string of packhorses carrying *food?* "From all this you can regulate your movements so as to allow the reinforcement to join you."[83]

Regulate their movements? The only direction they could move to allow Mountfort to join them was backward, toward Fort Brooke. Or did he mean to suggest that they sit here for two days? No matter, really. Whatever Belton thought no longer mattered—not to this detachment. Seminoles were all around, had been for days, probably since the moment they left the fort. Ahead, far out on their flanks, trailing them. Nothing Belton could do would help them now. A junction with Mountfort was out of the question, probably had been after the first day. Only stealth and darkness and a miracle had allowed Jewell to make it through. At moments like this it looked like the same might hold true for them all.

He wrote a brief response, letting Belton know that Jewell had gotten in, that they would push on in the morning. Holata Emathla's son could carry the message back. They needed an Indian boy about as much as they needed the slave. And better the boy go back than a soldier. If the hostiles started trouble he'd need every man he had.[84]

Chapter Four

The Fourth Day
Saturday, December 26, 1835

Before dawn a messenger was brought to Belton from Holata Emathla. An interpreter listened, thought, turned the Seminole words into English: Some of Holata Emathla's people had just come in from getting stock . . . among them were men who had wives among the hostiles . . . the women had heard scouts report that the major and his soldiers had crossed the Lokcha-popka-chiska yesterday morning . . . had marched on toward the Weewa-thlock-ko. Chief Yaholoochee (called Cloud by the white men), leading some of the Pea Creek band and the party who burnt the bridge, planned to attack the soldiers tomorrow night. Holata Emathla was anxious that this warning be carried by express to the major . . . and he urged that his son, if he was still with the soldiers, be allowed to return with the runner.[1]

God almighty. Dade had crossed the Hillsborough—was pushing on. Belton had taken for granted that the command would be delayed at the river, that Jewell would reach them there, that Dade would wait. Mountfort would have had only twenty miles or so to go, could have reached him today with a forced march. Still, Jewell should have reached the command last night, even beyond the river. With the knowledge that Mountfort was in, was leaving at dawn, Dade would surely hold up where he was. But now the distance was thirty, thirty-five miles—more than Mountfort could cover in a day. And the Seminoles *were* lying in wait. He had let himself believe it was only a rumor—Indian talk. At least Holata Emathla believed it, wanted to get his son back before the shooting started. And if he *were* to credit the warning, if the Seminoles were prepared to attack Dade, what of Mountfort with only fifty men? And if

Dade *didn't* wait, Mountfort could never reach him now. Have to send an express, warn Dade, let him know that Mountfort and . . . well, that Mountfort was on the way. . . . No, he couldn't do that . . . couldn't send him alone . . . have to wait for Greyson. But how long? . . . There had been no lights on the bay all night. Still, if Greyson *was* in the bay, could disembark his command quickly . . .

The sun finally rose with a clear morning light, the bay watched by every open eye. The light spread, Gadsden's Point visible more than five miles south, the open water of Tampa Bay beyond. Empty. It seemed impossible. Officers, soldiers, and civilians exchanged rumors. Most seemed to believe that Greyson was in the bay, though no one claimed to have seen his ship. But the peninsula jutting down into the bay from the north that terminated in Gadsden's Point split the upper part of Tampa Bay in half. The fort stood on the east side of the east lobe, called Hillsborough Bay, while the west lobe, or Old Tampa Bay, twice as large as Hillsborough, was concealed from view by the peninsula between. Looking west from the fort it was a good two miles across Hillsborough, another mile across the heavily wooded peninsula. Whether Greyson had sailed into the wrong branch or was still twenty miles or so south, just in from the Gulf, God only knew. But wherever he was, he wasn't *here*. That was all that mattered right now.[2]

Belton knew there were those who were saying that he should never have allowed *two* companies to march out, much less consider allowing a single company to follow them, suggesting even that he should have ignored the commanding general's orders for "a handful of men," as Lieutenant Casey put it, to attempt a march through the heart of the Nation. They pointed out that it had been months since Clinch had visited Fort Brooke, that they were here "without any instructions, authority or means," and that the command had been sent out "in opposition to our opinions, formed on the spot." Of course they were right, but it was all beside the point. Orders were still orders. As he saw it, his only option had been in the phrase "as soon as practicable." Given that the route was alive with Seminoles and a shortage of troops was endemic, December 23 had been as "practicable" a time as any other.[3]

On the other hand, he was *not* under orders to send another single company. And it looked like that meant no reinforcement today—which

THE FOURTH DAY 131

probably meant no reinforcement at all. Tell that to Dade, Gardiner, Fraser? He had already told them that Mountfort was pulling out at dawn—now. What if they were waiting? Jesus. Have to tell them how things stood with Mountfort. But wait—he could hold the express a little longer, give Greyson, Mountfort—Dade—every chance. A mounted courier would make better time, but when and if Mountfort and Greyson did leave they would need every horse, every mule he had, in addition to what the next transport brought. But even an Indian runner should reach the detachment around midnight, a little after—enough time to warn of an attack. But where was Greyson?

Noon finally came, but not Greyson. Time was left only for a letter. Belton went to his desk and took up his pen. It did no good to think of Dade out there waiting, listening—for attack, for reinforcement. No good at all. "Sir. I send this . . . to apprise you . . . that you will be attacked tomorrow night. . . . Holata just now urges that his son, if yet with you, should return with this express." Holata Emathla had been conducting himself with his band in a manner worthy of all praise. For whatever his son might be worth to Dade as interpreter, hostage, or one more gun, he felt obliged to pass on the chief's request.[4]

Then, in spite of his assurance of yesterday, he had to tell Dade that he was on his own, after all. "I have delayed Maj Mountford [sic] for the other company." But he hastened to assure him that when Mountfort and Greyson did leave they would still be bringing the extra rations he had promised. "Many flying reports about your movements but Nothing Certain, it is said that Powell has cut up a company of Georgia Militia 100 strong and with three waggons at the Ocklawaha; with small loss."[5]

He had no help to send—only a dire warning, promised help withheld, rumors, concern, nervous commentary, some New Orleans papers. Time was running out, a young Indian express was waiting to go. He closed abruptly with "Very Truly, etc., etc.," signed his name, continued writing.

"P.S. This night our courier sent to Micanopy, should get in. The old Tallassee is here—but I much doubt whether I shall leave—if I do I will write by Maj. M." Finally he blurted it out—what he had wanted to say from the beginning: "Shall you keep on?" He folded the note, sealed it, handed it to the runner. Good luck. Wait. What about Jewell? What if

he had run into trouble, hadn't gotten through? Better send a copy of
Jewell's letter in order for Dade to understand the references to Mountfort.
A copy was made, given to the runner. The man turned away, hurried
out.[6]

Osceola lay on his belly. The heavy rain of the day before had left the
sand damp, cool. Cradled in his arms was a silver-mounted rifle. Fronds
of dense palmetto rustled above his head. A breeze came toward him past
the sutler's nearby house and store, the agency beyond, and, farther on,
the fort. The morning sun was a glowing light behind the trees on his
left, the roof of the soldiers' barracks just visible above the tall, log walls,
damp flag barely stirring. A host of tassikaya, Seminole warriors, lay
scattered throughout the hammock, silent, intent, invisible among the
brown, loglike palmetto trunks, beneath the rustling green fans. The
Seminoles watched as the sutler and his people carried out boxes, crates,
and bundles from the store. It was clear that the goods were being removed
and carried to the fort, the store emptied. Stray dogs roamed the area but
did not come toward the hammock. Sometimes one would look their way,
raise his head, and, catching their scent, turn, slink away. The white men
paid no attention to the animals' behavior, unable to comprehend that
Indians knew how to control dogs, to keep them quiet. Of more interest
was the sound of drums coming from the distant fort, the faraway call of
orders.[7]

Many times had Osceola watched the soldiers during their practice and
preparation for war at Tampa Bay and here at Fort King. He had seen
the soldiers' willing submission to the orders of officers, the men who
wore the gold and silver marks upon their shoulders, the long swords. It
was easy to see the strength it gave the white men when, in battle, all
would move and fight on a series of commands. It was also clear that if
officers were killed early in battle the soldiers, leaderless, not thinking for
themselves, might be more easily overcome, like a snake without its head.[8]

He had also listened to their signals, whether by voice, bugle, or drum.
This morning he had heard the sound of reveille at dawn, then the "General"
had sounded telling the soldiers in the fort to pull down their tents,
load their wagons. And moments ago "Assembly" had been signaled,
calling the men to make formation prior to marching. Some of the soldiers

were going to leave. There would be fewer men around his "friend," Wiley Thompson.[9]

Osceola had known many white men in his life. An early memory was of the man the white people now called the president, Andrew Jackson. He could remember being taken captive with his mother, Polly, by Jackson's soldiers. He had been too young to be a warrior of his people, the Tallassee, a tribe of the Creek Nation. His mother had brought him south from the place called Alabama when he was only a che-paw-nee, a boy. There had been trouble. Polly and her husband, William Powell, a white man, had separated. Two sisters had stayed with their father when his mother had taken him to the Okefenoke Swamp, where they joined friendly Mikasukis. Later still they had come to Florida, traveling with a band under a man called Peter McQueen, related to his mother. The band had been in camp along the Econfina, between St. Marks and the Suwanee, when the soldiers attacked. McQueen and most of the warriors had escaped, but nearly one hundred women and children had been taken. He could still remember the terror of the attack, the fighting, killing, and capture.[10]

It was not long before an old woman of the band had somehow arranged with Jackson for the release of the women and children. She led them far to the south, beyond Tampa Bay to Peas Creek where McQueen and his Tallassee band, having eluded Jackson's soldiers, had established a village. In time Osceola, heir to no title or power, through personality, physical prowess, and capacity for leadership, had gained respect and a following among the young men of the Mikasuki. Then, about the time he himself had gained the age and position of tassikaya, he and his mother moved once more, to another Mikasuki settlement at the northern edge of the reservation, not far south and west of Fort King.[11]

Once again he was acknowledged the best athlete and hunter, the most expert at running, wrestling, and all physical challenges among the young Mikasuki warriors. In acknowledgment of his superiority they began referring to him as Tallassee Tustenuggee, or subchief. As a warrior Osceola recognized Holata Micco, Blue King, leader of the Mikasukis, as his immediate chief.[12]

During frequent visits to Fort King he had come to know the successive agents—Humphreys, Phagan, and now Thompson—as well as many officers and men. Once, acting as guide to a party of mounted white men, he had inquired about the cause of their slow pace. Informed that it was out of consideration for him, afoot, he dismissed their concern and urged them to proceed at whatever pace they chose. When the party spurred on he kept with them through the day's travel, arriving at their destination without any signs of fatigue. His lithe, nearly naked figure exhibited "the most beautiful development of muscle and power . . . the easy grace, the stealthy step and active spring of the tiger."[13]

In their efforts to maintain the increasingly uneasy peace, and "knowing his resolution and prowess . . . U.S. Officers, as well as the Indians, all looked to Oceola [sic] to secure offenders." It was a fact that Osceola had, in past years, urged the policy of remaining within the reservation, had taken more pains and endured more fatigue in pursuing those who had strayed, had induced them to return to the reservation, even to submit to punishment, than any other. "By his boldness and energy, he always succeeded in bringing them in." And by so doing he had earned not their enmity but their respect and subordination.[14]

As a young man he had thought that a promise was a promise, an agreement an agreement. But that was before the white men in all their numbers had come, had insisted on rules and boundaries, had drawn maps, written on papers, and convinced the Seminoles that it was a wise thing to make their marks. And after the confusion of a meeting, the endless words, the promises, the threats, there were always rewards: powder, knives, cloth. In those times it was possible to think of the white men as unwelcome intruders; they were blundering, rude, but not a danger. They would pass, like so many afflictions in life. And, finally, one could go away, east, west, or south, and leave the problem behind. Who could have imagined that one day there would not be enough room in Florida to get away from their strange and threatening ways, to go where an Indian could live in the way the Great Spirit had meant for him to live, with his own people?

No, by the time it became clear that with the white man only the *Indian's* promise must be kept, that only those things agreed to by the *Indian* must be carried out, by then there was no place to get away to, all but the swamps had been infected with whites. Osceola and his people had allowed themselves to be herded together like cattle in a pen by the treaty at

Moultrie Creek, then sent away by the papers signed at Payne's Landing and Fort Gibson. They had been as much fooled by good words as they had been forced by guns. Perhaps he should have understood the white men long ago. Like most Seminoles, he had believed, he had trusted. A warrior, he had thought himself a man.

At their first meeting with Thompson, Chalo Emathla had told him, "I view you as a friend, but if we differ in opinion, *I am a man, and have a right to express my sentiments.*" Osceola, neither chief nor subchief, did not have the right of speaking in council. He had attended the first day, the second, had listened as Micanopy, Ote Emathla, Halpatter Tuste-nuggee, and other chiefs demanded the provisions and protection from the whites due them under the Treaty of Moultrie Creek, provisions and protection for which they had given up all of Florida except the reservation. Thompson, brushing aside their demands, said talk of Moultrie was foolish and unreasonable, that he would talk to them only of removal as agreed to at Payne's Landing. Alarmed by his language and irritated by his response, his listeners put aside their usual solemnity, muttering quietly but in harsh words among themselves. As though speaking to unruly children, Thompson ignored their complaints, asking repeatedly if they wished to be paid in gold for their cattle before they left Florida or to be given equal cattle later? And did they wish to leave Florida by water or by land?[15]

Irritation turned to anger, and several chiefs protested with high words and violent gestures that they had signed the paper at Payne's Landing only under threat. Ote Emathla told the agent that those who signed had done so only to keep the white men quiet. Micanopy insisted that he had not signed the treaty at all. In mid-afternoon, refusing to listen any longer, Thompson had dismissed them, told them not to bring him anymore foolish talk when they returned.[16]

Later in the day the chiefs met with their own people in private council within the Seminole camp. Here anyone could voice an opinion. Osceola, furious with Thompson's insistence that the Seminoles must leave the land, alarmed by the faltering indecision of some chiefs, and desperate with the certainty that not words but war alone could save them, rose to speak.[17]

"My Brothers! The white people got some of our chiefs to sign a paper

to give our lands to them; . . . they [did] wrong; we must do right. The
agent tells us we must go away from the lands which we live on—our
homes, and the graves of our Fathers, and go over the big river among
the bad Indians. When the agent tells me to go from my home, I hate
him, because I love my home, and will not go from it."[18]

"My Brothers! When the [G]reat [S]pirit tells me to go with the white
man, I go; but he tells me not to go. The white man says I shall go, and
he will send people to make me go; but I have a rifle, and I have some
powder and some lead. I say, we must not leave our homes and lands. If
any of our people want to go west we won't let them; and I tell them that
they are our enemies, and we will treat them so, for the [G]reat [S]pirit
will protect us."[19]

The council chamber fell silent. Holata Emathla, a leading chief and
one of several who had no wish to struggle against the soldiers, who had,
like his brother Chalo Emathla, spoken for removal, did not speak now.
Among the crowd were several who listened, remembered, and would
report to the agent.[20]

Whites and Seminoles met a third time. Thompson asked for an answer
to his three questions. Ote Emathla said again that he did not wish to go,
that Moultrie gave them twenty years to live in peace, in Florida. Osceola,
seated next to Micanopy, spoke to him in a whisper, urged him to be
firm. The head chief, grown old and timid, listened, then spoke. "I say
what I said yesterday, I did not sign the treaty." There was silence for a
moment while the agent listened to the translation. He turned to the black
interpreter at his side. "Abraham, tell Micanopy that I say he lies."[21]

Thompson returned to his theme, reviewing *his* opinion of the facts,
driving home *his* view of the hopeless future for Seminoles in Florida. "I
stand up for the last time to tell you that you must go; if not willingly,
you will be compelled to go."[22]

The agent had been speaking, pausing, speaking, pausing, for half an
hour while Abraham struggled to turn the English words into his version
of Seminole. Before he finished Thompson's final words, "no more annuity
will be paid you here," Osceola was on his feet, eyes flashing, scorn upon
his upcurled lip, his voice clear and shrill: "I do not care if any more
annuity is *ever* paid!" Ignoring the outburst, not deigning to acknowledge
a response from a common warrior, Thompson continued, "I hope you

will, on more mature reflection, act like honest men, and not compel me to report you to your father, the President, as faithless to your engagements."[23]

Again Osceola was standing, arm raised, fist clenched. "*The sentiments of the [N]ation have been expressed.* THERE IS LITTLE MORE TO BE SAID! The [N]ation have consulted, have declared, they should *perform*— what *should* be, SHALL be! There remains nothing WORTH WORDS! If the hail rattles, let the flowers be crushed—the stately oak . . . will lift its head to the sky and the storm, towering and unscathed."[24]

Winter passed, and Osceola had continued to urge his views upon the people. Such was his growing influence that when April came and another meeting between Thompson and his charges was planned, a white visitor at the fort noticed that "the first question asked by those who had come to be present at the talk was, 'How is Powel [*sic*]—on which side is *he?*' To this we received for answer—'O he is one of the opposition; but he is fast coming round. He has given us much trouble—restless, turbulent, dangerous—he has been busy with his people, dissuading them against the treaty—and thus sowing the seeds of discord where his influence,— for, though young, and a sub-chief merely, he is manifestly a rising man among them—if exerted on our side would greatly facilitate our views. But he has cooled down latterly and we have great hopes of him now."[25]

James Simmons of St. Augustine was seated with friends on the piazza one evening "when a somewhat tall, slightly but well built Indian, came suddenly and quickly up the steps, taking us almost by surprise. His air was unassuming, but graceful and dignified; and his presence marked by great self-possession. He had a slight stoop in his shoulders, but carried his limbs as if their joints had been oiled. The play of his arms was singularly free and rapid, as, indeed, were the movements of the whole man; but the manner in which he used his arms we were particularly struck with—it was characterized by that ease and energy which may be observed in animals accustomed to spring upon their prey, but which we had never before seen displayed in the action of the human arm. . . . His waist was small, the whole figure elegant—and yet it inspired you with the idea of combined craft and power. He walked with his head down, which, together with the crouching of the shoulders, and that peculiar action of the arms, occasioned you, if in the same path with him, involuntarily to give way; yet, not without a certain feeling of admiration for the fine and flexible form that moved with an air of wild freedom so fleetly and silently before you.

"But if the figure of the man, which, without being at first striking, would yet gradually grow on the attention, presented an image of combined energy and elegance, the face was eminently worthy of a Raffael [*sic*]! The prevailing tone was that of profound melancholy, which rendered his smile the most wildly beautiful we had ever beheld. The eye, shrouded by long, dark lashes, appeared to sleep as within a shroud, but it was a shroud of thoughts, which you could not doubt had for their subject the sad fortunes of his race, hundreds of whom were there around him, reminding him by their presence of their impending doom—if indeed he ever could forget this—for did not the wing of that cloudy destiny which hovered over *them*, throw, too, its cold shadow upon *him?* It was an eye, then, full of fearful meaning; anxious, restless, when not fixed in thought, for then it riveted as if it grew upon the object on which its gaze had fallen. When in one of these moods of intense musing, the head would be partially turned on one side, as if looking over the shoulder, which gave an air of deeper abstraction to his manner, from which, whenever recalled by anything said or done by those near him, it was always with one of those beautiful and seemingly unconscious smiles that acted like a mysterious charm on the beholder; it fascinated while it freezed; you admired, and yet shrunk from it; for after all was it not the smile of a savage, a high souled Indian, without doubt; daring, dauntless; of amazing powers of mind and body; courage to bear, as well as act; but one, nevertheless, whose bloody code interposed a perpetual barrier between your sympathies and his. Perhaps, however, the most characteristic, as it certainly was the most marked, feature of the face, was the mouth. . . . The space between it and the chin was such as to give to the curled underlip an air of high disdain, of indignant energy; while a faint, perhaps, but indelible trace of ferocity played around that noble mouth, at each corner of which a speck of froth, white as the flaked snow, yet wrathful, as if it had been forced up there by the workings of the vexed spirit within, might generally be seen enhancing, in no small degree, the savage expression of the mouth. . . . There was a tremulous motion about the lips; it was but the faint breath from the whirlwind of that stormy soul that played upon them,

Osceola. Smithsonian Institution.

and gave to them their nearly audible vibration—they seemed as if they panted but to curse and kill!

"It was this contrast between the repose of one feature, and the constant and almost painful play of the other; between the quiet of the eye and the action of the mouth, that might be said to stamp its peculiar character upon the face of [Osceola]. The nose was Grecian, perfect! The chin ample, square, and firmly set. The head not large, though somewhat long, but with nothing of the 'retreating forehead and deprest [sic] vertex' which is believed to indicate an inferior grade of intellect. The head, on the contrary, was altogether a fine one. His dress was plain, though full—leggins; the hunting shirt and turban; with moccasins of fine soft leather, closely fitted to his feet."[26]

Then Thompson prohibited further sales of powder and lead. To both whites and Seminoles this was clearly a hostile act toward the Nation, virtually a declaration of war. Outraged, Osceola had gone to Thompson. "Am I a negro, a slave? My skin is dark, but not black. I am an Indian—a Seminole. The white man shall not make me black. I will make the white man red with blood; and then blacken him in the sun and rain, where the wolf shall smell of his bones, and the buzzard live upon his flesh."[27]

That was summer, half a year ago, when the world was green and he was young. Now it was winter again. The world was brown and Osceola was a man. From the fort the "March" rolled from the drums. At first all he could see were the soldiers' flags, then the column of men came in distant view, marching two by two, white crossbelts bright against blue coats, drums rattling out the step. Small, one-armed Lieutenant Colonel Fanning followed the advance guard, leading the main body, the peculiar ring of his shrill voice carrying clearly. One company, fifty men, passed the hidden Seminoles. A second, a third, then the rear guard. Only one company then was left at the fort, along with the sutler, a few Indians friendly to the whites, several slaves, and Thompson. They would be more cautious now, but they could not stay within the fort forever.[28]

Sixty-two miles south of Fort King, officers and men of Dade's command had been up before first light, struggling into boots, equipment, answering roll call, eating, ready or not. The sun had revealed a clear sky, a cool day. Today the first six or seven miles would continue flat, due north, in the afternoon dropping slowly but steadily through the spring and summer floodlands, a land of lakes, ponds, and marshes even in this dry, winter season. Two miles east of camp was the Withlacoochee River, parallel to the road, flowing north. About midday the road would turn northeast, the river northwest. By late afternoon they should reach the Little Withlacoochee, coming in from the east to join the main river.

Pacheco waited for his orders. The major was talking to Captain Fraser. "See here, Captain, I had a strange dream last night. It was one of the strangest dreams of my life. I dreamed that I was among all the old officers that died in the war." While Pacheco waited, Dade went on to give the officers' names, how each of them looked, what they did, and what they said. Finally taking notice of the slave, he said nothing further of sending him to Wahoo Swamp, told him instead to go on to the river, reconnoiter the area. Neither spoke of waiting Seminoles.[29]

Company drums rolled "Assembly," noncoms shouted orders, men took their places in the long, double column, grumbled, joked, adjusted their equipment, waited for the command. Flankers out, advance and rear guards in position, the order was given, they were under way.

Dade drifted up and down the column. He knew that men stared as he passed, trying to gauge their chances in his face, his bearing. He sat easy in his saddle, nodding confidently to an officer or noncom. The confidence was real. They faced nothing now that they hadn't faced from the time they left Fort Brooke. It was a gamble of one hundred men against whatever the Seminoles might do. Men who carried guns were always subject to being shot by other men with guns. The only difference was that the risk had been theoretical at Fort Brooke; here it was real.

Others were not so confident. Upton Fraser had labored mightily as commander of Fort Brooke to strengthen the defenses, had expected attack in spite of palisade walls, two six-pounders, and nearly two hundred men. If the fort had been in danger, what could be said of this detachment— half the men, one gun, and already forty miles from help? The unmistakable sounds of Seminoles in the night, every night, left no doubt that the command was being watched. But in spite of threatening, derisive taunts from the darkness, graphically translated by Pacheco and others, a sense of movement just beyond the range of vision through the day, and occa-

sional signs reported by Pacheco, there had been no real threat, only the
sense of a Seminole *presence*, the feeling that the odds against them were
growing with every mile they traveled. The sun was bright, the sky as blue
as kerseymere trousers, palmetto blossoms and flowering vines nodding
cheerfully in the southeast breeze, but dread was beginning to ride behind
Fraser. Often he rode apart from the column, taking small parties with
him, scouring the woods and hammocks sometimes for a mile or more
off, men calling to and running the dogs with cries of "Sooby, boy! Sooby!"
He watched for a flicker of motion through the trees, a flash of color in
the palmetto, the brown grass.[30]

While Fraser rode silent or apart, his noncoms kept order and control
under the aegis of lieutenants Mudge and Keais. Second Lieutenant Robert
Rich Mudge of Lynn, Massachusetts, was the oldest of eleven children,
ten of them living. His father, Benjamin, had followed the sea in his
youth, been captain of the artillery company in Lynn from 1813 to 1816.
Robert had early on shown a special interest in military affairs, in fact a
"conspicuous military ardor," in the opinion of Lt. John Child, a friend
and West Point graduate. With Child's encouragement, Robert had applied
for entrance in 1827, when he was seventeen. Turned down, he had
reapplied the next year, only to be passed by a second time. Accepted on
his third try, he had entered in July 1829 with Benjamin Mudge's "cheerful
assent." He graduated as brevet second lieutenant, Third Artillery, four
years later, fourteenth in a class of forty-three. He had served at Fort
Sullivan in Eastport, Maine, and for the past year as assistant instructor
of infantry tactics back at West Point.

"During his connection with the institution there, he made an excursion
with several other young gentlemen to Montreal and Quebec, visiting the
British officers in those places, examining their system of discipline and
tactics." In September he had received a promotion to full second lieutenant, along with a transfer to Florida and his first real field service. He
wore a black leather shako adorned with a gilt eagle, crossed cannons, and
a gold regimental 3 as well as red cockfeathers in a gilt socket. Beneath
the hat his black hair was short, curly. He wore no beard. White gloves
covered a chased gold ring on one finger. A young man of delicate features,
fine teeth, amiable disposition, and studious habits, he had time, as he
marched with the men, to compare infantry tactics as practiced in the

Second Lieutenant Robert Rich Mudge. From *Memorials: Being a Biographical and Historical Account of the Name of Mudge in America* (Boston, 1868).

field with those he had recently studied in Canada and taught at West Point.[31]

John Low Keais, "of a highly respectable family but unfortunately poor," was still second lieutenant by brevet only. Twenty-four years old, just six months out of West Point, he was a classmate of Henderson, who was marching up ahead with Gardiner's company. Though described as "a friendless orphan" when he applied for an appointment to the academy, Keais had nonetheless managed a letter of recommendation from Vice President Calhoun. At West Point he had earned friends as well as a commission. A month after graduation he had written to Bvt. 2nd Lt. Abraham R. Johnstone, classmate and friend, "I accepted the appointment, took the oath and wrote to my Genl. for orders. He has assigned me to Fort Brooke, Tampa Bay, Florida and it is likely that I shall set out for it in a few weeks. From what I can learn of the country, [going there] will be equivalent to intering [sic] myself alive. Indians for companions—alligators—deer—bears and whatnot for playthings."[32]

Perhaps it was the calm of furlough after the struggle of West Point, but in August, waiting for assignment, John had plunged into lethargy and felt that his situation was the most critical that he should ever occupy. From the dark side of a slump he attempted to assess the value of his military education and wondered if "the 4 years labor I have just accomplished was for something—or for worse than nothing." Three months later, at Fort Brooke, the black mood had passed. John could look back on it as an "impulse of the moment or dictated by some peculiar vein into which I had fallen—soon to get out of and never perhaps to fall into again."[33]

The long voyage down the east coast, around the Keys, and up the Gulf to Tampa Bay in October may have effected a sea change. John was certain it would "form an era in my life. The occurances [sic] [of the journey] might not have struck many people at all—but novelty gave them such a coloring that in my eyes they almost look like *adventures*. To be at sea in a little boat . . . the whole crew drunk—the passengers drunk and helpless and sick—the boat leaking like a riddle—I [as] Captain and Mate and Sailors—now steering—now pumping ship and now threatening to tumble all passengers overboard sick as they were if they did not assist me to free the ship of water. . . . [W]hen I remember this novel situation

I can't help thinking[, having] got out of it safely[,] that I had achieved an Adventure."[34]

The novelty of Indians, alligators, and deer had worn off soon after Keais's safe arrival at Fort Brooke, "this jumping off place of creation." By this expression he referred only to the fort's distance from where his journey had begun, "without making any allusion to the qualities of the place itself." Lt. John Casey, recently in from Pensacola, had assured him that Fort Brooke was "superior to [Fort Pickins] or any other post on the Gulf," in spite of the fact that they "had arrived at a more unfavorable time than any for the last 10 years." Did he refer to the Seminole threat? If John's heart started, Casey reassured him that he referred only to the last, severe winter, which had killed the fort's grove of oranges and limes. Captain Belton himself had told Keais that the fruit ordinarily "lay under the trees . . . in such heaps that the men chunked one another with them!!"[35]

In August Keais had complained that he did not like "La vie Militaire," neither the giving nor the taking of orders. In November, though the novelty of tropical frontier life was gone, he had not yet grown dissatisfied. "At present I like the service and have no intention of quitting soon." How long this mood would last he could not say, but "judging by the great thirst I have for change . . . I should answer not long." Change had come a month later with the order for his company to prepare for the march to Fort King. "What is to be my history of course is more than I can guess." For now it was enough to tramp beside the men, his new boots dulled by sand, new trousers snagged and limp from brush and wear, his shirt soaked with sweat beneath the heavy coat, the small pistol in his pocket just another burden. It looked like Belton was right when he said they might not find another orange tree within sixty miles of Fort Brooke. Here there were "nothing but pines and those fan like vegetables the Palmetto."[36]

Finding no sign but oddly unreassured, Fraser turned back toward the main body, attempting to summon thoughts of confidence, assume a cheerful mood, put on a good face for the men. According to Jewell, Mountfort should be on his way by now. He would understand their danger, would drive his men hard. His advance or his scouts *could* make contact tonight . . . well, tomorrow. From a distance, as he came in, the extended line of troops in double-file route step, winding through an open pine barren, white crossbelts upon a ground of sky blue, black leather caps glittering in the sun, seemed to flow along the little hills and turnings of the road.[37]

Closer, Fraser watched the men of his company marching stolidly, the young lieutenants confident in their knowledge and their innocence, his sergeants, older, wiser, enforcing orders with a look, the flat of a sword. The year young Lieutenant Keais had entered West Point, John Vailing, a German, had already served thirteen years, had been on the expedition against Black Hawk, made corporal. Now he was a sergeant, had served under Fraser for the last eight years, had been at Fort Brooke since *last* December. He was married, his wife Louisa and four-year-old daughter waiting for him back in Boston. And Sgt. Benjamin Chapman, enlisted in 1831. His five-year term would be up next October. Austin Farley, a farmer from Virginia, had volunteered in 1832, been assigned to Fraser's company. He had learned fast, worked hard, made corporal. In April 1834, at Fort Mitchell, Alabama, Fraser had promoted him to sergeant. He must have been waiting for it. Four months later he had married his sweetheart, Elsey. Good men. On recruiting service through the years, in St. Louis, Boston, and Old Point Comfort, Virginia, Fraser had re-cruited them one by one. They had trusted him then with their futures—their lives, for that matter. They were in it together now, all of them.[38]

Until the midday halt the road had continued north through high, first-rate pineland, bending only a little to skirt a pond or baygall. The afternoon road had made an abrupt northeast turn following the highest ground. It had become more apparent by the hour that the river was somewhere off to their right, that before many miles road and river would converge. More and more frequently the high ground and hammocks to the east had been invaded by swamp and grassy ponds. Soon wet, boggy land began to appear to the west as well. The road had been built upon the highest land in the area, an arm that was reaching toward the river.

"I flatter myself," Capt. Isaac Clark had written ten years before, "[this road] will be pronounced by judges to be the best road which has yet been opened in Florida." Orders had come down in March 1825 for Clark to take all the troops that could be spared from the cantonment for the purpose of building a military road north to the newly established Seminole Agency. The road would begin at Fort Brooke, enter the reservation midway down its west boundary, continue as far as Lake Thlonoto-sasa, then turn north for some seventy-five miles to the agency, splitting the reservation down the middle. It had been evident even before the Treaty of Moultrie Creek had been drawn up that the island created in the center of the Florida Territory by a Seminole reservation would be an inconvenience for the military as well as for the settlers who would quickly surround it. Yet Article IV of the treaty stated "the United States promise to guaranty to the said tribes . . . to restrain and prevent all white persons from hunting, settling, or otherwise intruding upon it [the reservation]." How then, some had wondered, could that same guarantor not only allow trespassers to come into the Seminole land but build the very roads that would bring them there? The framers of the treaty had deftly entered a caveat among the guarantees: "The United States . . . reserv[es] the right of opening through [the reservation] such roads, as may, from time to time, be deemed necessary." And if it came right down to it, there was another legal justification: "the United States *promise* to guaranty." A promise without an operative date had no more worth than the guarantors chose to give it. This promise had not been kept, never would be. Without that there *was* no guarantee. Legal semantics perhaps, but what was a treaty if not semantics? Civilized people had spent a thousand years developing the technical language of diplomacy. If Indians chose to remain uncivilized, it was on their own heads.[39]

Clearing a road through a wilderness of forest and swamp and bridging four rivers would require tools, tents, wagons and harness, mules, oxen, horses, and men. All Clark had on hand were the men. By the time equipment and animals arrived, the countryside had been completely inundated by unusually heavy rains. Assured by Colonel Brooke (as well as Seminoles and settlers) that "it will be impossible for men to live in the woods, owing to excessive heat and the rainy season" from mid-June to mid-October, Clark had put the task off until the fall.[40]

When Francis Dade had returned to Fort Brooke in May 1825, after almost a year of recruiting in the north, he found that Capt. Jeremiah Yancey and Lt. George McCall and their companies had been assigned the job of building the proposed road, under the direction of Captain

Clark. Dade did not have Clark's experience, and he outranked McCall
and Yancey. Relieved at missing fatigue duty but bored with garrison life,
he was grateful when a call to arms came down in July. Reinforcement
was needed at the agency, some trouble with the Seminoles. As senior
captain, Dade had been given command of two companies, his own and
McCall's Company D. The route for the new road had been blazed, but
that was all. There was nothing for it but to follow the old Indian trail,
skirting every tree, every mudhole, the path intersected with savannas of
tall grass and—at that season—decidedly wet. There were no bridges
then; they had forded every creek and river. But, unencumbered by a
cannon, they had made the trip to the agency in only five days.[41]

Dade and McCall had returned to Fort Brooke from the agency in
August, and the actual work of roadbuilding had begun in October. Captain Clark had divided the work party into three squads, the first employed
in cutting and opening out the road, the second in ditching and causewaying, and the third in grubbing and taking out stumps. Because of the
immediate need for opening a more effective communication with the
interior, the roadway had been limited to sixteen feet in width, but cleared,
ditched, and graded. At the beginning McCall had claimed that he was
glad to be in motion again, but by the time he returned to Fort Brooke
after three months of hard work he had "rejoiced at the termination of
our labors." He had also learned a basic fact of army life, one that Dade
had learned much earlier: "No soldier likes 'fatigue duty'! It stands on the
Roster below 'Duty under Arms'; and every good soldier's pride leads
him to rejoice when detailed on the latter, while he dislikes or even detests
the former." So McCall had got "fatigue duty," while Dade had managed
to get "Duty under Arms."[42]

Now, ten years later, they were four days out of Fort Brooke and had
covered less than half the distance to Fort King. The constant problem
of the narrow, iron-shod wheels of the gun carriage cutting into the sand,
combined with the snail-like pace of the plodding oxen, seemed to condemn
them to an endless journey. But it was not the roadbuilders' fault that
this part of the world was made of sand. No amount of filling, ditching,
and grading could alter that, while the logs used in causewaying had been
eaten up by white ants about as fast as they could be laid, leaving only a
sort of mulch, easy on the feet but tough pulling for the oxen, horses.

Within an hour they had crossed the last of the high land, the road beginning a barely perceptible downhill slope. Virgin pine still predominated, but now more frequently live oak, water oak, and sweet gum stood on hammocks that rose above the grassy ponds and low land that was thick with tall winter grass. In the wet season here the road would be the only ground above water, and there were plenty of seasons when it, too, would disappear.

Pacheco returned, reported to Dade that he had found fresh tracks in the hammocks ahead. The suggestion of danger was obvious and not what the major wanted to hear. He responded to the slave angrily: "Oh I'll go through if I have to fly sky-high."[43]

The horses sensed it first, tossing their heads, snorting, before the heavily timbered ranks of cypress along the river were visible above the hammock growth. Water. The Withlacoochee River. Spaniards crossing not far from here in the sixteenth century had given it the name Amaxura. By any name it was the southern border of the Seminole heartland, the Great Swamp. For the next dozen miles the road was the east boundary of the swamp, sometimes a half mile to the west, sometimes not a dozen feet. After that the road would angle away to the east for Fort King while the river and its attendant swamps turned nearly due west for the Gulf. If they could make it past the swamps to the Little Withlacoochee and cross and reach the high, open country beyond, they should be virtually out of danger, less than forty miles to safety. But if the Seminole threats meant anything, if they really planned to make mischief, this next stretch was the place to strike, between the dread "forks of the Withlacoochee."[44]

Captain Clark had brought the road to the edge of a gorge, a point where the river had forced its way through a pine bluff, "the first obstruction to its passage to the Gulf of Mexico met with in its descent from the fountain-head," McCall had observed. The banks ended abruptly fifteen or so feet above the swift water. The stream was narrow, the water surface no more than fifty feet wide, though it would fill and spread as much as two miles in season. The original bridge had long since been lost to the white ants and wear, and the fine, new bridge of a year ago, like the one over the Hillsborough, was a victim of recent Seminole arson. Perhaps this fire had not had as long to burn, for the structure, while charred, was still intact. Fire had consumed portions of the three-inch-thick sawed planking, but nothing that could not be patched and mended well enough to cross the wagon, cannon, and men.[45]

Privates Markham and Wagner were the only professional carpenters Dade could call on, but carpenters or not, virtually every man here knew how to handle a hammer and saw. Tools were brought from the wagon, and eager hands took them, fell to work. Guards were posted, and men not working stood down but with weapons near to hand. Patching only the largest holes, the mending was quickly done. The advance crossed, pushed on, flankers followed, fanned out. In route step the column began the crossing, men alternately watching their steps on the patched, blackened planks and looking up at the green wall along the bluff ahead, stretching far to the right upstream, on the left following the curve of the river down and around a bend a hundred yards away. Two by two they crossed, moving quickly up the road cut like a tunnel through underbrush studded with dense thickets of oak and hickory that arched overhead, crowded in on the road, scratching over leather hats and snagging at woolen sleeves. Men marched close and hard on the heels of the man ahead until all were over. Then the oxen were goaded carefully up the approach, only twelve feet from side to side, the four beasts towing the light wagon with no more effort than if they had been walking free. The sense of wood beneath their feet instead of earth, the hollow echo that bounced back from the rushing water below, made them uneasy. Keeping their attention with the crack of his whip, the goad, talking steadily, the driver kept them moving up, across, and down. Finally the horses with the limber and cannon, hooves clattering on wood, eyes rolling like giant marbles, struggled up the approach, guided step by step, restraining ropes slack just in case. Men swarmed around the gun, nudging, pushing, directing the exact course of the wheels lest they break through a weakened puncheon. There wasn't a man who didn't feel the energy of raw nerves, listening for a shot, a warning, a Seminole scream. Then the gun was across and down the far side, word was shouted up the line, the column jerked and shuffled. Drawn along by the advance, it straightened like a pulled rope and moved out.[46]

Within a mile they had left the river thicket behind, were hurrying through land that was beginning to show clearings again, little hills, pines. The sky was visible again, blue sky, sunlight splintering among the trees.

Fort King Road crossing of the Big Withlachoochee River several months after Dade's passing. Library of Congress.

Darkness would be coming soon, but they were dry and, so far, safe. Camp couldn't be far ahead, and with it fire, food, and rest. They could sense higher ground in the little extra effort of walking, bodies leaning forward, heels pressing harder against the back of their boots. They were leaving the twisted underbrush quickly, coming into pine woods, fallen needles carpeting the sand, a few vast live oaks, clumps of brilliant green palmetto, a clearer view. They had already come perhaps a dozen feet higher than the river bluff behind, could see other hills flowing out, away, diminishing.

Half an hour later came the command to halt, echoing down the column from company commander to first sergeant, squad leader to squad, reaching each man with a wave of relief. The distance today had not been as much as yesterday or the day before, a dozen miles maybe, easy marching, but the threat, the tension, had grown with each short mile, especially these last two miles since the river. Word was that Pacheco had brought report of Indian sign, crossing, recrossing the road, heading north. Some said he brought warnings, others that he said there was no danger. Private Ransom Clark didn't trust him. "Our negro interpreter Louis (a great scoundrel, I knew him well), said all along there was no danger, and that we should not be molested by the Indians. He repeatedly went off alone into the woods to hunt for signs, but always said he could find none." Strung out these past hours, each man alone, silent with the effort of the march, the creak of his leather musketstrap whispering in his ear, his mind conjuring images of Seminoles screaming, shooting, stabbing, it was a relief to join with other men in the homely tasks of camp, joking, cursing, being part of a crowd.[47]

Half a dozen sentinels were detailed off, posted a hundred yards and more out and around the knoll. The steady chunk! of axes and the crash of falling trees gave a comforting air of industry to the campsite. As quickly as the logs were limbed they were carried to the hilltop, notched down one upon another to form a low-sided box, enough to afford some little defense for men lying within. The horses and oxen were picketed, sinks dug, fires started with the lightwood knots lying to hand, supplies brought from the wagon, food preparation begun. Men were grouped by company and squad, lined against the walls as they would sleep, dropping their

knapsacks, haversacks, and canteens where they would lie, keeping muskets, swords, bayonets. Lines formed by the cook fires.[48]

Later, in the darkness, lying on the ground, musket by his side, head
on his knapsack against the wall, a man could watch the fires, the sparks
dancing up to join the stars, bright in the moonless sky. Men on either
side, the row continuing down the wall, fires in the center. A clear night,
mid-sixties, camp as quiet as a camp gets. Officer of the guard making
his rounds, checking his posts, quiet challenges, crackle of the fire, a little
talk, a groan, a snore. With his company, but alone, Captain Fraser sat
writing. Firelight flickered over his paper, his sharp features, gentle eyes.
The letter was addressed to his friend John Mountfort. He wrote, stared
into the fire, wrote again. He could sense them out there in the night,
Seminoles so close he could almost see them, slipping from tree to tree,
watching, waiting for their courage to build for the first shout, the first
taunt, perhaps a shot. He told Mountfort they had been beset every night
but were pushing on. What else was there to say? What else could they
do? He folded the paper, pushed it between the logs.[49]

A dozen miles ahead, a few miles west of the road, other campfires
burned on a hammock in the Wahoo Swamp. Flames leaped and flared;
restless energy, hot and hungry. Seminole warriors were swarming. Ote
Emathla waited.[50]

Extending far into the gloom and shadow of the distance on every side
were countless small cookfires, one burning before each lodge. Visible in
the glare were women dressing their coarse food. The lodges were made
almost entirely of materials taken from tala-la-kulke, the palmetto, and
large enough to sleep a family. Upright palmetto logs supported a platform
of split logs laid side by side, flat side up, one jump above the ground.
Even in wet weather the platform provided a dry place to sit or lie down.
Along the edges stood other logs, taller than a warrior, widely spaced,
unsplit and undressed, supporting the roof. Rafters rose from the walls
to a high ridge, heavily thatched with palmetto fronds, watertight and
durable, resistant to all winds except hutallay-cluccko-mast-chay, the very
great wind.[51]

This was Ote Emathla's home. Here were his wife, his son, friends, followers. A "town," the white men would call it. Abraham, the black man who spoke the white man's language, had gone far north to the towns of the white men, told of buildings of wood and brick and stone, told of the multitude of furnishings, of lamps that burned oil, of iron boxes for winter fire. Ote Emathla had seen such things himself in the place the white men called New Orleans. But what did white men know of living? With everything they built they took themselves further from the land. They scorned the earth, cursed the creatures that inhabited it, cut whatever grew and killed whatever moved, but still they coveted. There was no place so poor to the white men that the Seminole might have it, might be left in peace. They had promised that if the Seminoles gave up their country, came here to the swamps, a place that no white man wanted, the United States would take them under its care and patronage and afford them protection against all persons.

Ote Emathla himself had urged the abandonment of most of the Seminole country, had told the people that peace and life were better than land and death. "At the treaty of Moultrie, it was engaged that we should rest in peace upon the land allotted to us for twenty years. All difficulties were buried, and we were assured that if we died, it should not be by the violence of the white man, but in the course of nature. The lightning should not rive and blast the tree, but the cold of old age should dry up the sap, and the leaves should wither and fall, and the branches drop, and the trunk decay and die." It was agreed that all ill feeling should be buried, that if white or red should meet with a brother's blood upon the road they should not believe it was by human violence, but that he had snagged his foot upon a root or that a tree had fallen upon him. That they were always to meet as friends and brothers, without distinction of rank, so that if one was hungry the other should share his bread with him.[52]

Had he really believed what they said, Gadsden and the others? Had Richards, who made the white talk into Seminole, told them the truth of what the agreement said? It made no difference. He and the other chiefs had signed the paper because they had no other course. If the Seminole people were a forest of pines, white men were as many as the needles, too many ever to repel. Already they had nearly destroyed the game upon which the Seminoles were chiefly dependent for their subsistence. They could no longer live as hunters, wild and free. If they would live at all it would be on a reservation, by the white man's law. Their one hope had been that ever after they would be permitted to remain unmolested, that the country allowed them would be a permanent home for themselves and their posterity.[53]

The people had trusted him, had sold their horses, cattle, hogs, taken their possessions, given up their homes, their crops. Some traveled by river, drifting silently down dark water into this last redoubt. Hundreds walked for the last time through their forests, hammocks, and savannas. They came down from the north and up from the south, in from the ocean on one side and the great sea on the other. They lay down at night in the sweet grass upon the sand and held the children. They had come finally to the sand hills, the Great Swamp—the reservation. They passed between trees that had been marked to show the boundary, a living fence. With limbs secured across from tree to tree it would have served for penning cattle. It was told that white men were saying that this was the poorest land in Florida. White men said many things. This time they spoke the truth.[54]

Poor land and bad weather had brought starvation. The government ration of cattle and hogs was not enough to sustain life. Within two years people who had lived on the bounty of the earth were dying of hunger. They had eaten the conti-katke, or briar root, but it was soon gone. They ate of the talalocko, or cabbage tree, then their atchee, or seed corn. Two more years and there was not a bushel of atchee left in the whole Seminole Nation. Deprived of their cultivated fields and a region of country fruitful of game, placed in a wilderness where the earth yielded no corn and even the fortune of the chase was denied them, the Seminoles could starve within their limits or go outside the reservation and prey upon the herds of the whites who had rushed in upon the good land given up. Hungry Seminoles killed, and ate. Near Cabbage Swamp some who carried passes signed by their agent were fired upon by settlers, their rifles and many skins taken. Close to Kanapaha Pond five Seminoles who had killed a cow were discovered by whites who took their weapons, flogged them with cattlewhips. These had been called "accidents," but they were not. This was the plan. This was the law.[55]

The white people surrounded them now, could reach them from all sides. They had come into the reservation, demanding payment for cattle killed to feed starving people. They saw many iste-luste, black Seminoles, said they knew them, had owned them. Other men came with papers. Then the soldiers came.

It made no difference that most black Seminoles had been born in Florida like their parents before them. To Americans they were slaves because their skin was black. To the Seminoles they were men, and women, and children. It was true that the Great Spirit had made men of different colors and given them different employments, but such differences did not cause people of one color to be less human than the others. It was explained in the legends:

"The Master of Life said, we will make man. Man was made, but when he stood up before his maker, he was white! The Great Spirit was sorry; he saw that the being he had made was pale and weak; he took pity on him, and therefore did not unmake him, but let him live. He tried again, for he was determined to make a perfect man, but in his endeavor to avoid making another white man, he went into the opposite extreme, but when the second being rose up, and stood before him, he was black! The Great Spirit liked the black man less than the white, and he shoved him aside to make room for another trial. Then it was that he made the red man; and the red man pleased him.[56]

"In this way the Great Spirit made the white, the black, and the red man, when he put them upon the earth. Here they were—but they were very poor. They had no lodges nor horses, no tools to work with, no traps, nor anything with which to kill game. All at once, these three men, looking up, saw three large boxes coming down from the sky. . . . [T]he Great Spirit . . . said, 'White Man, you are pale and weak, but I made you first, and will give you the first choice; go to the boxes, open them and look in, and choose which you will take for your portion.' The white man . . . said, 'I will take this.' [The box] was filled with pens, and ink, and paper, and compasses, and such things. . . . The Great Spirit spoke again and said, 'Black man, I made you next, but I do not like you. You may stand aside. The Red man is my favorite, he shall come forward and take the next choice.' . . . The red man stepped boldly up and chose a box filled with tomahawks, knives, war clubs, traps, and such things as are useful in war and hunting. The Great Spirit laughed when he saw how well his red son knew how to choose. Then he said to the negro,

'You may have what is left, the third box is for you.' That was filled with axes and hoes, with buckets to carry water in, and long whips for driving oxen, which meant that the negro must work for both the red man and the white man, and it has been so ever since."[57]

Still, the blacks' only real bondage was ignorance. Blacks, like any men or women with no skill to offer, only their hands, their brain, could do nothing but manual labor. But being men and women, they learned. They put themselves under the protection of one chief or another and called him master, "and to whom, for this consideration, they render a tribute of one-third of the produce of the land, and one-third of the horses, cattle, and fowls they may raise. Otherwise they are free to come and go at their pleasure, and in some cases are elevated to the position of equality with their masters."[58]

The Americans always talked of freedom, of the two wars they had fought for their *own* freedom against the "English," who had come from across the great water. Yet the American soldiers took the black men, women, and children back into slavery. Sometimes they took away an Indian whose skin was darker than others. They had the power. They told the Seminoles that if white claims of ownership could not be proved the blacks would be returned. Proved? How? Returned? When? "We heard the same talk about the negroes which were taken from Nelly Factor, *twelve moons* since, but the negroes have not come back." Ote Emathla had not refused the soldiers, but had appealed to the agent: "The laws of the whites appear to be made altogether for their own benefit, and against the Indians, who can never under them get back any of *their* property; if it once gets, no matter how, into the white people's hands, we fear their laws will leave to us nothing. If we could see them work, so as to restore the property that has been stolen, and otherwise unfairly taken from us, and not so as to rob us of the little we have left, we should have more reason to believe them just, but as it is, the benefit to be had from them goes all to the white people's side."[59]

Ote Emathla had "signed" the paper at the camp called Moultrie. It had been read to the Seminoles by Richards. He remembered many of the words—they were the reasons he had touched the pen: "The United States will . . . afford . . . the Florida Indians protection against all persons whatsoever; The United States promise to guaranty to the said tribes the

peaceable possession of the district of country herein assigned them; . . .
and to restrain and prevent all white persons from hunting, settling, or
otherwise intruding upon it." Five years after Moultrie, Ote Emathla and
other chiefs had asked for a meeting with their agent, the man called
Humphreys.[60]

"We know you tell us what you think, and wish and hope that your
words may prove true, but it is discouraging, and makes our hearts sad,
to have the white people coming every few days, to wrong us out of our
honest property, when we can never get out of their hands that which
they stole from us many years ago. . . . It seems that the white people
will not rest, or suffer us to do so, till they have got all the property
belonging to us, and made us poor. . . . We have submitted to one demand
after another . . . but it seems that there will be no end to them . . . as
long as we have anything left that the white people may want."[61]

Ote Emathla remembered something else. Many times in the treaty it
was written "twenty successive years." Richards had explained to them
that if they gave up the land to the whites, went to the "reservation land,"
they were to receive money for "twenty successive years," a blacksmith
and gunsmith would be available to the Seminoles for "twenty successive
years." What meaning could a man make of this except that the Seminoles
would be secure within the reservation for "twenty successive years"? Not
half the years had passed when the white man called Gadsden had come
among them again. He told them that their father, the president, had a
new plan. It would relieve their distress, end their desperate suffering. He
had invited them to meet with him on the west bank of the Okle-wahaw,
at Payne's Landing.[62]

It was the time of miscostos, of spring. The meeting place was less than
a day's walk north of the agency, outside the reservation. On the west
bank of the Okle-wahaw, or muddy water, the grass was sweet, the flowers
bloomed. Chiefs and subchiefs of the Mikasuki and Alachua bands came
in, waited. There were not so many as had come to Moultrie. Again
Richards made their words into the language of the whites and the talk
of the man Gadsden back into Seminole. Their new agent, called Phagan,
was there, the sutler, Erastus Rogers, and two black men, Cudjo and
Abraham, who spoke both languages. These men, who had once been
slaves, could be trusted to speak the truth.

The white man Gadsden talked. Then Richards and Abraham and Cudjo. They talked, but they made no sense. If they were to be believed, the Great Father wanted the Seminoles to give up the last of their Florida home, to move again, far away, beyond the western river, toward the sunset. As the foolish words struggled from the mouths of the three men, Ote Emathla looked at Micanopy and Halpatter Tustenuggee.

Nor was this all. The name Taloph-ulke was spoken, spoken again, the name of people from whom the Seminoles had fled a hundred years ago, people who had fought against the Seminoles under the soldier Jackson, the people the white men called Creeks. The far country, called Ar-kan-sas, had already been given to those people, but Abraham and Cudjo and Richards were saying that the Seminoles were to share the land with the Taloph-ulke, their ancient enemies. A man, a chief, could not cry like a child, could not scream like a woman. He could only look at Gadsden, who spoke for the white president, the few soldiers who stood for so many, and he could feel his heart die.

There was more talk, a day, two days. What had seemed clear was no longer clear. Abraham, adviser to Micanopy as well as interpreter, urged them to visit the western country. It would please the president, and his pleasure was important. The president asked only that the chiefs go and see for themselves what a fine land was in that place and, upon their return, report to their people. Only then, and only if the people agreed to removal, would the paper, the compact, have force. So great was the concern of the president that his children, the Seminoles, should live in a country more suitable to their habits and wants than the one they presently occupied that he would provide transport for all the people, give them money and, to each man, woman, and child, a blanket and a frock. Go, see the land, take the gifts that would come their way. When they returned the present troubles might have passed. And if the Creek country was not good they would tell that to the people, the people would say no and that would be an end of it. After all, Abraham too was a Seminole, a farmer, a leader. He could talk the white man's tongue, could understand what would be good for the Seminoles and what would not. Sign the paper, visit Ar-kan-sas. The paper, the pen, the ink lay on the table. Gadsden and the soldiers watched and waited.

A white man picked up the pen, dipped it in ink. Hands reached out,

were withdrawn. Micanopy reached across Tuckose Emathla, pointed at
the pen. Gadsden spoke, then the interpreters. He must *touch* the pen.
He drew back. He had not meant to put his mark. He did not want to
move to the far country. No, only visit. Go, *see* the new land. That is all
the paper says. Chalo Emathla moved to the table, touched the pen. Others
waited for Ote Emathla. He rose, reached out. He would rather touch
chitta-micco, the rattlesnake. They could go and see. They could please
the president. Though their hearts might turn within them, they could
endure it for the Nation.[63]

Seven chiefs had gone to Arkansas, Ote Emathla and six others, with
their agent, Phagan, and Abraham. The party had traveled by water, by
horse, and by foot. The way was strange and long and hard. Winter had
come with cold and rain. Phagan was a man of violent passions, and as
troubles came there had been many quarrels. Horses were stolen and
chiefs were left to walk, to carry their belongings on their backs. When
a man became sick, his legs as broken reeds, he was abandoned by the
agent and left to catch up if he could.[64]

They reached the new country in the dead of winter. For another moon
and two and three they were led on, here and there, up and down, across
and along the boundaries of a barren, dreary land. So much time, yet the
land so small that an Indian child could have run the boundary in a week.
And just outside the boundaries, all around, were other Indians, among
them the hated Creeks; strange Indians, taken from *their* distant lands and
huddled here—bitter, vengeful men. If the Seminole people were to come
to this place they would be surrounded once again by bad and hostile
neighbors, and the fruit of bad neighbors is blood that spoils the land and
fire that dries the brook. Ote Emathla had said to Phagan, "You say our
people are rogues, but you would bring us among *worse* rogues, to *destroy*
us." Snow and freezing cold had chilled the bones of strong and healthy
men, men who had lived their lives in the sun. How would it be for the
old and the very young, the mothers-to-be and the sick?[65]

Finally, half a year away from Florida, from home, they were taken to
a fort called Gibson. More white men were there, more words, more
paper. As he had done at Payne's Landing, Abraham told the Seminoles
what the papers said. Even from their friend Abraham the talk was confus-

ing, sounding like the papers said first one thing, then another. There was talk of joining "with your brothers of the west," talk of agreeing to bring their people to this land, and Abraham told them that once again they must touch the pen, put their names to the paper. Ote Emathla had agreed to visit this new country, Micanopy and others had not, yet marks had been made by their names on the paper at Payne's Landing. Where had the marks come from? Would marks appear on this new paper, too, whether they touched the pen or not? Abraham was saying that their marks here would only mean that they had *seen* the new country, that it was a good land, that their marks would not oblige them to move there. Phagan had become very angry, threatened them, saying that he would not "proceed with them on their journey home" if they did not acknowledge that they had seen the land, that the land was good. Without white help they could never go home.[66]

Summer had almost come when they were brought back to Florida. Babies had been born who had not been begun when they left. They told the people what they had seen. Perhaps the land was good. They did not know the soil, the plants, the number and habits of the game. They did know something of the neighbors to the land, the Creeks, Pawnees, and Cherokees. Men who, even while the Seminoles were there, had stolen horses from other tribes, had brought scalps into the garrison. They had no wish to live among such people. And they acknowledged that they had signed their hands to a paper, "but we did no more than say we liked the land, and when we returned, *the nation would decide.*"[67]

A year and more had passed. Ote Emathla heard that Phagan was no longer their agent, that another man, Thompson, now spoke for the Great Father. Near the end of the year, the time that the white men called "October," the year "1834," Thompson had sent word to the chiefs that he wished to meet them, to have a "talk." Talk. As if given enough talk a man would overlook the loss of everything else. From disease, starvation, murder, and sickness of the heart the people had grown fewer in number, weaker in spirit. Those who wanted war instead of talk had grown stronger, young men like Osceola, men with the courage to risk death but not the strength to endure life—Ote Emathla had thought *that* the strength they must have if they were not to die in battle, to live in peace. So he had gone once more to talk. He hated to remember, but it was his duty. In the Great Swamp, the camp quiet now, he could not forget why he and the warriors were here, why they were going to kill the soldiers.

The talk had come down to this: the reservation land given them at Moultrie was to be taken away, all of the people sent west. Tricks and lies had been used to show that he and Micanopy and Halpatter Tustenuggee and the others had agreed to give up the land. In vain had they protested that they had no authority to do so, had never claimed to have such authority. The agent had claimed that authority had been given them by the treaty! How could a paper with the white men change the authority of a chief over the People? Perhaps the ruin of the People that now was clear before them had been there all along and he had not seen it, or seeing it had not wanted to believe it. Suddenly the blind were forced to see. Hope was dead, peace was dead. Killing was all they had left. Better to die here than leave the People to endure the hardships of the trip west, the survivors to die in a strange land. When Osceola had stood, his eye bright, his breath short, his fist clenched, he had spoken for them all: "The People in Council have agreed; by their chiefs they have uttered; it is well, it is truth, and must not be broken."[68]

Scouts reported to Ote Emathla that the "Big Knives" had crossed Weewa-thlock-ko, had made camp for the night. The time was close, the opportunity would not come again. From the swamp he could strike quickly, cut down the soldiers. If the fight should go against them the swamp would be a safe place of retreat. Another day, two days, and the favorable moment would pass, the soldiers gone to the north where open country would help them. He had no wish to help them. There was no longer any good blood between Ote Emathla and the white men. "Every branch that a white man hews from a tree on our soil, is a limb lopped from [my] body—every drop of water that a white man drinks from our springs, is so much blood drawn from [my] veins." Yet Osceola had not returned from Fort King, Micanopy had not come from Pelacklekaha.[69]

Both men were to take part in the attack. Here about him Ote Emathla had plenty of warriors, but Osceola could hearten the mildest of them and Micanopy carried the authority of the Seminole Nation. The old chief was fearful of trouble, but what trouble could be worse than that which they already faced—losing their world? Without Micanopy only the most reckless among the warriors might join the attack, but this blow against the soldiers was not planned to be a random act of a small, irresponsible group; it was to be a blow of Seminole against white. Even whites claimed to be sometimes driven by the spirit in them, the kind of spirit that many Seminoles had already lost. Killing the soldiers might make other whites lose the spirit that drove them to take this land, to enslave the blacks. It was only a hope, but it was the only hope left. He could lead them against the soldiers without Osceola, but victory would count for little without the presence of Micanopy. Pelacklekaha, where Micanopy lived with his wives and many blacks, was east of the swamp, beyond the soldiers' road. He was timid, had urged delay, but the time for delay was over.[70]

Chapter Five

The Fifth Day

Sunday, December 27, 1835

The town of York in Livingston County, New York, was a farming community. The Seneca Indians, a powerful tribe of the Iroquois, had cleared and cultivated much of the area before the arrival of white settlers from New England. In 1779 Gen. John Sullivan's army had subdued the Senecas. His men vowed to return to the rolling hills, waterways, and acres of high, cleared land.[1]

One farm a few miles outside York was owned by Benjamin Clark. He had come to the area shortly after the second war with England, and by 1830 had put together a farm of 250 acres. He raised potatoes and hay and kept a large stock of cattle. He sold frequently and rarely bought. He was "a shrewd, money-making man, especially in his trades," known to be a close man in a bargain. He was also known as a habitual drunkard. According to a York magistrate, "Mr. Clark was of that class of men who are made sharper and brighter and better qualified to do business after drinking moderately than if they had drank nothing." A man of violent temper when sober, he would grow so vicious under the influence of whiskey that his workers sometimes threw down their tools and left the fields. His hay, not cut in season, would be left to rot. He was described by his attorney and adviser, who was frequently called upon to handle controversies and lawsuits between Clark and his neighbors, as "the most harsh, coarse, brutal appearing man in his family that I ever saw." Neighbors on adjoining farms frequently heard his voice across the fields, raging in profane language toward his family, "for that was his common way of speaking [to] them."[2]

His family consisted of his wife, Catherine, and ten children—five boys

164

and five girls. Between Benjamin Clark and Catherine "there was an entire absence of all the feeling that we ordinarily see between man and wife." He had little use for any of his children. As the older girls married he refused to have anything more to do with them. Toward his oldest son, Henry, he had "manifested ill feelings" ever since Henry had interfered on behalf of his mother when Benjamin had struck her with his fist, almost knocking her down. His lawyer was accustomed to the sight of the younger girls and boys bringing whiskey to their father in a bowl or tumbler. As for his third son, Ransom, the lawyer stated simply that Benjamin "did not like him."[3]

On May 10, 1830, Ransom Clark, at the age of eighteen, had had enough of home life. Taking virtually nothing with him, for he had nothing, he left home. Benjamin immediately gave notice in the *Livingston Register* that he was no longer responsible for his son. Large for his age, skilled only in hoeing potatoes and making hay, handy with shovel, pitchfork, and gun, Ransom did whatever he had to do to survive. After three years with no particular gains, no particular goals, he turned up at the U.S. Army recruiting office in Rochester. On August 3, 1833, 2nd Lt. Abner Hetzel signed him up for three years with the Second Regiment of Artillery. Private Clark joined his regiment at Fort Mitchell, on the west bank of the Chattahoochee River in Alabama. His company commander was Capt. Francis Belton.[4]

Gold had been discovered a few miles south of Fort Mitchell on the Creek reservation. Belton's company, and a second under Capt. Upton Fraser, had been given the task of protecting the Creeks and their gold from white intruders. Already the whites had opened mines, built villages of log houses, and set up trade with one another. Captain Belton sent 2nd Lt. Walter Scott Chandler and twenty-five men, including Clark, to break up one such settlement. Clark described the encounter: "On arriving at the village, all the inhabitants, men, women and children, 50 or 60 in number, had marshalled themselves in battle array, armed with clubs, axes, hoes, brickbats and broomsticks, apparently ready to give us a warm reception. Our muskets, by command of the officers, had been loaded with blank cartridges—and on our arriving a few yards in front of this Spartan and Amazonian host, orders were given the detachment to draw the blanks and load with balls. No sooner was this order attempted to be put into execution, than the hitherto undaunted foe dropped their *weapons*, and scampered for the woods, as fast as fleet heels could carry them."[5]

In February 1834 Belton's company was ordered to Fort Morgan, at the mouth of Mobile Bay. They marched across the state to Mobile, boarded the steamboat *Sangumon* for the twenty-five-mile trip down the bay, and on March 7 were the first troops to garrison the vast new fortress.

Lieutenant Chandler, Belton's second in command, had been posted on recruiting service in January. He brought his catch to Fort Morgan in April, only to be sent out again, this time to Fort Gibson on ordnance duty. In November he finally rejoined the company after nearly a year's absence. Chandler was twenty-five years old, a graduate of West Point's class of 1830. He had served in Charleston, then at the academy as assistant professor of mathematics, in garrison at Savannah, followed by Fort Mitchell and service in the Creek Nation. He was quartermaster of the regiment in January 1835 when Belton assigned him the task of taking a crew up the bay to Mobile to draw pay and provisions for the post.[6]

Chandler chose for his crew Sergeant W. Grant and privates Leavenwise, Finn, and Clark. The bay was known for its suddenly rough water and capricious winds, called "Northers." Five men in a small sailing boat could have their hands full, but the trip to Mobile—five miles west across the bay, thirty miles north—was uneventful. It was a cold day, and clear once the morning fog had lifted. Heavy winter coats, wool jackets and trousers, and Jefferson boots kept the men warm, though a dash of spray felt like ice water on exposed fingers that held the tiller or worked the sail. The water, like the air, was nearly twenty degrees above freezing. The men were glad of the change. A boat trip and a night in Mobile were a rare treat, an adventure for men who were garrisoned in the most isolated post in the country, where fatigue duty was the order of the day. They kept well out of the channel, far from the risk of collision.[7]

They started back the morning of the twenty-fifth. A civilian messenger had joined them. They carried all the provisions the skiff would hold. There was little room left to move about and the six men took their positions with their feet among the bags and barrels. They had little freeboard, but the bay was calm, fog shrouding them like a winding sheet. By nine o'clock the fog was thinning, the sky bright, a breeze pushing them down the west side of the bay, choppy water slapping against the hull, six miles out of Mobile, two miles below Choctaw Point. They had passed the mouth of Mobile River and were coming up on Dog River. Without warning a freak of wind was on them, throwing the boat flat, catapulting the men into the bay along with the provisions and sacks of coin. Clark was in the water, clutching at the capsized boat, gasping with the shock. In an instant the water had penetrated his heavy clothing, seeming to squeeze the air out of his lungs. Around him the others floundered, shouted. The boat, unable to complete its roll because of mast and sail, unable to right itself with half a load of water, lay on its side, a low half-moon of planking that offered a place to hold on but nothing more.[8]

Lieutenant Chandler had regained the boat, was shouting to the others to swim, get to the boat. They floundered closer, struggling against the leaden weight of waterlogged clothing, Chandler and Clark grabbing for them. Then all six were together, clutching the boat, only heads and hands above water, hardly able to speak for the chattering of their teeth, splashed and choking on the waves that broke against the hull. Under Chandler's direction they tried to right the boat, but their efforts could only settle it further and risk losing its equilibrium, sending it to the bottom. Spontaneously, desperately, they shouted for help, singly, then together. The fog swallowed the sound, there was no reply. Silent then, the men looked at one another. They were far from shore, out of the channel. Who would see them, hear their shouts? Should the strongest swimmer strip, head for shore? In the fog they had lost all sense of direction. If their strength held until the fog burned away, if land was not too far. . . . But the cold was taking hold of them already, bodies shuddering, hands and feet, legs going numb.

A long time passed, or seemed to. The fog had faded, the shore was visible, impossibly far away. Even if a ship should pass in the distant channel they would never be seen. Talk dwindled to prayer, oaths. Suddenly a man was gone, vanished. Terror joined fear, cold. Clark held. He heard Chandler, others, silence, then a shout. Chandler was struggling with a man, trying to hold him to the boat. More time, and then the sky was darkening, night was coming. Clark looked down the boat, not sure where he was, what he was doing. He was alone. Night, and he knew only that he must hold on, must not let go. His mind was as numb as his body, feeling nothing, knowing nothing except that he must not let go, must not go down in the black water to die in the mud.

He heard something. He opened his eyes. The fog was back, thick and bright. Morning. The sound was almost on top of him, a persistent, mooing sort of sound. He had heard that sound before. The *Sangumon*, the steamboat that had brought his company the last leg of their march to Fort Morgan. The whistle. A steamboat whistle! He tried to move, to shout. Suddenly it was visible, side like the wall of a barn. Men were shouting, calling to him from the huge ship. They had seen him, he was saved.[9]

The steamboat *Watchman* from New Orleans, bound for Mobile, had gotten out of her regular channel on account of the fog, crewmen had seen him in the moments of passing the skiff, had hauled him aboard nearly frozen, and the captain had taken him back to Mobile, the only survivor. Recovered after three weeks, he returned to Fort Morgan, and in December he had come to Fort Brooke with Belton's Company B. Clark and ten others had been transferred to Gardiner's company to bring it up to strength.

Now Clark tramped along next to the leading file of the right column, breathing in the sour smell of wool still damp with sweat and rain, knees rubbed raw by his woolen trousers, cotton drawers bunched and damp against his thighs, his body hung about with bayonet and scabbard, knapsack, canteen, haversack, and cartridge box. He'd keep his eyes open and take it as it came.

As usual, Pacheco had been sent ahead to reconnoiter. "About this time I could see that the Major was anxious-like," but nothing further had been said about sending him on to the Wahoo.[10]

The officers gathered around Gardiner's map. The line of the road ran nearly straight north to the fourth and last river, the Little Withlacoochee. No more than four miles. If they could reach that and make the crossing, it looked like maybe another couple of miles to high ground, open country. They would leave the swamp, the wet feet, the danger behind them. No Seminole in his right mind would let them pass through jungle and swamp to attack them in open woods. From Dade to the newest recruit, there wasn't a man that didn't know that this stretch would be the place and time of greatest risk. Tonight, if they lived that long, they would have run the gauntlet, would sleep on high ground, only forty dry miles from Fort King.

They had left their log encampment behind, snug on its little knoll, Fraser's message wedged between the logs. Within an hour the long, double file in column of route had wound around and past a thousand wet spots from mudholes to creeks, the country more a jungle than a forest. Two miles to the west the Withlacoochee, dark and silent, haunt of Indians for a thousand years, hurried along parallel to the road. If the water level should rise even a couple of feet the land would be flooded into one huge swamp. Even now there wasn't a dry boot in the command. The sky was clear, the temperature sixty-two and climbing, a cool breeze coming nearly head-on. Overcoats were rolled and packed, short jackets left the men's arms free, muskets, powder, and bayonets easy to hand. They were alert, watchful, ready. An almost palpable sense of lurking Seminoles made men strain to hear a cry of warning, the sound of attack above the rumble, creak, whipcrack, and shouts of an army on the move.

The advance guard kept its distance, flankers out on right and left, alternately thrashing through palmetto and splashing through ponds, rear guard following, urging the crew on as they put their shoulders to the wheels of the gun, rolling deep in murky water, horses straining at their harness, pawing the earth for traction, while the dogs bounded through the woods, baying up anything that moved and much that didn't. On the map the road was straight, but in reality the twists and turns kept the column weaving back and forth so that a man could see only a short distance ahead or behind at any given moment. It created a feeling of vulnerability, and that in turn kept the ranks closed up, the pace quick. Men in Fraser's company, splashing through a creek bed churned to mud by the men ahead, glanced up to see the captain stop, his horse in the water, while he carefully split the end of a stick, fitted a folded paper in it and stabbed the stick into the creek, offside to the passing column. The captain had his ways about him.[11]

The sun, climbing slowly behind the filter of trees, cleared the oaks, even the towering cypress, reached the top of the sky. Their course, slightly east of north now, swung back to north, then west of north. When

they built the road, McCall and Isaac Clark had searched the banks for
several miles up and down the river before finding a place sufficiently
high for bridging the stream, had bent the road east to reach it. Spirits
rose, the silence of worry began to break into loud, rough humor. The
ground was rising a little, growing drier as they paced off their last mile
within the Cove of the Withlacoochee. Then they could feel beneath their
boots the incline of the causeway that rose the last hundred yards to the
crossing. The bridge would likely be gone, burnt by the Seminoles. They'd
have to patch it up, or, like as not, have to ford again. No matter, sooner
they got across the better. Like the major said: "I'll go through if I have
to fly sky-high."[12]

The advance reached the end of the causeway, the charred ruin of the
bridge before them. A command echoed down the line, bringing the
column to a halt. Dade, Gardiner, and Fraser joined the advance, stared
silently for a moment while their horses, reins loose, stretched their necks,
chomped noisily at the dry grass between their feet. The river, main
affluent of the Withlacoochee, wide only in flood, was now shrunk to its
winter size of eighteen feet, little more than a creek. The bridge was a
ruin, but there were trees in plenty. Fell a couple, trim them up, send
the men across dry, and ford the horses and oxen with the gun and wagon.[13]

Felling axes were brought from the wagon, swung with easy grace by
ready hands. A path was cut below and beside the causeway, pines along
the low, steep banks crashed across the water, shuddered as they struck,
broken limbs stabbing the earth. In a moment other axmen swarmed
across, clearing the way of standing limbs, chips launched like cockleshells
on the dark water, floating jauntily downstream and around a bend only
yards away.[14]

Again the inevitable problem of a crossing, of dividing their forces.
After the advance had crossed, one by one, the command, in single file,
muskets slung, filed forward. The first man stepped up on the broad log,
shuffled his hard leather soles against the slick, brown bark, started forward. Another, and another, while others watched and held their breath.
Not likely to slip—only get wet if they did—but very likely to be shot.
On the far bank the advance guard, quiet, muskets at the ready, kept
watch in all directions. If the Seminoles were hidden, waiting, they would
come at them on both banks, from upstream and down, but not quite yet.

Another hour, fifty men here, fifty there, horses and gun in the water. . . . The first man jumped down, a half-dozen on the log following, moving slowly, staring down, then up at the grey-green screen of foliage, down again, white-knuckled fingers gripping their muskets. Few spoke, everyone listened, watched. Dade nudged his horse to the water, crossed, then Gardiner. Henderson crossed on foot with the men, Basinger still at the rear with the cannon. Fraser, Mudge, and Keais waited with their company.

Ten years earlier, having completed construction of the first bridge over the Little Withlacoochee, Lieutenant McCall wrote that "we dashed into a dense thicket of oak and hickory with an undergrowth almost impenetrable to anything less potent than an elephant or the American felling-axe. Eighty stout axe-men, however, made everything fly before them, and in one day we made our way through all impediment, and were again in the pine woods." The path they had cut looked today more like a hole cut through a haystack than a road. As Gardiner and Henderson formed up their men and began to move them out behind the advance, the way was an arcade of overreaching limbs, the sides a wall of interwoven branches, close and narrow. Yet, while a man felt confined, even trapped, the tunnel offered a certain protection. If a soldier couldn't see through the mask of growth, no serious Seminole attack was possible, either. The plunge of a knife, perhaps, a shot from a hidden rifle, but no more than that. A snake could hardly reach them. And as for lying in wait at the end—that worked both ways, too. When they came to the egress, when the thicket would begin to give way to less frenzied growth beyond the floodplain of the river, if the Seminoles should be bunched for attack, *they* would be the easy target, while the soldiers, protected on either side by the growth, could hold them off as long as needed. And then, safely out of the tunnel, they would soon reach what McCall had described as "the sweet balsamic atmosphere of [the pine woods] which is so exhilarating in the early mornings of our cloudless days: nothing could be more health-inducing."[15]

Meanwhile, half the command was now on one bank, half on the other. Where the first men to cross had been anxious and slow, the remainder trod on one another's heels. Noise was rising, Basinger urging on the gun crew, the teamsters goading the lumbering, stubborn oxen with their foolish wagon. And then, finally, the last were over. The command, forming up in column of route, had begun moving up the road with the animals, streaming water as they struggled up the bank and into column, lurching after them. The rear guard followed. Flank guards had not been posted north of the crossing, for no man could make his solitary way through the fastness beyond the road. At least no white man. Fresh sign had been found just north of the crossing: Indians, three of them, but the general opinion was they were runners sent to Fort King. Three hundred yards beyond the river the road swung back from northwest to northeast, the course it would take from here to Fort King. Another half mile and they came to a Seminole town set in a clearing near a large pond on the left of the road, a collection of palmetto log and frond structures. There were no signs of life—Seminole, horse, or dog.[16]

The first two miles had been spattered with ponds. Then these coalesced into lakes, and for the first time in hours a man could look past the green wall and across open water. One, on the right, stretched south a half mile, the near shore reaching almost to the road. Scattered willows stood along the shore, leaves spattered white with the droppings of snowy egrets and giant blue herons, hundreds settled quietly now on the treetops for their afternoon naps. In the water, coots and wood ducks paddled along, dipping their heads for tidbits. Water turkeys popped their heads above the surface for a quick look around, then submerged, leaving barely a ripple. Here and there an alligator lay on open shore, warm sun on his cold hide, indifferent to their passing, a million years of patience in its unblinking eyes. The land was drying out, the road rising so gradually that it couldn't be felt, and then, far ahead, pine tops could be seen above the oak. High ground, open woods, safety.[17]

By late afternoon word drifted down that Pacheco had returned but had found no sign of Seminoles. It was amazing, incredible. The Seminoles had let them pass. Men told each other that they would soon be in the clear, that them Indians was all bluff. Twenty-seven Irishmen in the ranks might have nodded in agreement with the Pat who exclaimed, "The baists, and shan't we have a rap at them for our pains? By the Holy Spoon, and are we not to have some diversion for the honor of ault Ireland, boys?"[18]

They had come not quite eight miles since morning. Much time had been lost in pushing and pulling cannon and wagon, bogging down again and again. The strain on minds and nerves of crossing the Cove of the

Withlacoochee had been as exhausting as the days when they had made twice the distance, but now the valley of the shadow was behind them. Dade and others who had passed this way before remembered a watering place surrounded by pines just ahead. The westering sun was slipping down the sky, the hard winter light glittering through the trees, heaven's blue turning dark with overcast and evening, the temperature dropping from the seventies to sixties. Soon camp, and fires, to dry boots and trousers, to cook a meal and warm the heart.

Never had men been so glad to reach a pine barren. Here, as in most of the Florida Territory, the giant virgin pine ruled the land. The massive fall of needles covered the ground like a brown blanket, suffocating nearly all other growth, leaving it virtually barren of all but pine. The needles, or pine straw, cushioned the feet and, bunched together, made a fine, fresh-smelling bed. The long, clean trunks made a sturdy barricade that would provide some small defense in case of attack. And finally, "lightwood" or "lightwood knots" of fallen trees lay scattered about, perfect for starting a fire. The hard, pitch-soaked heart of a pine tree remained for years after the tree died, the bark and punkwood long since rotted away. A man had only to stop the vent in his musket with a wooden plug to save the powder and ball, then ignite the lightwood with the flash of powder in the pan.[19]

A hundred feet east of the road was a fine pond of good water. Lieutenant Mudge referred to it as "the round clay sink," a natural and common geologic feature in areas underlain by limestone, but not known in his native Massachusetts. Hard, blue clay banks led down to leaf-green water, the pool almost a perfect circle more than one hundred feet across. It was a "limestone sink," commonly known as a "clayhole," a place where the porous earth had collapsed into the caverns that ran beneath the land. Some caverns, like this one, were deep enough that they never ran dry, part of the vast seas that lay beneath the earth like honey in a comb.[20]

Once more they posted guards, brought up the wagon and gun, built a stout barricade, made fires, dug sinks, picketed the animals. Never had they felt safer since leaving Tampa Bay. This was white man's country, high, dry, open. Within the redoubt the fires were big and bold, flames lighting a hundred young faces, tired, dirty, confident. Each man was entitled to the balance of his daily ration, three-quarters of a pound of pork or one and a quarter pounds of beef, twelve ounces of hard bread, a few ounces of peas or beans, rice, coffee, and sugar. "Standard daily meals were soup, stew and hash and often the only difference between the three was the amount of water used." With the pleasant lassitude that comes with warmth, food, and security, they began to find their places, lie down, and pull their blankets about them against the chill that was coming with the night. There were no stars to see as they lay on their pine straw beds, rubbing grainy eyes, staring up. Clouds had gathered. There was a smell of rain in the air. No matter. Fort King was only two, three days away. Tattoo rattled from the drums.[21]

It was dark when Fanning, driving hard, reached Fort Drane with his three companies, 150 men. The twelve-foot-high picket walls loomed up in the evening light, 150 yards long, 80 yards wide, a small cannon mounted on a square blockhouse in the east wall. Inside was a throng of militia, settlers, and dogs. The place was a moil of activity, with supplies of every kind being readied for a march to the river. He saw to food, space for his men, then reported to Clinch.[22]

It was plain to see that the old general was relieved. He had already sent couriers to bring in two detachments out scouring the country for Seminoles. When they returned, plus Drane's company, and now Fanning's three, he would have a battalion of regulars—an army, not a mob. Preparations were well under way; food for a week were being cooked, and ammunition, forage, and medicines were ready to be loaded on some twenty-seven wagons. As things stood they should be ready to march the morning of the twenty-ninth. That would leave Call's men just three days to serve, but he couldn't help that. General Call had given his volunteers a pledge that they would be permitted to leave for home on January 1. Day after tomorrow, the combined force would march out eight hundred strong, but if there was to be an encounter at the river it would be the regulars who would have to carry it.[23]

Clinch had no guide who knew the intricacies of the area beyond the river, which, like "all the difficult parts of Florida were, to the whole army, one *terra incognita*. Government gave . . . no topographical information, nor had any to give; and the booksellers' maps only afforded outlines filled up with unlucky guesses." "*The Cove*, a Cretan labyrinth, [with]held from the knowledge of the white man, as the sacred groves of the Druids were never entered except by the initiated." He was counting on the Seminoles to challenge a crossing.[24]

In the Great Swamp the hosts continued to gather. Micanopy had finally joined. There was no word from Osceola, only that he was at the agency. It was the time. It would be a fine thing if the subchief could be with them, lead the young men with the fire and the spirit that would take them against the "Big Knives" and their gun. But with him or without him, it was the time.

Scouts reported that the soldiers had crossed their last river, were encamped now an hour's march north of it. Ote Emathla knew the place as he knew most of the land in Florida. The land was clear there, open and easy to travel. The white man's road continued on a little toward the sunrise, then soon it swung back toward the place where the sun went to rest. If he and his warriors left the swamp at dawn they should reach a spot where the road swung close around a pond. An attack there would leave the soldiers no place for retreat, while the Seminoles, if not successful, could return to the swamp. They would have time to choose their places, prepare themselves, and wait.

Chapter Six

The Last Day
Monday, December 28, 1835

Word was brought to Belton at dawn that a sail had finally been sighted. He reacted as though it still mattered, as though Dade and his command were not five days out, fifty miles and more away. He sent a message to Lieutenant Greyson, in command of Legate's company on board the vessel:

> Fort Brooke, Decr 28th 1835
> Sunrise
>
> Sir
>
> I understand . . . that your vessel is in sight in Old Tampa [Bay]— I have directed a signal to be made on the beach[:] a white and red flag to signify that you may land a Detachment of troops there and march over a distance of about 3 miles[,] leaving the baggage to be delivered by the Transport on her arrival. It is unfortunate that the error has been made. . . . [W]e are anxiously awaiting your arrival to move with Maj. Mountford [*sic*] to Fort King.
>
> In haste reply
>
> > I remain etc., etc.
> > F. S. Belton
> > > Captn. 2d Art.
> > > Commanding[1]

Along the high, west rim of a pale green pond, two companies of U.S. soldiers stood quiet, in double file, waiting for orders. Water dripped from the bills of their leather forage caps; the smell of wet wool and woodsmoke hung in the air. The light rain that had come in the night was almost gone, and the sky was turning bright grey in the east. The rain had brought cooler weather, and here and there a man shivered in his damp clothes. Overcoats were buttoned over belts and cartridge boxes or bags to protect them from the damp. The nervous grumbling of other mornings was gone, and men were smiling. Clark thought "the officers and men were in fine spirits, and I should judge, apprehended no danger." They looked to the major as his horse moved slowly along the column.[2]

"I can not tell you to place your guns on the cart, for that would be unmilitary, but as it is raining you may hold them under your great coats." Confidence surrounded Dade like an aura. Five days of traveling through country that was made for ambush and there had been nothing but night-time shouts, threats, a shot or two. Excessive caution could become a burden, even induce fear. Nerves had been strained enough, now it was time for relief. From here on in, speed was more critical than caution. As far as Dade was concerned, the question up to this point had been whether he could run the gauntlet posed by the hostile Seminole Nation. That question was fairly settled. Now they could get on with the real purpose of their mission, the speedy reinforcement—or rescue, if it came to that— of Clinch and his men at Fort King.[3]

Advance and rear guards would lead and follow, but Dade would post no flankers. They could still make no better speed than what could be driven from the oxen, but flankers struggling through underbrush, watching for rattlesnakes as well as Seminoles, could be slower than oxen, and in open country like this they would not extend his vision beyond what could be seen from the column itself. From horseback he and Gardiner, Fraser, and Basinger, even the men driving the wagon, riding the lead horse for the limber, could see further out through the trees than a flanker on foot a hundred yards out. If Seminoles tried an ambush on such unlikely ground the dogs would flush them out. He directed that the hounds be set loose again, the men urging them on with cries of "Sooby, boy, sooby!"[4]

Dade sent for Pacheco. In high spirits, or perhaps prompted by the opportunity to taunt Fraser and his abolitionist concern, he said, "Louis, I have concluded not to send you to [Pelacklakaha] this morning, (the remainder in a loud voice, intended for Capt. Frazier) [sic], but I will send you ahead into Ft. King tomorrow, though!" Pelacklakaha was Micanopy's

town, one of the most prosperous in the Seminole territory, where the
old chief lived with his two wives, a few other Seminoles, and a great
many blacks, believed to be mostly escaped slaves from Georgia. It lay
four miles ahead, four miles east. If Micanopy or Abraham had messages,
they could meet him where the road to Pelacklakaha joined the military
road.[5]

The advance guard moved out, a sergeant and five men in single file
led by Lieutenant Mudge and under the command of Captain Fraser.
Pacheco was with them, sticking near the captain. When the advance had
a lead of two hundred yards, the drummer began the marching beat and
the main column followed in double file, Captain Gardiner leading. Rested
and eager, the men stepped out smartly, left, right, left, the line stretching
longer and longer until proper spacing was achieved, followed by horses,
limber, gun and crew, then the lumbering oxen and their wagon with two
drivers, another interval and last the rear guard, both gun and guard
commanded by Lieutenant Basinger. The mounted officers drifted up
and down the line, watching, listening, the laughing call of a pileated
woodpecker, the chatter of squirrels breaking the silence of the flatwoods.
Well under way, the command for route step was given and the drumming
stopped, the men broke cadence, keeping their rank and file position at
their own step. The yelping of the dogs was a carefree chorus of sound,
like the cries of children in a school yard. Marching with Company C,
Second Regiment Artillery, young Lieutenant Henderson could reflect
that, even with his resignation already accepted, he had managed to have
one real adventure in the army, had risked danger, had faced the threat
of Indian attack. It was an adventure he would never forget.[6]

With each mile the sun climbed, the sky brightened. The land was
open, pleasant, a breeze from the northeast carrying the smell of damp
and pine. Overhead limbs swayed, needles shook, water fell. Another
hour and it would be dry enough to roll and pack their coats, unlimber
muskets. Then the road was bending toward the west, the woods on the
right thinning as the land sloped down, thick brush, small trees, and marsh
grass giving evidence of swamp or pond ahead. The sharp, nasal "yap-
yap" of the ivory-billed woodpecker came occasionally from the high
branches of a pine. Suddenly, through the trees and underbrush a dog

gave a bay of discovery. Others joined, rushing toward the sound. Captain Fraser left the advance to investigate, told Pacheco to join him. They moved out of the road, Pacheco on foot, Fraser on horseback, man and animal walking warily through the trees, finding only an ancient grey horse gumming at the stiff grass. Relieved, they turned back, coming up with the main column, going on to rejoin the advance. Pacheco thought the dogs seemed chastened after their false alarm, coming into the road close to the marching men. They "were sent out again but persisted in remaining in the road. They did not hunt through the woods nor bark with any spirit." Then, ahead and off fifty feet or so to the right, a large pond was visible through the trees, the edge thick with broom grass, the silver sheet of water no more than three or four feet lower than the road.[7]

Dade rode alongside the column, footfalls of horse and men alike a muffled beat, cushioned by a carpet of pine needles thick as a mattress, the column moving in almost total silence down the aisle of a pine cathedral. Another false alarm. Fraser worried too much with his concern for the welfare of a slave, his little notes left behind like messages in a bottle. As if Seminoles would let them pass the rivers and the swamp, only to attack here. Nonsense. As if to offset the alarm caused by the dogs, he turned in his saddle, called out to the men as he passed: "We have now got through all danger; keep up good heart, and when we get to Ft. King, I'll give you three days for Christmas!" And again: "Have a good heart; [our] difficulties and dangers [are] now over; and as soon as [we] arrive at Ft. King [you shall] have three days rest, and keep Christmas gaily." His confidence and the promise of reward brought smiles, shouts, hurrahs. He passed the head of the column, continuing up the road after Fraser and the slave, who were only partly visible through the screen of pines. The road sloped down, crossed a shallow ditch that must have carried water to or from the pond in times of heavy rain. The ditch was grass-grown, a few inches of stagnant water stirred to mud by the passing of the advance.[8]

Another half a mile and they would pass the road to Pelacklakaha branching off to the east. On their way to Fort King ten years ago Dade and McCall had visited the town, only to find it abandoned. A black man had come out to meet them, told Dade that "the inhabitants, on hearing approach, had taken to the swamp, and would fight if followed." Dade had assured the man "that our object was to prevent fighting, and that they had no cause to regard us other than as friend."[9]

Twenty yards west of the road Micanopy and Ote Emathla lay side by side in the tall grass, rifles in their hands. Halpatter Tustenuggee was nearby. "Every warrior was protected by a tree, or secreted in the high palmettoes." South, along the road, other warriors waited. The soldiers were coming. Six men first, one an officer. He wore a tall, black hat with a red plume and the number 3, a white stripe down his trouser leg, a red sash around his waist, a short sword at his side. They were followed by an officer on horseback, near him a black man on foot. A second officer on horseback was coming up the road behind them, a tall man with a black beard. Micanopy said he was the leader, "he knew him personally; had been his friend at Tampa." His name was Dade.[10]

Last night, in the swamp, Ote Emathla and Micanopy had argued about the attack planned against the soldiers. Halpatter Tustenuggee listened. "Micanopy was timid, and urged delay. [Ote Emathla] earnestly opposed [delay], and reproached the old chief for his indecision. He addressed the Indians, and requested those who had faint hearts to remain behind; he was going, when Micanopy said he was ready." Before dawn the camp had come alive, the warriors preparing for battle. Some dressed only in loincloth and paint, others wore captured bits of uniform, decorations of feathers, medallions beaten from silver coins. "Just as day was breaking we moved out of the swamp into the pine barren." Each warrior was required to hand in a stick representing himself. "I counted, by direction of [Ote Emathla] one hundred and eighty warriors." One of them was Ote Emathla's son, another was his cousin. A black man named August was with them.[11]

There would be no more delay. Ote Emathla held the muzzle of his rifle against Micanopy. "If you do not fire the first shot, I will." His small eyes set in a swollen, pockmarked face, Micanopy sighted in on the tall officer. "I will show you," he said. The rider was clearly visible above the grass, his horse slowed to a walk. He was nearly opposite now, just at the rear of the advance guard, behind the black man. He reached in his haversack, took out a biscuit, raised it to his mouth. The snap of the

Halpatter Tustenuggee ("Alligator"). Smithsonian Institution.

rifle sounded like the breaking of a dry stick. They heard him cry out
"My God!" and then he was gone, shot through the heart and dead before
he touched the ground.[12]

The crack of Halpatter Tustenuggee's rifle came like an echo of the first
shot. In an instant every warrior in the grass and palmetto rose, every
man behind a pine stepped out, leveled his rifle, fired. The other officer
on horseback was wounded, leaning, falling. The ragged crashing of the
guns rolled through the woods. Then the soldiers and the black man were
all down. The officer with the black hat, the red plume, had been struck
in the right breast, from which blood was seen to flow. "He for a moment
leaned against a tree, and was finally seen to fall." The horses stood
riderless, then one was hit, stumbled down, Dade's horse in terror dashing
into the midst of the Seminoles. A triumphant shout ripped from Ote
Emathla's throat as he leaped to his feet, a scream of retribution taken,
of battle joined.[13]

Pacheco, with Captain Fraser, had nearly overtaken the advance guard
when he "heard a single rifle shot, and looked back to see if some one was
shooting game, but just in time to see Major Dade fall just in front of me,
shot in the breast." Immediately, "I looked off . . . and saw the Indians
rise up like a string of pepper in a streak of light. They had on only breach-
clouts and moccasins. Their bodies were painted red, and when they fired
it looked as though lightning flashed along the whole length of the line.
Every man of the advance guard fell. Consternation filled the troops. You
could see them waver and tremble. Then the voice of a command rang
out and they remained firm. I thought I had seen the last day of the world.
I . . . laid close down behind a pine tree, beating my head against it and
praying."[14]

Ransom Clark was second man in the right file of the main column.
The dogs stayed close. No birds sang, no squirrels chattered. He reckoned
the time at eight o'clock. The sharp crack of a rifle was as unexpected as
a bolt of lightning. The U.S. Army had rifles, somewhere, maybe one to
every twenty muskets. The only men in *these* woods with rifles would be
Seminoles. Other shots followed, so close as to be almost continuous. A
flush of danger shot through his body, his teeth clamped, hands grabbing
for the musket under his coat. He stared ahead looking for the major in
time to see him, through the trees, lean, fall. "I had not time to think of

Micanopy. P. K. Yonge Library.

Gene Packwood, "First Fire." Drawing depicting the first moments of the
assault. Courtesy of the artist.

the meaning of these shots, before a volley, as if from a thousand rifles, was poured in upon us from the front, and all along our left flank. I looked around me, and it seemed as if I was the only one standing in the right wing. Neither could I, until several other vollies had been fired at us, see an enemy—and when I did, I could only see their heads . . . peering out from the long grass, far and near, and from behind the pine trees."[15]

Seminoles seemed to spring up from every bush, step out from every tree. Unable to think, to comprehend what was happening, Clark could only watch, mesmerized, as they leveled their rifles, taking easy aim, and then the crash of fire rolled across the grass, bullets bursting through wool and flesh and bone to the applause of savage screams. Then the fearful faces were gone and only smoke was left. Numbed, the firing of the rifles, the cries of wounded men roaring in his ears, Clark tried to sort it out. Ahead the road was clear, behind him there were more men down than standing. Men were sprawled on the ground, clawing at their wounds, fingers seeming to squeeze the blood from arm and belly and leg. Others, their faces or necks a splash of red, lay still. Agonized voices rose in screams and curses, a medley of pain. Some standing men, still clutching their muskets at the ready, aimed at the sky, fired. Others, ramrods forgotten in barrels, fired them through the woods like unfledged arrows. He heard a voice behind him bellowing a curse, turned. Captain Gardiner stood in the road, plain frock coat still belted around his short, thick body, sword stabbing the sky, his voice a cannon roar of rage.

Halpatter Tustenuggee had run south through the pines, shielded by the tall grass, the palmetto, to a position opposite the main column. The soldiers had become a screaming mob. Half of them were down, others staggered blindly, clutching their wounds, muskets dropped and forgotten. One man stood alone. Dressed more like a settler than a soldier, he carried no musket, only a sword. He made no attempt to take cover, "a little man, a great brave, who shook his sword at the soldiers and said, 'God damn!' [N]o rifle ball could hit him."[16]

Clark, his fingers suddenly finding the buttons of his coat, tore it open, threw it aside, swung his musket up under his right arm to rest on his hip, pulled the heavy hammer to half-cock. No time here for the full twelve steps of the firing command. With his right hand he jerked open his cartridge box, snatched out a cartridge, and bit off the twist of paper

Ken Hughs, "The Dade Massacre." Courtesy of the Historical Museum of Southern Florida.

at the end with clenched teeth. Opening the pan, he poured in a pinch of black powder, shut the pan, grounded the musket. He poured the rest of the powder down the smooth barrel thick as his thumb, followed it with a one-ounce lead ball still in the paper cover, powder, ball and paper rammed home with the flared end of the rod. He raised the musket to his shoulder, drew the hammer to full-cock, aimed, and fired. Suddenly aware of his danger, he ducked, ran to the nearest tree. In the chaos he looked around, tried to make sense of the scene before him.[17]

The captain's cursing was as explicit as a command, driving the soldiers into action, taking cover, muskets beginning to open a sharp fire. Facing the attack, their backs toward the marshland surrounding the pond, "the Indians . . . scattered round, in a semicircle, on our left . . . and in advance—reaching . . . to the edge of the pond; but leaving an opening for our entrance on the path, and a similar opening on the other extremity for the egress of our advanced guard, which was permitted to pass through without being fired upon, and of course unconscious of the ambuscade through which they had marched."[18]

Gardiner stood his ground. Ahead there was no sign of the advance guard, Dade, Fraser, or Mudge. Six men, three officers, down and likely dead. To the rear, maybe half the rest were down. It had been his command to start with, and now, broken and bleeding, it looked like it was his again. In an instant he was shouting orders, calling for his remaining officers. Henderson, his left arm broken, was handling a musket with one hand. Keais was nowhere in sight, Gatlin would be at the rear with Basinger and the gun. The gun! He bellowed at the nearest men: The gun! Bring up the gun! The words were thrown down the road like a lifeline: Bring up the gun![19]

George Gardiner had learned long ago that a cannon was more than a weapon—it was a symbol. "The gun is the rallying point of the detachment, its point of honor, its flag, its banner. It is that to which men look, by which they stand, with and for which they fight, by and for which they fall. As long as the gun is theirs, they are unconquered, victorious; when the gun is lost, all is lost." If there was any salvation, it would be in their gun. Canister and grape would find Indians that no musket ever would, solid shot shattering a tree would shower them with splinters as deadly as arrows, while the sound and fury of the blast would encourage the men and terrify the Seminoles.[20]

The horses drawing the gun would be the principal and easiest target. Standing higher than the grass, they could have no cover. Basinger knew the value of the gun, would bring it up if he was able, the horses still alive. But no good waiting here, losing more men every minute. It looked like half the command was down already. Nearly all recruits received some infantry drill training in the "School of the Soldier" and "School of the Company," but the men of his and Fraser's companies had moved on to specialize in the handling of artillery, and it was that training that would save them now if anything could. His job was to get them to it. Sword slashing the air, commands cutting through the sounds of battle, he herded men down the road, soldiers dodging from tree to tree, back through the ditch, stepping over the dead as well as the living. Time for the wounded later—if there was a later. Nothing mattered now but staying alive, and life depended on the gun. And there it was! The horses, plunging, screaming, blood streaming from their flanks but still pulling, whips cracking over their ears, just coming up opposite the pond. Basinger, dismounted, sword drawn, his spare figure showing no wounds, shouted commands to his crew.[21]

Then the horses were lurching, huge eyes staring in fright, lips curled in a rictus of pain and effort as they tried to keep their feet while bullets continued to burst their taut hides. Now they were stumbling, going down with a crash one after the other in a tangle of harness. Enemy fire was coming most heavily from the north and along the west side of the road, a glimpse of turbans and muzzle flashes haloed in smoke showing a line a quarter of a mile long. The pond was the only break in the encirclement. It was as good a place to make a stand as any.[22]

The gun crew, eight enlisted men and one noncommissioned officer, marched in two columns behind their weapon. At Basinger's command— "Posts!" "Right and left oblique!" "March!"—the ranks veered apart, halting at their assigned positions alongside and facing the gun, eighteen inches from the ends of the axles. Cannoneers numbers one and two, from their positions on opposite sides of the muzzle, grabbed up the implements, thrust them at the crew. Basinger's shout of "Attention!" "Unlimber in

Scene from an annual Dade battle reenactment.

battery!" was hardly given before cannoneer number five, standing by the right wheel of the limber, stepped to the middle of the limber pole lying between the stricken horses, raised it, lowering the trail. The gunner of the right unhooked the lashing chain, and with the help of the gunner of the left raised the trail, lifting the lunette from the pintle. Numbers five and six, unable to advance the limber the prescribed three paces because of the horses' bodies, pulled it away just enough to allow the trail to be put down. The two gunners grabbed the ammunition box from between the flasks and placed it on the limber, the gunner of the right cried "March!" and numbers five and six dragged the limber west twelve paces, inclining to the right, then wheeled it to the left-about, the pole toward the gun. At the gun, number four had unhooked the handspikes from the carriage, passed one to number three, each fixing one in the pointing rings. Immediately the two gunners stepped to the pointing handspikes, lifted the trail as numbers one, two, three, and four went to the wheels. Working together, the six turned the gun right-about to face the attack, lowered the trail to the ground, returned to their posts.[23]

Far from being a time to ignore the lessons of the "School of the Gunner" or "Manual of the Piece," this was the type of exigency for which they were taught. Without the minutely choreographed routine of the drill, the knowledge that the life of each man was dependent on the moves of every other, the crew would be no more than a terrified mob. And only through belief in the catechism of the gun, that his responsibility was to the piece and not to himself, could a man ignore the smack of bullets striking tree and gun and flesh and listen only for the commands given by the chief of the piece.

Basinger, from his position midway between the limber and the trail handspikes, shouted "Attention!" "To action!" Cannoneer number one, back in position on the right of the muzzle, facing the piece, stepped to the left with his left foot, held the six-foot sponge and rammer-staff horizontally with both hands. Number two, on the left of the muzzle, ammunition pouch on his belt slung from right shoulder to left hip, stepped out with his right foot, ready to receive the cartridge. Number three grabbed the water bucket from its hook on the carriage, put it under the end of the axle-tree, half faced to the left, stabbed his lint-stock into the sand. The lint-stock was a forked stick wound with a cotton rope and soaked in a solution of saltpeter treated with lead acetate. It was a slow match, burning only four or five inches an hour, and it was already alight. In his right hand number three held the portfire-stock, a staff tipped with the portfire itself, a paper tube containing a fast-burning mixture of gunpowder, saltpeter, and sulphur moistened with linseed oil. He touched the portfire to the slow match, withdrew it, held it steady, fire down, four inches from the ground. Standing left of the cascabel, number four pulled off the vent cover, or lead apron, as the gunner of the right stepped between the handspikes, directed the lay of the piece as commanded by Basinger, and resumed his place outside the trail, facing the gunner of the left. Number six came from his position with number five and the noncommissioned officer in charge of the ammunition box to stand behind number two, handed him a cartridge, a flannel powder bag tied to a wooden sabot and iron shot, and returned to the limber.[24]

Basinger shouted "Load!" The gunner of the left, wearing a finger-stall, a buff leather cover for the middle finger of his left hand, stepped to the breech and put his finger over the vent. At the same moment, cannoneer number one, on the right of the muzzle, raised his sponge, took a long step with his left foot, put the sponge in the tube, pushed it to the bottom, twisted, withdrew it in a single stroke, threw the sponge-end to the right, letting the shaft slide through his right hand almost to the sponge, dropped the staff near the rammer-head into his left hand. The moment the sponge was withdrawn, number two stepped forward one pace, placed the cartridge in the bore with his left hand, stepped back. As he did so, the gunner of the left took his finger from the vent, seized the elevating screw with his right hand, and adjusted for level fire. Number two raised the rammer and, throwing the weight of his body on his right arm, pushed the cartridge home with one thrust. He withdrew the rammer, reversed the staff, and resumed his position. Number four was standing on the left of the cascabel, holding the priming wire in his right hand with his thumb through the ring, the tube-box buckled around his waist, an ammunition pouch hanging on his left side. He stepped forward one pace, with his right hand pushed the wire through the vent hole to breach the cartridge, placed the priming tube in the vent with his left, stepped back, and signaled number three to fire by raising his right hand above his head. Without bending his wrist, number four, his back to the enemy, raised his right arm and, careful not to hold the portfire directly over the vent, applied the flame to the tube. The first crash of the cannon was shockingly loud, a great roar of outrage in a burst of sulfurous smoke. With one and a quarter pounds of powder and zero elevation the range was 318 yards. In less than one second the ball had hurtled across the grass to strike a pine, momentum bursting the trunk, sending out an explosion of splinters as the top fell into the arms of the next tree and crashed to the ground.[25]

Halpatter Tustenuggee was sure that the first volleys had "laid upon the ground, dead, more than half the white men." As for the rest, he and the other warriors had concentrated their fire on the officers when they could find them, then the horses that brought the gun. Now the horses were down, the gun manned, the crew moving and a bad target. "The cannon was discharged several times, but the men who loaded it were shot down as soon as the smoke cleared away; the balls passed far over our heads." As the gun was heaved this way and that, warriors in the line of fire moved to either side, taking cover behind a tree or lying flat, prepared to fire the moment the smoke of the explosion lifted.[26]

At the beginning each warrior, ready, lying in wait, had taken his time, aimed carefully, and fired with deadly effect. The bullets, though smaller caliber than those of the soldiers' muskets, and were sufficient for the work at hand. But shooting at men in line who were unaware of danger was one thing, moving targets that shot back another. And itchacluccko, the big gun that bellowed like hulputta, the alligator, and could sting men to death like chitta-mico, the rattlesnake, did not allow time for care. From his sukchahoo-che, the bullet pouch that hung at his side, a warrior had only time to dump an unmeasured charge of powder in his barrel, spit in a ball from several carried in his mouth, come to one knee or stand exposed, fire toward anything that moved, and give a war whoop— a growl that rose to a scream—before he dropped flat, rolling on his left side to reload.[27]

The fierce gun squatting in the road continued to belch metal, flame, and smoke. The bearded young officer behind it shook his sword and swore, driving the soldiers to take up the tools and positions of the crewmen as quickly as they were struck down. Warriors who had been moving in from tree to tree, screaming of their courage, their hate, had stopped, did not expose themselves to fire as gladly, began moving farther and farther out, away from the gun. The solid balls were bursting trees, throwing pine spears in all directions. There was little danger from the ball itself, for every man watching threw himself to the ground as the fire was applied, but when the many small shot were fired they scattered in all directions as they left the barrel—even down, striking men lying in the grass. Ote Emathla and Halpatter Tustenuggee saw that the warriors, though clearly victorious, would not hold, were beginning to slip back, away from the gun. It was vain to shout at them that if they held, cut down the remaining men as they were driven to the gun, it would soon cease to speak. Each man had come to battle on his own initiative and was bound to leave the same way. But even if all left now, a great victory had been won.[28]

Louis Pacheco still lay with the dead of the advance guard. He had thrown down his gun as he dropped to the ground. Seminoles had passed, stepping between the bodies that filled the road, grabbing up a musket here, a sword there, going on to crowd the soldiers who, under the little officer's commands, were retreating in order back toward their gun. Several times he was noticed. A warrior stopped, leveled his gun. Pacheco spoke in Seminole, begged for his life, said he was a slave and doing as he had been told. The warrior put up his gun, moved on. More came, and passed. Pacheco lay still. Two young warriors came within ten feet of him, realized he was alive, jumped back and cocked their guns. "One aimed at me, but an old Indian knocked the gun barrel up and said: 'Don't kill him.' They passed on by, and three more saw me; but this time the son of Chief Jumper saved me. He said: 'That's a black man. He is not his own master. Don't kill him.' Still another Indian wanted to kill me, but I told him Jumper's son said not to. A moment later this Indian threw his arms in the air and fell dead. One of the bucks who passed me got a bullet fastened in his gun and ran back. All the Indians saw him run and not knowing what he ran for, followed him."[29]

His view confined to a short stretch of road, the woods blocked by grass, Pacheco was unaware that more than half of Dade's command were down, most of them dead. Finally he had heard the six-pounder begin to return the fire, had heard nearby Seminoles at first mock the gun "with derisive yells and 'Puff! Ugh!' and they answered it with bullets which hummed like bees about my ears." Then the gun had evidently been heaved around, aimed toward the Seminoles coming down the road, the elevation raised to increase the range, for suddenly "the grapeshot tore up the ground all about me." This had brought the Indians back, drawing out of range. Ote Emathla's son, passing back with the others, again took notice of the black man lying in the road. He put him under the guard of an "old crippled colored man," told him to bring Pacheco along with them, a prisoner.[30]

Captain Gardiner, "God of War," stood his ground with drawn sword, cursing, encouraging, commanding one man after another to join Basinger, take up the position left at the gun by the last man down. With no more protection than the smoke of each firing, men were fearful of leaving the cover of a pine to join the crew, to join the dead and dying. Totally exposed to enemy fire while serving the gun, several men were already down, others bleeding, and still Gardiner drove them on. Basinger seemed to be losing a man with every round fired, but it was still their only hope. If they could hold out a little longer, keep the gun firing, some might survive. Without it the fight would be man to man, and he was outnumbered at least ten to one. Move, damn you!

And, miraculously, the Seminole fire *was* slowing. Basinger had directed the lay of the gun from west to north to west, gone from zero elevation to one and two degrees, used solid shot, grape, and canister. The field of fire was ripped and plowed, trees shattered, stumps cut from ground level to twenty feet high, fires smoldering here and there. The only rifle shots were coming from a distance. As the Seminoles pulled back their aim grew worse, bullets cutting through the limbs far overhead or smacking into trees instead of men. Basinger commanded, "Cease Fire!" The woods were suddenly silent, empty, as though a nightmare had ended. Deafened by the almost continuous rattle and crack of musket and rifle, punctuated by the explosions of the cannon, the fighting men only now began to hear the pleas, the prayers and curses of the wounded. Calls for Dr. Gatlin, for water, entreaties to Jesus and Mother came from men convulsed with pain, men who clawed at their wounds as though desperate to reveal the source of their agony. Gatlin was working from man to man, tending the wounded with improvised tourniquets, his instrument case open with its saws and lancets, the crimson velvet lining sinister in the sunlight.[31]

A little ways off stood the stave-topped, canvas-covered wagon, oxen shot down in their traces, their yokes still on, lying as though they had fallen asleep. Without oxen or horses for the wagon they had no way to carry the wounded should they attempt a retreat. They could not be left. Gardiner sent men to bring the axes, had others drag back the wounded and dead from the gun, the area around it. He directed that trees be dropped, trimmed, stacked in a barricade around the clearing. The smaller trees—eight inches at the butt, sixty feet long—were as much as fifteen men could carry into position. As fast as desperate hands could swing an ax they cut into the pines, one man on either side, fast cutting a wedge until one, then another, and another trunk began to lean, fall faster, crashed to earth. They'd barely struck ground when they were topped, the remaining high limbs taken off with a whack and the shorn trunk grabbed up by at least a dozen pairs of hands. The first two logs were laid north and south of the clearing, a third across the west ends of the others like a rail fence, two more stacked north and south, another on the west ends, forming an isosceles triangle. There was time for only a perfunctory chop or two in an effort to notch the joints, rudely size the trunks. There were eight-inch gaps between the logs, but perhaps it was better than nothing, a place for men to crouch and fire and wait their turn at the cannon should the need arise. The open, east side was narrow, seven or eight yards wide, facing the pond. Three large pines were left standing within the work. The limber and chest were brought inside, the gun placed outside the north wall, its field of fire north and west.[32]

While the barricade was being built, Ransom Clark was one of a dozen sent forward to gather ammunition and bring in the wounded. They made their way up the road, moving from tree to tree, their movements rousing wounded men to pleas for help, for water. Later, later. The dead and dying were clustered more thickly as they reached the point where the head of the column had been when the attack came. For the moment the wounded were ignored in favor of the dead. The wounded could carry their own cartridge boxes or bags; the ammunition of the dead must be taken. The black leather box of 1833 design carried the letters U and S separated by an eagle embossed on the flap. Within was a wooden block

drilled for twenty-six rounds. Beneath was a shallow metal tray divided
into three sections, the middle holding flints and small tools, each side
designed to hold twelve rounds. The boxes of the men who had not been
cut down at the first fire were only partially filled. They'd have better
luck with the men of the advance. Using their forage caps as bullet pouches,
they gathered every round they could find, moved on.[33]

Beyond the head of the main column, the road was abruptly empty,
silent, beyond the painful cries of the wounded. Then the faint but distinct
sound of voices made them pause, look toward the west. At a distance
through the trees movement that could only be Seminoles was visible. On
foot and horseback, they were gathering on a rise a quarter of a mile away.
Clark and the other men hurried on, more quickly now.[34]

Another fifty yards, through a shallow ditch, and they could see another
cluster of bodies in the road. Captain Fraser first, east of the road, a rope
lying near him. Then Major Dade, blood from the bullet wound in his
chest clearly visible. Just ahead of them a sergeant and five enlisted men.
"They had, evidently, all been shot dead, not a man had moved from the
place where he fell . . . each man occupying the position in which he had
marched." They came upon another man, an officer, sitting, his back
against a large pine, a glove by his side, "his head fallen, and evidently
dying." It was Lieutenant Mudge. "I spoke to him, but he did not answer."
A sergeant lay near him, and a private, dead. There was nothing Clark
or the others could do, except take their ammunition.[35]

There was no sign of the interpreter, Louis. They darted from man to
man, snatching open cartridge boxes, dumping the paper twists into their
forage caps, trying not to look at the dead, staring eyes of fellow soldiers,
friends, glazed and already drawing insects. No need to take swords,
muskets, pistols. Plenty of those and to spare back with the captain at the
gun. Together they turned back. Now they could take time for the
wounded as they made their way down the road, giving water, getting
men up, heading back to Dr. Gatlin, the captain, the gun.[36]

The breastwork had been raised two and three logs high on north, west,
and south. Men drenched with sweat and fear, coats discarded, hands
black and gummy with pitch, still labored to cut and trim another pine,
and another, create a bulwark against destruction. Clark and the others
brought their wounded in through the east end, helping them to whatever

Replica of the log barricade set up during the battle. Courtesy of the *Sumter County Times*.

crowded comfort they could find, lying down or sitting with their backs
to the log walls. Clark looked around. Outside the dead lay as they had
fallen or been dragged to make way for the breastwork. The gun was
being positioned, readied for renewed action. Sharpened pine stumps
dotted the ground. Several dogs lay dead. The scene within the meager
barricade looked more like a hospital ward than a fortress. There were
more men wounded than not. "Captain Gardiner, Lieut. Basinger, and
Dr. Gatlin were the only officers left unhurt by the volley which killed
Dade. Lieut. Henderson had his left arm broken, but he continued to
load a musket and to fire it, resting on the stump," and all the while "he
bravely kept up his spirits and cheered the men. Lieut [Keais] had both
his arms broken in the first attack; they were bound up and hung in a
handkerchief, and he sat . . . reclining against the breastwork, his head
often reposing upon it, regardless of everything that was passing around
him."[37]

Gardiner directed the disposition of those men able-bodied enough to
take positions of defense—Clark, DeCourcy, Wilson, Sprague, at best no
more than forty men, many of them already wounded. Another crew was
put together for the six-pounder. With Basinger they took up their positions
outside, around the gun. Gardiner made it clear that if the Seminoles
should return the gun would be kept firing as long as there was ammunition
and a man on his feet to fire it. As men were wounded, others were to
take their places. The barricade was not a place to hide—only to give
some protection to the supernumeraries, and that was every man here.
And if they came to the point of no more supernumeraries, no one on
their feet except the final crew, then the "Manual of the Piece" specified
that the duties of the first man disabled without a replacement would be
taken over by number four, *his* duties taken by the gunner of the left. The
gunner of the right would replace the second man disabled, and so on.
No matter if there wasn't a full crew—four men, even three, two, could
man it—every man here knew the drill. And if it came to that, Lieutenant
Basinger, the chief of the piece, would perform the duties of gunner and
the noncommissioned officer those of purveyor. As to ammunition, they
had started with fifty rounds. A dozen and more were gone, thirty to
forty left. Take your time, make them count.[38]

Inside the barricade, Gardiner placed his men either kneeling or extended on their bellies parallel to one another, particularly behind the north and west walls, muskets resting on the logs. Here they could give the best covering fire to protect the men at the gun. The last of the ammunition was brought from the wagon and distributed. Dr. Gatlin had his two double-barreled shotguns brought, placed ready to hand. The walls already crowded, Gardiner directed Clark, Sprague, and a few others to extend as light infantry, or skirmishers, taking up positions behind pines along the road. They would provide cover for the gun from the north.

Ote Emathla and Halpatter Tustenuggee rallied the warriors, encouraged them to return. The wounded had been helped, the dead buried. If there had been meaning in the attack, there was the same meaning in the destruction of the survivors. Yes, a victory had been won, but a greater victory was at hand. More than half the soldiers were dead, many of the rest wounded. Those who lived were not moving on, spread out, alert, ready. Then the risk would have been great, seeking them out one by one, but the sound of tree cutting could be heard by all. The soldiers were building a box, and they could be seen gathering around it. To go back would be less dangerous than the first attack. And here, more warriors had joined, many of them mounted. The soldiers at the gun were unprotected, could be shot down quickly, the great gun silenced. Then, if any of the "Big Knives" were still alive in their log box they could be encircled and killed.[39]

An hour passed and still they talked. Halpatter Tustenuggee would not let up. Some say no! Are you drunk, or sick, or women, to be afraid of a few white men? Have we forgotten why these soldiers are here? They are here to take our land, our homes, our lives. They will enslave our blacks. They come to "round us up" like cattle, pigs, put us on their boats, send us to the western land. *This* is our land. We did not come here today to leave it, but to fight for it. Then fight, until we kill these soldiers! Let their death carry the message to "The Washington Micco, the Great Father," Andrew Jackson, that though he may despise us for being Indian, for being Seminole, yet he still must look upon us as men. Go back! Go back and kill them all![40]

Protected by a massive pine, Ransom Clark watched them come. "We had barely raised our breastwork knee high when we again saw the Indians advancing in great numbers over the hill to our left." This time there were mounted warriors in addition to those on foot, more than there had been before, while the soldiers' numbers had been reduced by more than half. At best forty men to face what looked to Clark like a thousand Seminoles. They swarmed down through the woods "like devils, yelling and whooping in such a manner that the reports of the rifles were scarcely perceptible. . . . They came on boldly until within a long musket shot, when they spread themselves from tree to tree to surround us." In practiced hands a rifle had an accurate range of over one hundred yards, while a long musket shot might *reach* one hundred yards, but experience had shown that only 15 percent of such shots would be effective, the bullet having lost both force and accuracy at that range. In addition, one musket shot in every six and a half could be counted on to misfire. Clark considered himself "a pretty fair shot," but he had not fired more than a dozen live rounds in practice since he had entered the army. Along with the other artillerymen, he had been trained as a cannoneer, not a musketeer. About the only time he had been obliged to fire live ammunition was coming off guard duty when, to clear his piece, he had fired at a fixed target or simply into the air. He had supplied himself with forty or fifty rounds. Now he could practice in earnest.[41]

Muskets and cannon had opened a brisk fire. Clark looked toward the gun, the breastwork beyond. Every man, wounded or not, was going about the duty of killing in a steady, methodical way. At the gun Basinger shouted directions for each round, then "Load!" The crash of the firing was a roar of triumph. No man could stand behind it without hope. No man could stand before it without fear. Basinger calculated the effect of each shot while the crew readied for the next. Beyond the gun, Captain Gardiner stood near the center of the enclosure, directing the action, his stocky figure as much the embodiment of controlled fury as the cannon was. Under his command, every man had taken position behind the lattice-work of logs, loading, firing. To Clark they looked "as cool as if they were in the woods shooting game." "The woods rang with [Seminole] war-whoops; and the crack of their rifles was as one incessant peal of sharp ringing bells, to which the loud reports of musketry and the booming of the artillery formed a fitting though fearful accompaniment."[42]

Clark looked along the barrel of his musket across the tall grass, through the woods, squeezing off a shot each time the head and shoulders of a Seminole appeared. He tried to cover each man carefully, afraid to waste a single round, confident that he killed one, then a second, finally a third. "I had stationed myself in a clump of pine bushes and had several times fired off my piece, doing deadly execution each time." Then suddenly he felt a blow to his head, a searing pain. He stumbled back from his tree, his hand at his right temple, shielding the hurt. Fearfully he drew his hand away, stared at his fingers thick with blood. As he stood, unable to think what to do, another ball struck him in the groin, his right leg below the hip. From the force of the blow, a massive pain, he staggered, fell to the ground, his lap already sodden with blood. Gasping, terrified, with awareness of what had happened, what it meant—capture, torture, death—he struggled to get back to the cover of the tree, bring up his musket. Trembling with pain and weakness, he tried to focus, find an enemy face, dark skin, stiff black hair. He got off a shot, fumbled to reload, keeping himself shielded as best he could behind the pine, lifted the gun again.[43]

When a bullet ripped through his right arm above the elbow his fingers flew open, the musket fell, his left hand grabbing at the wound. He was on his back, struggling over to his side, off the injured hip, his left hand frantically going from bleeding temple to arm to thigh, clawing at the sand for balance, movement. Got to get inside, get behind the logs. At the end, hand to hand, won't have a chance out here, alone. He crabbed along, pushing with his good leg, pulling with his good arm, inches at a time, the left side of his face nearly touching the ground, past the thundering, screaming action at the gun, around the bodies of fallen crewmen dragged back from the piece. Then he was past the gun, foot by foot, a yard, eyes fixed on the breastwork ahead, the flashes of fire that came between the logs, the blanket of grey smoke that lay over it. Too far to go to the left, reach the open end. Straight ahead, up on one knee, pull with one arm, go over the side. "I saw an Indian, a few rods off, attentively observing me. I drew up my rifle as well as I could to shoot him—but he being too quick for me in my then condition, discharged his piece first at me—and his ball passed through and broke my right arm between the elbow and shoulder." One-third of the head of the right humerus was fractured, and the scapula fragmented. "I then scrambled over the breast-work." He lay inside among the dead and dying, pulled back from the wall by men who still had work to do. Pain was the only message he could understand, beyond sound, beyond fear.[44]

But pain would not save him. He groped through it, reaching for compre-hension, for life. He became aware of noise, of the parts of noise—the crack of rifles, the dull, heavy discharge of muskets, the boom of cannon, shouts of soldiers, screams of Seminoles. Battle, got to fight, bleed to death lying here. Pain. Ignore the pain. On his side, pulling feebly with one arm, his left foot pawing the ground. Bodies, muskets all around. Get to the wall, push a musket through the cracks, kill them. Kill them before I die.

He lay on his belly and looked between the logs. Behind him Gardiner was shouting orders, encouragement. He heard Dr. Gatlin's voice some-where along the wall. He turned his head. "The last I saw of him whilst living was kneeling behind the breastwork with two double guns by him, and he said 'Well, I have got four barrels for them!'" Other men lined the walls, some kneeling, some lying prone, some calm, some desperate, some streaked with sweat, some with tears. Some men cursed and others cried, but all who could fired, and loaded, and fired again. Sand was everywhere, on faces, hands, clothing, muskets, glued with sweat or blood. Clark, holding his musket with his left hand, leaning on his left elbow, barrel between the logs, saw a Seminole, fired. He pulled at the weapon, managed to draw it back, struggled to load with one arm. Outside, from the direction of the gun, there was a cry, then a shout. Nothing he could do. Load. Fire. Load. Basinger inside, talking with the captain. Only a flesh wound, I'm all right. Got to keep the gun firing. Gardiner going to the gun. Soldiers shouting, cursing. Lying on his left side to load, Clark could see between the logs forming the north wall. Like the steps of a macabre dance, each crewman changed position and duties every time a man was struck down. Sponge on the ground. No time for that. The precaution of swabbing and worming had given way to the urgency of the moment. The servicing of the gun had become almost as great a danger as Seminole bullets. Gunners often lost fingers, hands, eyes through improper loading, but that meant nothing now. Premature explosion or Seminole bullet—either way, the price was life. Bodies around the gun, only a couple of soldiers on their feet, shouting at the captain, refusing to stand there as "mere marks." Gardiner swung his pistol away from the attack, toward the crew, assured them, "You must fall in the discharge of your duty, or at my hand!" A moment later the cannon roared out again.[45]

The world was pain and noise. Time and again Clark slipped away to peace, only to return to nightmare. Several times he thought the cannon had been silenced, only to hear it erupt once more. Later one or two men tumbled over the wall to the inside—Gardiner came in. Last round in the gun, portfire match had gone out. Spiked the gun with a ramrod. Basinger, still standing in spite of his wound, directing musket fire. Gardiner, supporting his exhausted frame against a tree, was handling a musket. Then: "I can give you no more orders my lads, do your best!" Clark managed to turn his head. The captain had dropped his musket, blood coming from half a dozen wounds, one in his chest. He fell, lay still.[46]

Gun gone, and now the captain. Of 108, maybe a dozen men firing. Clark, Wilson, DeCourcy, Lieutenant Basinger. "I am the only officer left, boys; we must do the best we can." The rumble of musket fire had slowed to single shots. Ammunition—and time—were running out. The crack of rifles was louder, closer; the smack of bullets hitting the logs was steady. Then Basinger took a bullet through both legs, blood running down his trousers like a red stripe of rank. He staggered, went down. Clark revived, faded, revived again. "I was about the last one who handled a gun, while lying on my side. At the close I received a shot in my right shoulder which passed into my lungs—the blood gushed out of my mouth in a stream, and, dropping my musket, I rolled over on my face." The ball, carrying a piece of his coat with it, had traversed obliquely downward to lodge in his right lung.[47]

A voice. English. A white man. Clark opened his eyes, moved his head, slowly, slowly. Basinger, whispering urgently. He spoke of living, and dying. He had read of Indian battles where wounded men had escaped massacre by pretending to be dead when the Indians came to strip them. Pretend to be dead. That shouldn't be hard to do. "I looked through the logs and saw the savages approaching in great numbers. A heavily made

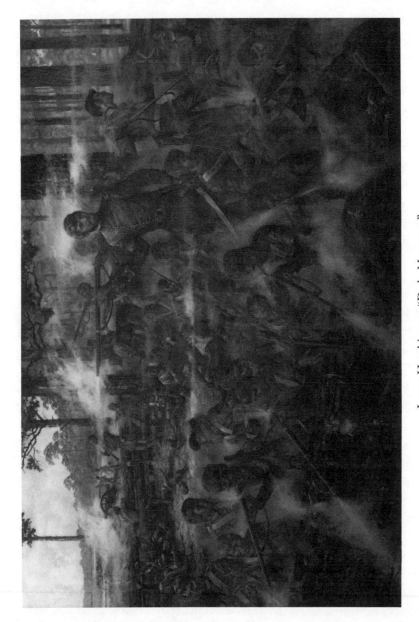

James Hutchinson, "Dade Massacre."

Indian, of middle stature, painted down to the waist . . . seemed to be the chief. He made them a speech, frequently pointing to the breastwork."[48]

Ote Emathla and Halpatter Tustenuggee, with Micanopy, the black man, August, and ten warriors, approached the last redoubt. Micanopy and then Ote Emathla reminded the warriors that the plan was to kill, not to steal. The soldiers' weapons were the fruit of victory, but taking money or jewelry was no more than thievery. Halpatter Tustenuggee and several others stepped over the low barricade. As if waiting for that moment a soldier, a young, bearded officer wearing a blue frock coat struggled to his feet, his trouser legs dark with blood. He stumbled forward to meet them, offered his sword, asked that his life be spared. One of the Seminoles brought up his rifle, shot him at point-blank range.

Clark lay still, listening, watching when he could as the Seminoles began to move about among the bodies. "There was none to offer resistance, and they did not seem to suspect the wounded of being alive—offered no indignity, but stepped about carefully, quietly stripping off our accoutre-ments and carrying away our arms." One bent over a body, searching for ammunition. Suddenly the soldier leaped to his feet, grabbed the barrel of the Seminole's rifle, snatched it from his hand, swept it into the air and down across his black-haired skull, spilling bone and brains onto the sand. Private Joseph Wilson, musician, leaped the north wall and ran for his life.[49]

"There was a brave man in the pen; he would not give up; he seized an Indian, cousin [of Ote Emathla], took away his rifle, and with one blow with it beat out his brains, then ran some distance up the road; but two Indians on horseback overtook him, who, afraid to approach, stood at a distance and shot him down."[50]

Only three or four of the soldiers had fallen backward into the pen. The rest lay, as they had fought, at right angles to the three log walls. The Seminoles went from man to man, offering no further injury, no indignity, picking up a musket here, a sword there. "They had guns, but no powder; we looked in the [cartridge] boxes afterwards and found they were empty. . . . The firing had ceased, and all was quiet when we returned to the swamp. . . . We left many negroes upon the ground looking at the dead men."[51]

The blacks had not the status of warriors, had not been given the privilege of joining the attack. Now, the fighting over, they had been allowed upon the field. Out of slavery, clothed in little more than freedom, for the first time they looked upon white men at *their* mercy. The anguish of the wounded was barely noticed by men who had borne the anguish of slavery. Deaf at best, vicious at worst, they moved from man to man, taking satisfaction, leaving jewelry, pins, brooches, gold watches, and hundreds of dollars in paper, silver, and gold. Clark lay still, what blood he had left pounding in his veins. "Having been wounded in five different places myself, I was pretty well covered with blood, and two scratches that I had received in my head gave me the appearance of having been shot through the brain, for the negroes, after catching me up by the heels, threw me down, saying 'damn him he's dead enough!'" Here and there blacks removed sweat-soaked jackets and trousers, while others took boots and forage caps. One drew a knife and cut off the genitals of a soldier, crammed them into the dead mouth. Another crushed a skull; several took scalps. "I last saw a negro spurn [Capt. Gardiner's] body, saying with an oath, 'that's one of their officers!'"[52]

From the wagon they took whatever the Seminoles had left of food and blankets. Using broken muskets and bayonets, they pried the cannon off its carriage, carried it east to the pond, and heaved it in. Waves rolled across the surface, through the high broom grass that covered it, lapping at the pale, stricken face of Pvt. Joseph Sprague. A thirty-two-year-old farmer from Vermont, Sprague had taken a wound, crawled to the pond, and concealed himself in the water and broom. The blacks turned away, set fire to the gun carriage, banking the flames against the wheels and beneath the axle. With the flames spreading slowly through the sparse, dry grass, they left the battle site, going north along the road, gathering more clothing, leaving white, half-naked bodies tumbled in the sand. They paid no attention to the bullet holes, the blood. They passed by broken muskets, ramrods stuck in the sand, bayonets, belts. They came to a young officer, his body propped against a tree. A white glove lay near his body, a cap with the number three. He wore a gold ring on one finger. They stared, turned away. Stopping where the advance guard lay sprawled in the road, they took time only to remove the coat, vest, and shirt from the body of one officer. Another they ignored. They tossed the vest aside as useless, the white body handled roughly by black hands, and they were done. Later, in the swamp, there would be a celebration. Seeing the bodies of white soldiers was celebration enough for the blacks. This victory would bring war. War would bring continued freedom, or death. Only peace was to be feared. Peace would bring slavery. There would be no peace now.[53]

Osceola waited. Two men were coming closer, further from the fort. It was afternoon, the sun slanting in through the pines low and bright, the sky clear, the day cool, the breeze from the west. Earlier he had seen soldiers leave the fort, carrying tools. He had heard orders shouted; the men had moved around to the south and east. He could no longer see them; they could not see him, even if he stood.[54]

To the right, through the windows of the sutler's house standing close by the hammock where he lay, he could see men sitting at a table, others passing back and forth. The sutler and his people slept within the distant fort but took their meals in the house. They were there now—Rogers, the storekeeper, his clerks, servants, a boy, a black woman. He could hear them talking, laughing. "In advising the warriors, when starting upon a war-party, [Osceola] always enjoined them to spare the women and children. 'It is not upon them . . . that we make war and draw the scalping-knife, it is upon men; let us act like men.'" He could enjoin, but he could not command.[55]

One of the men strolling along the road toward him was an officer, a young man. The other was tall, grey haired, old, smoking a cigar. His name was Wiley Thompson. Closer. Closer. The two reached the crest of a small hill in full view of the fort, perhaps twice the distance that Osceola had come when Thompson had arrested him, put him in chains. Osceola stood, aimed, fired. Thompson jerked back as though offended at the sound. In the moment before he fell other shots struck him. His chest was spotted with red. The last sound he heard was the peculiar, shrill war cry of Osceola. Two bullets struck the officer, Lt. Constantine Smith. Osceola and fifty others rushed toward the two fallen men. He cared nothing for the officer. Thompson was his. Lest the dozen bullets in his body not ensure the agent's death, he drew his hunting knife, stabbed him in the right chest. He jerked the red blade out, circled the scalp with a shallow cut, twisted the grey hair in his fingers, ripped the skin cap from the skull.[56]

Alerted by the firing, several people had broken from the house, were running for the fort. Ignoring them, the warriors surrounded the house, firing on the inhabitants through the windows and door. Some of the white people were down, bleeding, others screaming, rushing about, some in their panic attempting to get out of the windows in the face of the Seminoles, some running to other rooms. Leading the way, Osceola entered the building. He had no grudge against Rogers, who was still alive. He stepped in front of him, blocked Rogers's body with his own. Warriors behind him, raging against the whites, *any* whites, knelt, fired between his legs. Rogers fell. The only other white man, Kitzler, had two bullets in him, was already down, his skull smashed, brains spilled. Osceola turned away, went through a doorway into the storeroom, kicked aside empty boxes, used his rifle butt to batter aside furniture that stood in his way. The sutler's supply of wine and liquor had been stored here, hundreds of bottles. In the days of waiting and watching he had not seen them removed, but they were not here now. The shelves were nearly empty. Nothing but a counter and, under it, empty barrels. He saw no one. Suddenly the shooting ended.[57]

He returned to the dining room. Most of the men, the boy, lay dead. Rogers had been shot seventeen times. All but the boy had been scalped, and several skulls besides Kitzler's had been smashed. Broken dishes, scattered food lay everywhere. He went outside, looked toward the fort. He could hear shouts, but there were no soldiers in sight, the gates still closed. They would come soon. He gave another shout, motioned. Followed by two other chiefs, every warrior, half a dozen scalps among them, he moved into the woods, headed south.[58]

Five miles north and west of the battlefield, in the Cove of the Withlacoochee, the Wahoo Swamp, the only haven left, Ote Emathla, Halpatter Tustenuggee, Seminole men, women, and children exulted in victory. Aside, in the dark, some grieved for men who had not come back, but around the fires trophies of battle gleamed in the vast fires: muskets, swords, pistols. Exultant warriors strutted in soldiers' tunics, officers' coats with gold braid and epaulets over bare, bronzed chests streaked with paint. Soldiers' short, heavy boots were passed around, woolen trousers with strange flaps and pockets with buttons of bone and metal, shirts heavy with the stink of the white man's sweat, his life's blood.

Suddenly Osceola was with them, he and his warriors thirsty with the heat of travel, the weight of trophies. Some men wore the still-wet scalps of the enemy on their heads, foreheads streaked with blood. Again and again they told their stories of vengeance and victory: Thompson dead and not one Seminole lost.

Some liquor had been found on Dade's wagon, a few bottles at the sutler's. Joyful drink made the rounds. Scalps were given up to the medicine man, "who arranged them upon a pole ten feet in height, around which they exultingly danced till daylight, accompanying their frantic mirth by songs, ridiculing and defying the white men. . . . Speeches were addressed by the most humorous of the company to the scalp of General Thompson, imitating his gestures and manner of speaking to them in council."[59]

Thoughtful men might stare into the flames and wonder. Victory had been won in a daylight battle between armed men. Seminoles were not children to be lied to, tricked, herded like cattle. The sly wink of the white man would no longer be met with reluctant concession. Nothing more would be given away. But would the white men understand the message of the dead soldiers? Would the white man give up, leave the Seminoles in peace?

Cold. Pain. Thirst. Sound of crickets, an owl, the distant howl of a wolf. Mouth so dry his tongue dragged, throat too dry to swallow. Taste of blood. Ransom Clark opened gummy eyes. Darkness, terrible odors of violent death. Moonlight, enough to see shapes, bodies, the log wall, dark trees against a lighter sky. The chip of moon was nine o'clock high. "The sensation on waking . . . in the wilderness at night, it would be difficult to convey . . . to one who has never experienced it. The first thought is— is all *safe?* An object, though but a few yards from you—a cart, or a horse—will for an instant startle you—for all is strange and still! And yet the mound and the morass appear to whisper! and if there be a breeze abroad—though but a breath—it seems to moan in accents almost human! the senses grow thick; they labor—and the fall of a leaf has its fear!"[60]

Could die here. Got to move, got to go back. He thought he knew pain until he tried to draw up his right leg. Even the impulse was agony. Try the left. And left arm. Finally, gasping, sitting, he could see other soldiers, three or four sprawled like thrown dolls toward the center, near the captain. "The rest lay as regularly at right angles to one or the other of the top three faces of [the] little fort, the head lying on the top log . . . or immediately below it, as if they had been toy-soldiers arranged by a child in his sport." Leaning on his left hip, pushing with his left foot, pulling with his left hand, right arm hanging across his chest, Clark began to work his way across the enclosure. Near the south wall the bodies were too close to pass between. There was nothing to do but crawl over them. They were cold, already stiff. He dragged himself across. Then, "I put my hand on one man, who felt different from the rest—he was warm and limber. I roused him up, and found it was [Edwin] DeCourcy, an Englishman, the son of a British officer, resident in Canada." Compared to Clark, DeCourcy's wounds were slight; only his left arm and one side were bleeding. Struggling together, they made their way clear of the breastwork, passed the body of Dr. Gatlin, evidently dragged outside by the blacks. By the road lay the horses in their harness, a little further the oxen in their yokes. "As [DeCourcy] was only wounded in the side and arm, he could walk a little." The blacks had gone off to the north. They would head south, back to Fort Brooke. Clark insisted that "the danger appeared to be over, and we might fall in with some assistance."[61]

The danger over? DeCourcy heard the words but could not comprehend what Clark meant. The man should be dead. The side of his face was covered with blood from a scalp wound, an arm and a leg broken, a bullet in his lung, bleeding like a stuck pig. Fort Brooke was sixty miles, four rivers away through hostile territory. They had no food, no water, were coatless and barefoot. Walk? He could hardly crawl.

Clinging to one another, arguing, cursing, weeping, they started out.

Epilogue

The crescent of light in the sky was better than nothing at all. By moonlight and starlight the two men struggled on. Clark, at twenty-three, was two years younger than his companion, taller, with dark hair and dark complexion compared to DeCourcy's fair hair and pale skin. The Englishman was only slightly injured in one side and arm. With Clark's good arm—the left one—across his shoulders he could provide enough support for the crippled man to stand, touch his right foot to the ground, and swing his left leg forward. The agony of the bullet in his right pelvis, the hole through his right shoulder, his shattered shoulder blade, and the chunk of lead in his lung had to be ignored if he was to live. Men with less than mortal wounds lay behind in the barricade, doomed because they did not believe that life could pass through a barrier of mortal pain.[1]

Through the night the temperature barely dipped below sixty, cold enough for men who were barefoot, half naked. The chill and their slow progress helped to staunch the blood loss. Exhausted before they started, they could find little relief in rest, the pain for Clark in sitting and rising even worse than going on.[2]

"We got along as well as we could that night, continued on till noon, when, on a rising ground, we observed an Indian ahead, on horseback, loading his rifle. We agreed that [DeCourcy] should go on one side of the road, and I on the other." The Englishman ran off to the left, Clark hitching himself to the right on left hand and knee, right arm hanging, leg dragging, into a palmetto hammock close to the road. Curled into a knot of pain and fear, he could see nothing, could only hear the rustling of the horse's legs through the brush across the road. "Shortly afterwards

I heard the crack of a rifle and a little after, another." Then the Indian "came riding through the brush in pursuit of me, and approached within ten feet. . . . Suddenly however he put spurs to his horse and went off at a gallop." Taking no time to wonder at his own survival, Clark dragged himself across the road, found DeCourcy. He was dead.[3]

"I made something of a circuit before I struck the beaten path again. That night I was a good deal annoyed by the wolves who had scented my blood and came very close to me." "[I] crawled and limped through the nights and forenoons, and slept in the brush during the middle of the day, with no other nourishment than cold water." He would not give up. He would not die.[4]

At Fort Brooke, Captain Belton was still waiting—for attack, reinforcement, supplies, orders. On January 1 he reported, "Yesterday Pr. Ransom Clark . . . with four wounds, very severe . . . [came in]." It was evening. The apparition at the gate was clothed in rags, blood, and dirt. He had staggered and crawled sixty miles through Seminole country in three days.[5]

Private John Thomas had come in the afternoon of the twenty-ninth. He had known nothing of the command since the twenty-fifth, when he had begun his slow, painful return from the Big Hillsborough. As far as he had known they were fine. He had seen only a single warrior. The man had threatened him but then recognized him as the soldier who had put a new handle to his ax a few days before at the fort. He had taken the six dollars Thomas carried but left him his life.[6]

Clark, raving and cursing, was taken to the hospital. The log building, 116 feet long and 20 feet wide, contained two wards, a kitchen, and a dispensary. Each ward held four double bunks and four singles and accommodated twelve patients. Surgeons Heiskell and Reynolds examined the wounded man, the six windows of the wardroom open to the year's last bright sunlight.[7]

Private John Bemrose, hospital orderly, had never faced Seminoles in battle, had never felt the agony of torn flesh and broken bones. He thought Clark "a fearful fellow, swearing most terribly and continually whilst under the surgeon's hands, and when any broken bones were removed from his lacerated shoulders asking if they would not make good soup. He seemed thoroughly bad, turning his own misfortunes into a burlesque."[8]

Clark's wounds, inflamed and festering, were cleaned of dirt and blood, probed for bullets. The injury to his right temple proved to be only a flesh wound, but the others were not. The surgeons found him "severely wounded in the right shoulder, forever depriving him of the use of his right arm—also in the right thigh—in the right arm, above the elbow . . . and in the back." The path of the bullet through his shoulder was still open, bits of shattered bone working their way to the surface. They administered an emetic in an effort to determine whether the ball was in his lung. In the resulting coughing and vomiting he threw up a piece of his coat carried in by the ball. The wounds were inoperable, irreparable. Shaking their heads, they could only attribute his not dying to the fact that he had "bled a great deal, and did not partake of any solid food during the first [five] days." They bound him up, fed him, and gave him drink. "Here, then, I was again safe."[9]

Crowding into the hospital, spilling out onto the porch, milling back and forth across the two hundred yards to the barracks were officers, soldiers, and civilians; men, women, and children. Again and again Clark was made to tell the story. With vivid detail he recounted the march, the attack, the battle, and finally his own struggle in returning to Fort Brooke. One officer wrote that "he related [the story] in a quiet, simple way that would have carried conviction of his truthfulness to the most skeptical listener."[10]

Word of Clark's arrival, his condition, and his story was on every lip. Dismay, horror, and grief were in every heart. Fellow officers of the dead were appalled, many enraged. Widows of officers and enlisted men alike wailed out their anguish while scores of orphans tried to comprehend what they heard and did not hear. Through the night arrangements were made for the families of the fallen men to be put aboard the transport *Atlantic*, bound for New Orleans.[11]

In the morning, New Year's Day, a second survivor of the battle came in—Pvt. Joseph Sprague, wounded in one arm. He agreed with Clark's account but could add little to it. A member of Fraser's company, Sprague confirmed that the captain was dead with the rest, having fallen with the advance guard. Sprague brought with him the message Fraser had left in a cleft stick along the road, addressed to Major Mountfort. It merely said the command "was beset every night and pushing on." Mountfort hurriedly penned a note to a friend in New Orleans, informing him that "the whole command of Major Dade, officers and men, have been cut to pieces." In answer to the inevitable question, he protested that "this result could not have been prevented had my command gone on, and we should only have been cut up in detail."[12]

At the same time, Belton was writing the first official report of "the catastrophe of this fated Band." A week later Augustus Steele left Fort Brooke by ship to carry the report to Governor Eaton in Tallahassee, arriving on the seventeenth. The next day Eaton sent an express to Clinch at Fort Drane. The messenger arrived on the twenty-second, the report of the Seminole victory explaining their confidence and ferocity in his own clash with them only three days after the destruction of Dade's command, as well as indicating the probable source of the military coat Osceola had been seen wearing.[13]

Delayed in its sailing, the *Atlantic*, commanded by Captain Sawyer, reached New Orleans on Sunday, January 10. The next day Mountfort's letter was published simultaneously in the *New Orleans Bulletin* and the *Mobile Register*, the first word of the disaster to reach the public. From there the news was picked up and carried to Charleston, Washington, New York, and across the nation. Somehow hope was sustained briefly that Gardiner had escaped. A little later an officer who accompanied Gaines suggested that Fraser had been taken prisoner and tortured before being put to death. The only evidence for this assertion was "the position of the body, and a rope lying by it."[14]

With each telling the story became less of a battle lost and more of a massacre, even murder. Newspapers began to demand that government and people "Up and be doing! Send . . . armed volunteers . . . to Florida; and extirpate the Seminoles." Belton set the tone when he wrote, on January 5, "The best in the army lie bleaching in the air, defaced by Negroes and torn [by] obscene birds—Rouse up Florida."[15]

Not only was Florida roused, but the nation as well. In the name of revenge the Army, Navy, and Marine Corps (in addition to the militia) brought in troops or increased their number in the Territory, beginning with General Gaines's force of more than a thousand coming into Fort Brooke only six weeks after the destruction of Dade's command. For seven years the military cleared roads, built forts, fought Seminoles (or tried to), and brought captured blacks to slavery.

By August 14, 1842, when Col. William Worth announced "that hostilities with the Indians within this Territory have ceased," some two thousand military men—and perhaps an equal number of Indians—had lost their lives. Most of the surviving Seminoles had been deported to Oklahoma, the few hundred remaining had fled to the Everglades. Black families who had lived free for generations with the Seminoles had been returned to slavery. The door to freedom was closed. The future of Florida was in white hands.[16]

Appendix One

The Battleground

On December 28, 1980, a program was presented at Dade Battlefield State Historic Site to commemorate the 145th anniversary of the battle. Several distinguished speakers were followed by a first-person, "eyewitness" account of the battle by a man in the full uniform of the period. A small military encampment of tents and equipment, manned by a few reenactors, stood just outside the reproduction of the barricade.

Each year thereafter the program has been continued and enlarged. The 1993 production included nearly one hundred reenactors in the part of Dade's command and almost an equal number in the part of Seminoles, all authentically equipped to the last weapon and item of clothing. The officers were mounted, horses drew the six-pounder, and two oxen were harnessed to the supply wagon. Visitors were able to watch the forty-five-minute battle from a graded mound that provides space for five thousand spectators. The program is presented each year on Saturday and Sunday of the weekend nearest the actual anniversary. Reenactors create period military as well as Seminole encampments where visitors can experience in detail the sights and sounds of men preparing for war in 1835.

In recent years the museum on the grounds of the battlefield has been reorganized and the displays expanded. An officer's sword taken from the battlefield by Gaines's men is on loan from the Smithsonian Institution. The museum maintains a growing reference file on all aspects of battle-related material, and copies of research material are available for a small fee.

Just east of the museum are the graves of the men of Dade's command. For nearly sixty years the area has been surrounded by a cement replica of the last redoubt, incorrectly open on the west side rather than the east. This structure has recently been replaced with actual logs, cut to the original length, "rudely sized," stacked in open style (rather than notched down as in the corners of a log cabin), and, most important, closed on the west side (facing the attack) and open on the east. Today's visitor can instantly sense by its construction the desperate urgency of the men who had no way of knowing how long they might have before a second attack.

The barrel of the six-pounder, which had been placed over the officers' grave in February 1836, has not been found. In March 1836 Belton wrote: "This gun, the last weapon of their death agony . . . become[s] their monument, till country or comrades shall proudly place their name in full relief in the frequented paths of men . . . where devotion's eye may dim for the fate, and petition for the souls of these unshriven dead." Perhaps more effectively than any monument, the reenactment of the battle year after year will commemorate the courage and the loss of the soldiers who died here. Equally important, every visitor shall be reminded of the courage of the Seminoles, who won this victory, only to lose their world.

The impetus, funds, and arrangements for the continuing development of this historic site and the annual reenactment are provided by the Dade Battlefield Society, in cooperation with the Florida Department of Natural Resources, Division of Recreation and Parks. The society is a nonprofit organization whose purpose is the preservation and conservation of this battlefield. Dade Battlefield State Historic Site lies just south and east of Bushnell, Florida. Visitors traveling on Interstate 75 should take county road 476 east one mile to South Battlefield Drive, then south one mile to the park. From U.S. 301 take county road 476 east one-half mile to South Battlefield Drive, then south one-quarter of a mile. The park is open 365 days a year from 8:00 A.M. until sundown. Inquiries and information requests should be addressed to the Dade Battlefield Society, Inc., P.O. Box 309, Bushnell, Fla. 33513.

Appendix Two

Maps of Dade Battlefield

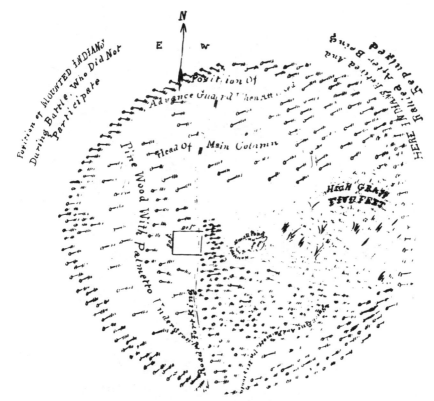

Battle Ground of Maj. DADE
7 Miles from Little.WITHLACOOCHEE
Decem 28ᵗʰ 1835

Map accompanying Maj. Francis Belton's official report of the battle.
National Archives.

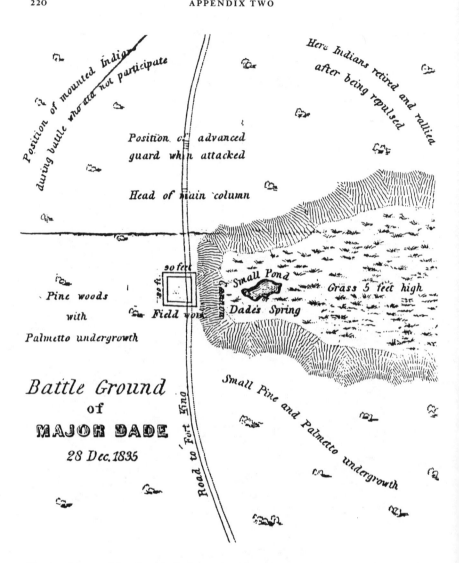

Position of mounted Indians during battle who did not participate

Here Indians retired and rallied after being repulsed

Position of advanced
guard when attacked

Head of main column

Pine woods
with
Palmetto undergrowth

90 feet

Field work

Small Pond
Dade's Spring

Grass 5 feet high

Battle Ground
of
MAJOR DADE
28 Dec. 1835

Road to Fort King

Small Pine and Palmetto undergrowth

Prepared by 2nd Lt. Joseph E. Johnston, March 20, 1836. From *American State Papers*, vol. 7.

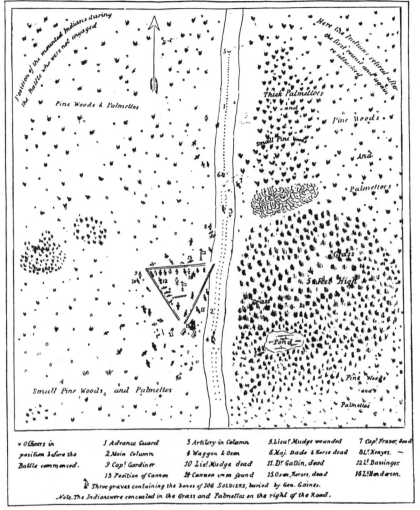

Prepared by 2nd Lt. Woodburne Potter, February 18, 1836. From Potter, *The War in Florida* (1836).

From the diary of 2nd Lt. Henry Prince, February 20, 1836. P. K. Yonge Library.

Sketch of Major Dade's Battle Ground taken upon
the spot by E. Rode U.S. Arty.

References

1 Position in which Maj Dade was found after the massacre in the road
2 Capt. Fraser and advance guard
3 Lieut. Mudge
4 Capt. Gardiner
5 Lieuts. Keais & Henderson
6 Lieut. Basinger
7 Dr. Gatlin
8 Burial place of the soldiers
9   "   "   Officers
10 Cannon found in pond
11 Breastwork made by felling pine trees three logs in height

------ Position of troops when first attacked

I I I Supposed position of the Indians, judging from the manner in which the trees are marked

11 Position of 6 pdr. in breastwork.

75 yds from marsh

Open Pines with Palmetto

undergrowth

Marsh connecting the ponds

Musket and Grape shot

Palmetto scrub

Trees Marked

Ft. King & Tampa Bay Road

From 9 to Breastwork is about 130 yds

Ground is nowhere elevated more than
3 or 4 ft above the level of the pond

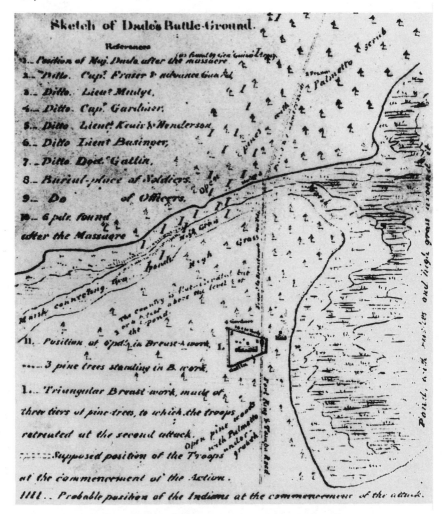

Prepared by Lt. Benjamin Alvord. National Archives.

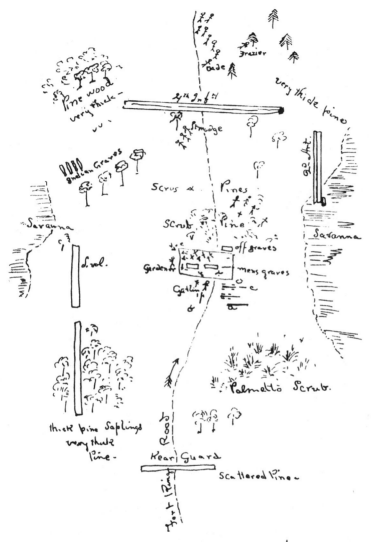

a Gun Carriage.   c Ox Cart.
b Limber   d pit when guns was buried.
e Basinger Keyes-and Henderson.

Prepared by an unknown artist.

Appendix Three

Soldiers and Seminoles

It is doubtful whether there is another instance in relatively modern times when the dead of a battle have lain untended on the field for as long as the men of Dade's command. Fifty-four days after the battle, on the morning of February 20, 1836, Gen. Edmund Pendleton Gaines and an army of one thousand reached the field. During the nearly eight weeks since the battle the temperature had often reached into the seventies.

Gaines deployed a guard and set the rest of the command to the task at hand. Every officer was identified, and all eight were put in a common grave outside the northeast angle of the barricade. Every body and bone of enlisted men was placed in one of two identical graves dug within the log enclosure. The excess dirt was piled in mounds over the graves of the enlisted men, and the cannon barrel was put over the officers' grave. "The graves were dug[,] the remains collected[,] tumbled in their receptacles and covered over in the shortest possible time, the whole having been accomplished, and the march resumed in little more than one hour." It was not a place to tarry.[1]

There is no reference to coffins, boxes, or even rough wrapping of the bodies, not surprising under the conditions of field service. When, in 1842, the bones were taken up and moved to St. Augustine, the only categorizing suggested in the related orders and reports was that the bones be "placed in the boxes in such manner as to keep the officers separate from the men & to mark the boxes accordingly." The remains were taken to St. Augustine where, on August 15, 1842, they were finally put to rest.[2]

Except, possibly, Captain Fraser.

By 1883 Fort Brooke had become militarily irrelevant. "The War Department relinquished title to the Interior Department and the reservation was opened to homestead applications." The remains of some twenty men known to be in the military cemetery were taken up and moved to the Barrancas National Cemetery at Pensacola. "The most famous remains to be moved was that of Captain Upton Fraser who had been killed at the Dade Massacre in 1835." The present director of the Barrancas Cemetery supplied the author with a photograph of the inscribed headstone.[3]

If Upton Fraser lies beneath that stone, how did he get there? Every reference to the burial of the officers at the battlefield in 1836 indicates that all were buried in one grave. For Fraser to have been separated from the rest at that time suggests that someone gathered his remains apart from the others, then carried them on to Fort King—and eventually back to Fort Brooke—for burial, all without making reference to these actions in the reports. Although this is theoretically possible, it seems extremely unlikely in a practical sense, and it would be difficult to imagine a motive for such a macabre effort. The same circumstances apply to the mass exhumation and removal in 1842. It is much more likely that Fraser rests under the cement pyramid at St. Augustine with his fellow officers, while an unknown soldier lies beneath the Pensacola headstone.

During the seven years of the Second Seminole War, the name of each of the fallen officers of Dade's command was given to one of the many forts built in Florida during that struggle, beginning in 1837 with Fort Dade on the south bank of the Withlacoochee River, just east of the Fort King Road. Within a decade a civilian community had grown up ten miles south of the river, and the soldiers sent up from Tampa Bay each year to reactivate Fort Dade began to make the civilian area their headquarters, referring to it as the "Fort Dade Community" and finally as "Dade City." Francis Dade is remembered also in the town of Dadeville, Alabama, and in the south Florida county of Dade, as well as counties in Georgia and Missouri. Neither stick nor stone of forts Dade, Gardiner, Fraser, Basinger, Mudge, Keais, Henderson, or Gatlin remains.

Of the officers, only Dade, Gardiner, and Basinger were married. Basinger had no children, and Dade's only child, a daughter, died unmarried in 1848. Captain Gardiner is the only one with direct descendants still living. His great-great-great-grandson, Thomas Forman of Joshua Tree, California, graduated from West Point in the class of 1959.

Lieutenant Benjamin Alvord, one-day member of Dade's command, continued in the army until 1880, serving with distinction in the war with Mexico and in the Civil War, rising to the rank of brigadier general. The only known public statement he made concerning Dade's march and battle was an address before the Dialectic Society of the Corps of Cadets at West Point in December 1838, "In Commemoration of the Gallant Conduct of the Nine Graduates of the Military Academy, and Other Officers of the United States Army, Who Fell in the Battles Which Took Place in Florida. . . ." General Alvord died in 1884.

Captain Belton, though not a member of Dade's command, merits mention here. Beginning December 12, the day after his arrival at Fort Brooke, Belton had reported what he believed to be the dire and immediate threat to the fort and all within it posed by the Seminoles: "sick reports are large," "the supply of ammunition is scanty," "provisions may hold out," "in expectation of an attack every night." His officers, almost without exception, urged delay in the execution of Clinch's request for reinforcements. This reluctance to take the field carries no stigma of cowardice but rather exemplifies wisdom: marching to meet an enemy who is known to be in the field (*his* field), with more than twice your number, and when the cause for the march itself is uncertain, is not courageous but irresponsible. Belton had the authority to delay the departure, and he knew before Dade left that 250 hostiles were lying in wait, yet he sent them out: "And the doomed band went forth to die," in the bitter words of Col. Alexander Fanning.[4]

No evidence has been found that any official inquiry was made nor censure given. On the contrary, Belton was promoted to major in 1838, lieutenant colonel in 1845, breveted colonel in 1847 for gallant and meritorious conduct in the battles of Contreras and Churubusco, Mexico, and died a full colonel in 1861.[5]

A second officer, not of the command, but whose death will always be associated with the Dade "Massacre," is Gen. Wiley Thompson. His body was interred in the Fort King burial ground, but, like the men of Dade's command, was not to rest easily. His widow, in Elberton, Georgia, was concerned about the care of his distant grave, and some months after his death sent Edward Roberts, a local contractor, to Florida to bring the remains back to Georgia. Three months later Roberts returned with the general's bones packed in a long, wooden box.[6]

"Mrs. Thompson removed the bones, one by one, and measured them to make sure, as she often stated, that they were in reality the bones of her husband. Having fully satisfied herself on this score and having been greatly attached to the General she refused for more than a year to inter the bones, but kept them beneath the bed in which she slept. Finally, however, her husband's nephew, Captain Gaines Thompson, prevailed upon her to bury them." For more than a century the remains lay undisturbed in the garden of their home, but they were moved once more in 1960 and rest now under an informative and imposing monument in Forest Hills Memorial Park, south of Elberton.[7]

Private Ransom Clark? He, of course, survived. He recuperated (except for the wound in his right shoulder) at Fort Brooke, where he remained until May 1836, when he was discharged. He made his way slowly, painfully home to Greigsville, New York, by way of New Orleans, Charleston, and Washington, D.C. His pension of eight dollars a month would not start until September. "Totally disabled from obtaining his subsistance [sic]," Clark attempted—with unknown success—to earn money by giving talks about his adventures in Florida. In spite of his disabilities, and in spite of his father, Benjamin's, total rejection (in 1833 Benjamin changed his will so that Ransom would only receive one dollar upon his death), Ransom married and had a child. The shoulder wound never healed, and when death came (probably from infection) on November 18, 1840, we can be sure that Ransom Clark did "not go gentle into that good night."

It now seems questionable whether Pvt. John Thomas, a member of Dade's command but not a participant in the battle, lived on until 1883, as was previously believed. The St. Augustine *Herald* of September 21, 1837, stated that Thomas "died this morning at the U.S. Hospital in this city, from diseases caused by the wounds received in [Dade's] encounter." Also in St. Augustine in that month, Capt. Nathan Jarvis, assistant surgeon, wrote that "in the early part of September many of the soldiers who had been laboring under chronic Dysentery and Intermittents dropp'd off. 12 died in the Genl. Hospital, among whom was John Thomas, one of the 2 [sic] survivors of Dade's massacre. His death was hastened by intemperance." Certainly this is strong evidence that Thomas died in 1837, but if this is the case it was certainly not as the result of wounds, as the *Herald* indicates. And a final doubt still clouds the probability of his death in 1837; Thomas's certificate for pension, signed on June 28, 1837, by Capt. Charles L. Merchant, commanding officer of Company E, Second Regiment Artillery, in Picolata, Florida, states that Thomas was discharged there on that day. This being so, how is it that Thomas, as a civilian, was in a *military* hospital nearly three months after his discharge?

Private Joseph Sprague served three more enlistments in the U.S. Army for a total service of twenty-five years, his final discharge dated March 6, 1843. The following year, living in White Springs, Florida, he applied to the secretary of war for "a spot of Land . . . somewhere in Florida." No evidence has yet been found that this wish was granted, but Sprague was "inscribed on the Pension List Roll of the Tallahassee Agency at the rate of Eight dollars per month to commence on the twenty fourth day of November," 1843. The last payment he collected under this pension was on September 4, 1847. It is assumed he died within the next six months. There is no indication that he ever wrote or spoke for the record of his experiences.[8]

What of the Seminoles?

On October 21, 1837, nearly two years after Thompson was killed, Osceola and other Seminoles were taken prisoner (by order of Gen. Thomas Jesup, then commanding U.S. troops) while meeting under a flag of truce with Gen. Joseph M. Hernandez one mile south of Fort Peyton. Osceola was taken north seven miles to Fort Marion (Castillo de San Marcos), where he remained until December 31, when he was transferred to Fort Moultrie in Charleston Harbor, South Carolina. There, on January 13, 1838, Dr. Frederick Weedon signed a contract with the government agreeing to perform the duties of "surgeon attending emigrating Indians." Already suffering from some form of fever when taken, Osceola's health continued to decline. On the twenty-sixth "he was attacked with 'violent quinsy' [tonsillitis complicated by abscess]." He died at 6:20 P.M. on January 30, 1838.[9]

Like those of Thompson and of Dade and his officers, Osceola's remains were not to rest in peace. His body was buried on the grounds of the fort the day after he died, and lay undisturbed for one hundred and thirty years. Questions of desecration, even furtive removal, prompted the National Park Service to begin an archaeological investigation in October of 1968. This exhumation confirmed that the body *was* there and, as clearly, that the *head* was not. Osceola's head had secretly been removed by Dr. Weedon at some time during the twenty-four hours between his death and burial. There are indications that Weedon may have anticipated selling the head, but several years later it was in the possession of a Dr. Daniel Whitehurst, who passed it on to Dr. Valentine Mott of New York City, who added it to his collection of one thousand anatomical specimens. At Mott's death in 1865 he left Osceola's head to "the Medical College on Fourteenth Street." The college burned down soon after, and all the specimens were lost.[10]

The bones found in the alleged grave of Osceola were subjected to thorough forensic examination in 1968. The evidence was conclusive; the remains were his. Osceola has been returned to the earth in South Carolina.[11]

Micanopy, along with Cloud and eleven other chiefs and more than a dozen warriors, also under a flag of truce, attended a peace conference with General Jesup on December 3, 1837, at Fort Mellon on Florida's east coast. A week earlier Jesup had written to the secretary of war, "If the council have [*sic*] no other effect, it will cause the Indians, who are now much dispersed, to reassemble, when they can be more readily attacked." The Seminoles were taken prisoner and sent to Fort Marion, where they joined Osceola. On February 22 Micanopy and the other surviving Seminoles were put aboard ship and taken to Fort Pike, near New Orleans. Four months later the survivors reached Fort Gibson, Indian Territory. Micanopy died there ten years later.[12]

Ote Emathla, with his family and other Seminoles, Indian and black, some 250 in all, surrendered to Gen. Zachary Taylor somewhere along the Kissimee River south of Tampa on December 19, 1837. A month later they were put aboard ship at Fort Brooke and sent to Fort Pike, where they were confined in barracks. While there, awaiting shipment to Indian Territory, Ote Emathla died of consumption on April 18.[13]

Halpatter Tustenuggee continued to fight until March 1838, when he, too, surrendered to General Taylor near Lake Okechobee. Taken with 360 other Seminoles and blacks to Fort Brooke, he and thirty of his followers escaped on June 4. Soon captured, he was returned to Tampa Bay with his family in July (see Appendix 4), then to Fort Pike, and finally to Fort Gibson. He accepted relocation as an unalterable fact, and worked

to improve conditions for the several thousand expatriate Seminoles encamped near Fort Gibson and Fort Smith in Arkansas. Returning to
Florida in 1841, he induced other Seminoles to put down their arms. He
went to Washington in 1844 to demand better treatment for his people.
Once more he received promises. In 1850, convinced that the government
would never permit the American Indian anything other than extinction,
accompanied by Coacoochee ("Wildcat") and other Seminoles, Indian and
black, he fled the reservation to Mexico. That government gave them farm
tools and land in the Santa Clara mountains, and they worked with the
Mexican army to bring peace to the border. It is believed that Halpatter
Tustenuggee's descendants, perhaps even he himself, may have eventually
returned to the United States.[14]

Appendix Four

Testimony of Survivors of the Battle

Among the survivors of Dade's battle, only one soldier, one Seminole, and one black later gave accounts of the circumstances and the action. The first to appear in print was that of Pvt. Ransom Clark.

Ransom Clark

Private Ransom Clark gave several brief depositions on January 8, 1836, only a week after his return to Fort Brooke, testifying to the deaths of Dade, Gardiner, and Basinger. Questioned often and in more detail by anxious officers, he gave a straightforward account. Captain James Barr, an officer of volunteers then at Fort Brooke, wrote down Clark's story on March 16. It formed part of his "Correct and Authentic Narrative" of the war, published later in that year. Another officer took down a detailed account and sent it to a friend in Portland, where it was published on March 13, 1836, in the *Portland (Maine) Daily Advertiser*. In July 1836 Clark was interviewed by the *Charleston Courier*, and on June 5, 1837, he gave an interview to the *Boston Morning Post*. His last published description of the battle, as far as is known, is contained in his *Narrative of Ransom Clark*, published in 1839, one year before his death. These five descriptions of the battle are the only distinct and different recollections given by Clark, all others found being duplicates or condensed versions of the above.

Clark's accounts of the battle prior to the site's being revisited were proven accurate in virtually every detail, leaving no doubt that he had endured the entire battle. With each telling of the story, however, his descriptions of the treatment of the wounded by both Seminoles and blacks after the battle grew more harsh, leading one to suspect that he was encouraged to cast unwonted guilt upon both groups and thereby justify harsh retribution.

The following is an extended excerpt from the first published account of the battle given by Clark, as printed in the *Portland Daily Advertiser:*

"I was next to the leading file of the right wing, (head of the column). It was 8 o'clock. Suddenly I heard a rifle shot in the direction of the advanced guard, and this was immediately followed by a musket shot from that quarter. Capt Fraser had rode by me a moment before in that direction. I never saw him afterwards. I had not time to think of the meaning of these shots before a volley as if from a thousand rifles was poured in upon us from the front, and all along our left flank. I looked around me, and it seemed as if I was the only one left standing in the right wing. Neither could I, until several other vollies had been fired at us, see an enemy,—and when I did, I could only see their heads and arms peering out from the long grass far and near, and from behind the pine trees. The ground seemed to me an open pine barren—no hammock near that I could see. On our right and a little to our rear, was a large pond of water some distance off. All around us were heavy pine trees, very open particularly towards the left, and abounding with long high grass. The first fire of the Indians was the most destructive, seemingly killing or disabling one half of our men. We promptly threw ourselves behind trees, and opened a sharp fire of musketry. I for one, never fired without seeing my man, that is his head and shoulders—the Indians chiefly fired laying or squatting in the grass. Lt Bassinger fired five or six rounds of cannister from the cannon. This appeared to frighten the Indians, and they retreated over a little hill to our left, one half or three quarters of a mile off, after having fired not more than 12 or 15 rounds. We immediately began to fell trees, and erect a little triangular breastwork. Some of us went forward to gather the cartridge boxes from the dead, and to assist the wounded. I had seen Major Dade fall to the ground by the first volley, and his horse dashed into the midst of the enemy.—Whilst gathering the cartridges, I saw Lt Mudge sitting with his back reclining against a tree— his head fallen, and evidently dying. I spoke to him, but he did not answer. The interpreter Louis, it is said, fell by the first fire. (We have since learned that this fellow shammed dead—that his life was afterwards spared through the intercession of the Chief Jumper, and that being an educated negro, he read all the despatches and letters that were found about the dead, to the victors).

"We had barely raised our breastwork knee high when we again saw the Indians advancing in great numbers over the hill to our left. They came on boldly until within a long musket shot, when they spread themselves from tree to tree to surround us. We immediately extended as light infantry, covering ourselves also by the trees and opening a brisk fire from cannon and musketry. The former I dont think could have done much mischief, the Indians were so scattered.

"Capt Gardiner, Lieut Bassinger, and Dr Gatlin, were the only officers left unhurt by the volley which killed Dade. Lieut Henderson had his left arm broken, but he continued to load his musket and to fire it, resting on the stump, until he was finally shot down towards the close of the second attack, and during the day he bravely kept up his spirits and cheered the men. Lieut Keyes [Keais] had both his arms broken in the first attack; they were bound up and hung in a handkerchief, and he sat for the remainder of the day, until he was killed, reclining against the breastwork—his head often reposing upon it—regardless of everything that was passing around him.

"The enemy by degrees surrounded us, and we, who had been behind the trees, being uncovered, fled to the breastwork. The cannon was fired in all forty-nine times. The last round, the cannister of which had been lost, was in the piece when she was taken. Lieut Bassinger first tended the piece; when he was disabled, Capt G [Gardiner] supplied his place. It is not in my power to say that we did the enemy much mischief. I know well that I killed three men. I fired also forty or fifty rounds, and never, as I have said, without covering my man, and I am a pretty fair shot.

"Our men were by degrees all cut down. We had maintained a steady fight from 8 until 2 P M thereabouts, and allowing three quarters of an hour interval between the first and second attack, had been pretty busily engaged for more than five hours. Lieut B [Basinger] was the only officer left alive, and he severely wounded. He told me as the Indians approached to lay down and feign myself dead. I looked through the logs and saw the savages approaching in great numbers. A heavily made Indian, of middle stature, painted down to the waist, (corresponding in description with Micanopy), seemed to be the Chief. He made them a speech, frequently pointing to the breastwork. At length they charged into the work—there was none to offer resistance, and they did not seem to suspect the wounded of being alive—offered no indignity, but stepped about carefully, quietly stripping off our accoutrements and carrying away our arms. They then retired in a body in the direction from whence they came. Immediately upon the retreat forty or fifty negroes, on horseback, galloped up and alighted, tied their beasts, and commenced, with horrid shouts and yells, the butchery of the wounded, together with an indiscriminate plunder, stripping the bodies of the dead of clothing, watches and money, and splitting open the heads of all who showed the least signs of life with their axes and knives, and accompanying their bloody work with obscene and taunting derisions, and with frequent cries of 'what have you got to sell.'

"Lieut B, hearing the negroes butchering the wounded, at length sprang up and asked them to spare his life. They met him with the blows of their axes and their fiendish laughter. Having been wounded in five different places myself, I was pretty well covered with blood, and two scratches that I had received in my head gave me the appearance of having been shot through the brain, for the negroes, after catching me up by the heels, threw me down, saying 'd—n him he's dead enough!' They then stripped me of my clothes, shoes and hat, and left me. After stripping all the dead in this manner, they trundled off the cannon in the direction the Indians had gone, and went away. I saw them first shoot down the oxen in their gear and burn the wagon. One of the other soldiers who escaped says they threw the cannon into the pond, and burnt its carriage also. Shortly after the negroes went away one Wilson, of Capt G's company, crept from under some of the dead bodies, and hardly seemed to be hurt at all. He asked me to go with him back to the Fort, and I was going to follow him, when, as he jumped over the breastwork, an Indian sprang from behind a tree and shot him down. I then lay quiet until 9 O'clock that night, when De Coney [DeCourcy], the only living soul beside myself, and I started upon our journey. We knew it was nearest to go to Fort King but we did not know the way, and we had seen the enemies retreat in that direction. As I came out I saw Dr G [Gatlin] lying stripped amongst the dead. The last I saw of him whilst living was kneeling behind the breast-work with two double guns by him, and he said 'Well, I have got four barrels for them!' Capt G, after being severely wounded, cried out, 'I can give you no more orders my lads, do your best!' I last saw a negro spurn his body, saying with an oath, 'that's one of their officers!' (G was dressed in soldier's clothes).

"My comrade and myself got along quite well until the next day, when we met an Indian on horseback with a rifle coming up the road.—Our only chance was to separate,—we did so. I took the right and he the left of the road. The Indian pursued him. Shortly afterwards I heard a rifle shot, and a little after another. I concealed myself amongst some scrub and Saw Palmetto, and after awhile saw the Indian pass looking for me. Suddenly, however, he put spurs to his horse and went off at a gallop towards the road.

"I made something of a circuit before I struck the beaten track again. That night I was a good deal annoyed by the wolves who had scented my blood, and came very close to me; the next day, the 30th, I reached the Fort."

Halpatter Tustenuggee

An account of Dade's battle was also given by Halpatter Tustenuggee ("Alligator"). Captured in March 1838, this Seminole leader was held for some time at Fort Brooke prior to exile in Oklahoma. While there it is assumed he gave this eyewitness account to 2nd Lt. John T. Sprague, later the author of *The Florida War*, in which it first appeared.

"We had been preparing for this more than a year. Though promises had been made to assemble on the 1st of January, it was not to leave the country, but to fight for it. In council, it was determined to strike a decided blow about this time. Our agent at Fort King had put irons on our men, and said we must go. Oseola said he was *his friend, he would see to him*. It was determined that he should attack Fort King, in order to reach General Thompson, then return to the Wahoo Swamp, and participate in the assault meditated upon the soldiers coming from Fort Brooke, as the negroes there had reported that two companies were preparing to march.

He was detained longer than we anticipated. The troops were three days
on their march, and approaching the Swamp. Here we thought it best to
assail them; and should we be defeated the Swamp would be a safe place
of retreat. Our scouts were out from the time the soldiers left the post,
and reported each night their place of encampment. It was our intention
to attack them on the third night, but the absence of Oseola and Micanopy
prevented it. On the arrival of the latter it was agreed not to wait for
Oseola, as the favorable moment would pass. Micanopy was timid, and
urged delay. Jumper earnestly opposed it [delay], and reproached the old
chief for his indecision. He addressed the Indians, and requested those
who had faint hearts to remain behind; he was going, when Micanopy
said he was ready. Just as day was breaking we moved out of the swamp
into the pine-barren. I counted, by direction of Jumper, one hundred and
eighty warriors. Upon approaching the road, each man chose his position
on the west side; opposite, on the east side, there was a pond. Every
warrior was protected by a tree, or secreted in the high palmettoes.

"About nine o'clock in the morning the command approached. In advance, some distance, was an officer on a horse, who, Micanopy said, was
the captain; he knew him personally; had been his friend at Tampa. So
soon as *all* the soldiers were opposite, between us and the pond, perhaps
twenty yards off, Jumper gave the whoop, Micanopy fired the first rifle,
the signal agreed upon, when every Indian arose and fired, which laid
upon the ground, dead, more than half the white men. The cannon was
discharged several times, but the men who loaded it were shot down as
soon as the smoke cleared away; the balls passed far over our heads. The
soldiers shouted and whooped, and the officers shook their swords and
swore. There was a little man, a great brave, who shook his sword at the
soldiers and said, 'God-dam!' [N]o rifle-ball could hit him. As we were
returning to the swamp, supposing all were dead, an Indian came up and
said the white men were building a fort of logs. Jumper and myself, with
ten warriors, returned. As we approached, we saw six men behind two
logs placed one above another, with the cannon a short distance off. This
they discharged at us several times, but we avoided it by dodging behind
the trees just as they applied the fire. We soon came near, as the balls
went over us. They had guns, but no powder; we looked in the boxes
afterwards and found they were empty. When I got inside the logpen,

there were three white men alive, whom the negroes put to death, after a conversation in English. There was a brave man in the pen; he would not give up; he seized an Indian, Jumper's cousin, took away his rifle, and with one blow with it beat out his brains, then ran some distance up the road; but two Indians on horseback overtook him, who, afraid to approach, stood at a distance and shot him down. The firing had ceased, and all was quiet when we returned to the swamp about noon. We left many negroes upon the ground looking at the dead men. Three warriors were killed and five wounded."

Louis Pacheco

The following statement by Louis Pacheco, interpreter for Major Dade's command, is found in D. B. McKay's *Pioneer Florida* (vol. 2, pp. 480–81). McKay attributed the interview to the Austin (Texas) *Commercial Journal*, August 1861, but research indicated that the journal did not begin publication until 1877 and ended in 1881. The same interview (with minor differences) *was* published in the *Sunland Tribune* (Tampa) on May 6, 1880, no source given. The text of the statement indicates that it could have been made anytime between 1852 and May 1880.

"I was born in the year 1800, on my master's plantation, about thirty miles west of St. Augustine and about fifteen miles northwest of Picolata, Florida.

"In 1821 my master, Francis Philip Fatio, sent me with the mail to Amelia Island, in which Tumas Lorento, who had command, was recalled from further prosecution of war, and the Spanish claims in Florida relinquished to the United States government.

"In 1824 I was caused to run away by the action of my young master, Lewis Fatio, but I was found at the Spanish Fisheries, on the Gulf coast, taken to Tampa and, at my own request, sold to Col. Brooke, who was the officer in command at that place. I was afterward sold to Col. Clinch, by him to Maj. McIntosh, and by him to Antone Pachaco [*sic*], who carried me to Sarasota Bay, where he died soon after.

"In 1835 or 1836, still living at Sarasota with my master's widow, she employed me to Major Dade at $30 per month as guide from Tampa to

Fort King, Major Dade assuring me that there was no hostility on the part of the Indians. I think Major Dade did me wrong, for he always sent me ahead to places of probable danger to examine, although Capt. Frazier [Fraser] told him in my presence that he was endangering my life to a considerable extent. He sent me ahead to examine at the Hillsborough bridge, about seven miles above Tampa, where I found the bridge burned, a cow killed and cut open and other signs of Indian hostility. He also sent me ahead at the Withlacoochee, where I found the bridge burned and Indian signs, etc. The morning after crossing the Withlacoochee, and the morning before the massacre, Major Dade said; "Louis, I have concluded not to send you to Philathlacaha this morning (the remainder in a loud voice, intended for Capt. Frazier,) but I will send you ahead into Fort King, to-morrow, though!" About 10 o'clock, while I was with the advance guard, Capt. Frazier and I turned aside to examine an old gray horse we found by the road, and finding it worthless had returned to the road and had nearly overtaken the advance guard when I heard a single rifle shot, and looked back to see if some one was shooting game, but just in time to see Major Dade fall just in front of me, shot in the breast. Although this was a perfectly open country, and I had looked carefully for Indians ahead, the country was now filled with large numbers of them on our left, coming for us with the war whoop. I immediately threw down my gun and laid down behind a tree, very much frightened. As I could speak the Seminole language, I begged each one for my life as they leveled their guns at me, and they were not a few, telling them that I was a slave and was doing as I was bidden, etc. Finally Jumper, the chief in command, interfered and ordered, as well as he then could, that I should not be shot; but even after this one Indian was determined to kill me, but fortunately another Indian got his rifle ball stuck in his gun and ran, when the other Indians, seeing this one run, became frightened and all run, when Jumper again took me and put me under a guard. This same Indian, though, still assured me that when he came back he would kill me yet, luckily for me, he was shot by the whites. The battle lasted from about 10 o'clock in the morning until nearly sunset. They never carried me near the battle ground, but from what I could learn they thought they killed all the whites. They let me keep my road intending to leave as soon as dark and try to return to Tampa, but very late an Indian came along and carried me to a negro cabin, an Indian slave, and father of Aunt Hetty, who is with me now. The negroes made me quite at home, but I learned very soon that I was supposed to have news important to the whites and being a guide would probably be shot at any time, and the Indians themselves told me often that I would not live long if I misbehaved, which kept me in constant dread as long as I was with them, and even after I was in the Indian Nation, for while there one tried to stab me.

"Several nights after the battle Oceola [*sic*] returned from an expedition against the whites, and overheard me talking from the next room and called to me, 'Do you say that Jumper saved your life?' and I answered 'Yes,' when he replied: 'No human being has power to save you. You are a lucky negro or a long lived man for we Indians claim to save no one,' and pointed above with both hands. He then, to prove his theory, gave an account of his expedition, stating that he had tried to save the life of storekeeper Rodgers [*sic*], but his men killed him by shooting under them and between their legs. He also stated that they had killed Gen. Thompson, but no attempt was made to save him.

"Once I stole a canoe from them at the head of the Peace Creek and travelled in it by night to the mouth of the same, where I was recaptured and brought back, and probably would have suffered at their hands had not affairs of war interested them more deeply then.

"In about two years after Dade's Massacre I was sent into Tampa with the Indians, and, by order of Major Gen. Jessup [*sic*], in command there, was sent with them to the Indian Nation, a short distance above the junction of the Arkansas and Grande rivers, around Ft. Gibson, commanded by Gen. Arbuckle. On the wharf at New Orleans, while on our way, I asked Capt. Runnels, the agent on Indian affairs, whether I was being sent as Indian property, and he said, 'No; you, Remeo and Primus (two other negroes in my condition) do the best you can; you are free.' I lived with them there until the year 1849, when I was purchased of the Indians by Marcelus Duval, the agent there on Indian affairs, for $50, as also were Aunt Hetty and about thirty others. He moved us to Van Buren, Arkansas, where he kept us until 1852, when I was carried with the others to within five miles of where we now live, and have been in this neighborhood ever since."

Notes

Introduction: The Battlefield

1. Sprague, *Florida War*, 107. (Sprague mistakenly refers to Belton as "Major"—his rank in 1836 was captain.) Sprague's history is a cornerstone for any study of the Second Seminole War; McCall, *Letters*, 321. McCall was a member of the expedition under Gaines. His book is an invaluable source.

2. Belton to Jones, December 22, 1835, Orderly Book, Company B, Records of U.S. Regular Army Mobile Units, National Archives and Records Service (NA) (hereafter cited as Orderly Book). Reference has been found in Monthly Post Returns (Fort Brooke), NA, for December 1835, to Belton's Order Number 132 of December 23, 1835, but not the order itself; Belton to Jones, March 25, 1836, Orderly Book.

3. McCall, *Letters*, 321; Sprague, *Florida War*, 107.

4. Duncan, February 13–19, 1836, Diary, U.S. Military Academy Library (hereafter cited as Diary); McCall, *Letters*, 321.

5. Except for occasional mention of the weather by a writer of the period, weather conditions have been re-created based on U.S. Weather Bureau climatological records. These include the Fort Brooke Weather Diary and the Fort King Weather Diary (Environmental Science Services Administration), beginning as early as 1823. The diaries report the temperature at 7 A.M., 2 P.M., and 9 P.M., as well as wind direction, general weather conditions (fair, cloudy, rain, and so on), and, frequently, pertinent "Remarks"; McCall, *Letters*, 324; Duncan, Diary, February 19, 1836.

6. Guild, *Old Times*, 124; Belton to Jones, March 25, 1836, Orderly Book.

7. Duncan, Diary, February 19, 1836.

8. Hitchcock in Sprague, *Florida War*, 108–9.

9. McCall, *Letters*, 305.

10. Duncan, Diary, February 20, 1836.

11. Ibid.

12. Sprague, *Florida War*, 108; Frances Basinger to Mrs. Elizabeth Basinger, March 12, 1836 (in Lawton, *Saga*, 140); McCall, *Letters*, 305.

13. "Sketch of Major Dade's Battleground taken upon the spot by E. Rose, U.S. Army," January 18, 1837, NA; Guild, *Old Times*, 125.

14. McCall, *Letters*, 306; the presence of this survivor here, now, will become even more surprising as subsequent events unfold, yet McCall is unequivocal. Though his *Letters* was published in 1868, more than thirty years after the fact, the letters are given verbatim as they were written. Thus his description in a letter of May 6, 1836, regarding the circumstances of the battlefield (and the survivor's presence) on February 20, 1836—"Clark, who was with General Gaines on this occasion . . ."—must be accepted as accurate, though amazing; Bemrose, *Reminiscences*, 65.

15. *New York Times*, July 16, 1836.

16. Belton to Clinch and Eaton, January 5, 1836, Orderly Book.

17. *General Regulations*, 1825, Article 34, no. 265; Belton to Jones, March 25, 1836, Orderly Book.

18. Belton to Jones, March 25, 1836, Orderly Book; Belton to Dade, December 26, 1835, Orderly Book.

19. Excavation, March 6, 1964, carried out under the direction of the author with the aegis of the Florida State Board of Parks and Historic Memorials; Belton to Jones, March 25, 1836, Orderly Book.

20. Duncan, Diary, February 20, 1836; McCall, *Letters*, 315; Belton to Jones, March 25, 1836, Orderly Book.

Chapter One: The First Day

1. *Columbus (Ga.) Inquirer*, February 20, 1835; Cullum, *Register*, 220, cadet number 589.

2. Fort Brooke Weather Diary, Environmental Science Services Administration; Frances Kyle Basinger to Mrs. Peter Basinger, March 12, 1836 (in Lawton, *Saga*, 140).

3. Clinch to commanding officer, Fort Brooke, November 13, 1835, NA; Belton to Clinch, December 22, 1835, Orderly Book; Alvord to Clinch, January 23, 1836, Record Group 391, NA; Bemrose, *Reminiscences*, 64; Hitchcock to Gaines, February 22, 1836 (in Sprague, *Florida War*, 109), states "eight officers"; Belton to Jones, March 25, 1836, Orderly Book, gives the names of eight officers. Dade had not

yet joined; Hitchcock to Gaines, February 22, 1836 (in Sprague, *Florida War*, 109), refers to "102 non-comd. offrs. and privates." Since each company at normal strength would have numbered fifty men for a total strength of one hundred, and it is known that more than one joined the first day, it is assumed that two must have joined. Both Hitchcock and Belton (Belton to Jones, March 25, 1836, Orderly Book) state that ninety-eight bodies were interred, though four are known to have left the battlefield. Again, this seems to confirm that one hundred men were mustered for duty on the morning of December 23; Belton to Dade, December 26, 1835, Orderly Book; Prince, June 1, 1836, Diary, P. K. Yonge Library of Florida History (hereafter cited as Diary); Clinch to commanding officer, Fort Brooke, November 13, 1835, NA.

4. Monthly Post Returns (Fort Brooke), NA, November 1835; Belton letter, December 12, 1835, Orderly Book; Monthly Post Returns (Fort Brooke), December 1834-October 1835; Nourse letter, January 5, 1836, NA.

5. Belton letter, December 12, 1835, Orderly Book.

6. Ibid.; Meek, "Journal," March 6, 1836; Frances Kyle Basinger to Mrs. Peter Basinger, March 12, 1836 (in Lawton, *Saga*, 140).

7. Belton letter, December 12, 1835, Orderly Book; Belton to Clinch, December 22, 1835, Orderly Book.

8. Casey to Thomas Basinger, January 2, 1836 (in Lawton, *Saga*, 139); Belton letter, December 12, 1835, Orderly Book.

9. Brooke to Captain (U.S. Revenue Cutter Fla) John Brown, July 27, 1825, and Brooke to Brown, August 14, 1825 (both in the *Sunland Tribune* [Journal of the Tampa Historical Society] 1, no. 1 [July 1974]: 12).

10. Monroe, Sixth Annual Message to Congress, December 3, 1822 (in Richardson, *Messages and Papers* 2:190); Duval, Gadsden, and Segui to Calhoun, September 26, 1823 (in Carter, *Territorial Papers* 22:747–51).

11. Duval, Gadsden, and Segui to Calhoun, September 26, 1823 (in Carter, *Territorial Papers* 22:747–51).

12. Powell, *Fourth Regiment*, entries for 1822, 1824; Brooke to Brown, April 6, 1824 (in Carter, *Territorial Papers* 22:845); ibid., February 5, 1824, 22:918.

13. Covington, "Life at Fort Brooke," 319; Brooke to Calhoun, January 18, 1825 (in Col. George M. Brooke, Jr., "Early Days at Ft. B.," *Sunland Tribune* 1, no. 1 [July 1974]: 7).

14. Meek, "Journal," March 6, 1836; McCall, *Letters*, 133; Powell, *Fourth Regiment*, entry for 1824.

15. Meek, "Journal," March 6, 1836; McCall, *Letters*, 139.

16. Research to determine the exact course of the Fort King Road began with reviewing the original government survey maps of Florida, which were begun in

1840. Previous research (Frank Laumer, "The Ft. Dade Site," *Florida Anthropologist* 16 [June 1963]: 33–42] had shown that these township plats, together with the field notes, gave the exact point at which the Fort King Road crossed each section line and a close approximation of the road's course from one section line to the next. By studying each township plat (as well as the field notes pertaining to it), it was possible to make up a composite showing the entire route from Fort Brooke to the battleground, a distance of 61 3/4 miles (as measured with a planimeter). We next obtained a modern set of maps (U.S. Geological Survey, Washington, D.C., 1943–75) covering the same townships, which in this series included the following quadrangles: Tampa, Thonotosassa, Antioch, Sulphur Springs, Zephyrhills, Dade City, Lacoochee, St. Catherine, Bushnell, and Wahoo. Using the specifications of the older survey, we superimposed the Fort King Road on the modern maps (Goza, "Ft. King Road"). With few exceptions, we found that each bend and turn of the road on the old maps matched still-existing features of the terrain, ponds, lakes, and so forth. Field trips to spot-check various locations revealed that, away from development, the old road was still there. In addition, a study of aerial photographs covering many sections of the road showed it winding like a dark thread across the modern countryside. In order to familiarize myself with the route traveled by Dade and his command, I set out from Tampa with two friends and walked the road to the battlefield in December 1963. In 1988, after twenty-five years of additional research, I made the hike once more, gaining new insight into the journey of Dade and his command; Fanning letter, December 16, 1835, in pension file of Frances P. Gardiner (found in the Gardiner pension file, NA).

17. Sprague, *Florida War*, 143.

18. *American State Papers* 6:58.

19. Thompson to Zantzinger, September 6, 1835, Record Group 391, Records of U.S. Regular Army Mobile Units, NA; Belton letter, December 12, 1835, Orderly Book; Fanning to Clinch, November 27, 1835 (in Carter, *Territorial Papers* 25:200).

20. Thompson to Zantzinger, September 6, 1835, Record Group 391, Records of U.S. Regular Army Mobile Units, NA; Belton letter, December 12, 1835, Orderly Book.

21. Winfield Scott to Belton, August 10, 1826 (Reel 34, Andrew Jackson Papers, Library of Congress).

22. *Fort Morgan, 1833 Bastion*, 7.

23. Fannin to the president of the convention of Texas, November 6, 1835 (in Jenkins, *Texas Revolution* 2:337); Belton to Fannin, September 23, 1835 (in ibid., 1:483).

24. Belton to Fannin, September 23, 1835 (see note 23); ibid.; Belton to Clinch, December 22, 1835, Orderly Book.

25. Belton to Clinch, December 22, 1835, Orderly Book.

26. Lt. F. D. Newcomb to Jesup, February 14, 1832, Record Group 092, Quartermaster General's Vessel File: U.S. Army Schooner "Motto" 1832–37 (Key West, Fla.).

27. "A Sea Coast Artillerist," *Army and Navy Chronicle* 2 (January 9, 1836): 79; Letters to Harriet Tracy Axtell, edited by Jean Rumsey (1964, in author's collection), 80.

28. McKay, *Pioneer Florida* 2:477; *Dade City Banner*, June 1, 1923 ("Nephew Describes Major Francis Dade").

29. Long, *Florida Breezes*, 175–76.

30. Newcomb to Jesup, February 14, 1832 (see note 26); Heitman, *Historical Register* 1:161; Cullum, *Register*, 223; Clinch to Dade, October 17, 1835, Collection of Joseph Rubinfine, Pleasantville, N.J.

31. Alvord to Clinch, January 23, 1836, Record Group 391, NA.

32. Registers of Enlistments in the U.S. Army, roll 19, p. 201, NA. The Registers of Enlistments give name, age (at the time of enlistment), eye color, hair, complexion, height, place of birth, occupation, when enlisted, where, by whom, period of enlistment, regiment and company, cause of death, date of death, date of desertion (if any), date of apprehension, and remarks. Under "remarks" are sometimes given particulars of death and reference numbers of applications for bounty land by the widow, applications for pension, and so on. These files in turn often give many details concerning the soldiers' life and death; Alvord to Clinch, January 23, 1836, Record Group 391, NA.

33. Dade to Jones, December 14, 1835, Record Group 391, NA.

34. Assistant Surgeon Nourse letter, January 5, 1836, NA.

35. McCall, *Letters*, 145–48; Quarterly Report of the Sick and Wounded at Key West, Florida, for the Quarter Ending December 31, 1835, Surgeon General's Office (SGO), NA; Belton to Clinch, December 22, 1835, Orderly Book.

36. Heitman, *Historical Register* 1:289; Cullum, *Register*, 219; Casey to Thomas Basinger, January 2, 1836 (in Lawton, *Saga*, 139); "Statement for Mrs. F. P. Gardiner . . ." in Gardiner pension file, NA.

37. Belton to Clinch, December 22, 1835, Orderly Book; Statement in Gardiner pension file, NA.

38. Simmons, "Recollections," in *Saturday Evening Post*, August 20, 1836; Belton to the adjutant general, January 1, 1836, Order and Letter Book, Records of U.S. Regular Army Mobile Units, NA (hereafter cited as Order and Letter Book).

39. Barr, *Authentic Narrative*, March 13, 1836.

40. McReynolds, *Seminoles*, 132; Belton to the adjutant general, January 1, 1836, Order and Letter Book.

41. Bemrose, *Reminiscences*, 42; Statement in Gardiner pension file, NA, referring to the morning of December 23. Circumstances of the previous thirty hours indicate that this was the likely time and place that such a conviction was formed in the minds of the chiefs. This event is referred to by Belton in his letters of December 22 to Clinch and January 1 to the adjutant general (Orderly Book). In the former he places the meeting "last night" (December 21), and in the latter "the evening of the 22nd." I have accepted the first date because Belton could not have described on December 22 an event that would not occur until the same evening. The letter of January 1 was written ten days after the event, and I believe his recollection of the exact date was in error.

42. Belton to Clinch, January 1, 1836, Orderly Book; Statement by Halpatter Tustenuggee ("Alligator") in Sprague, *Florida War*, 90–91; Clinch to Dade, October 17, 1835, from the collection of Joseph Rubinfine (see note 30); Belton to Clinch, December 22, 1835, Orderly Book; Belton to the adjutant general, January 1, 1836, Order and Letter Book.

43. Farr, *Tampa's Earliest Living Pioneer*, 11; ibid., 10 (italics added).

44. Alvord, *Address*, 41; Statement in Gardiner pension file, NA; Farr, *Tampa's Earliest Living Pioneer*, 11; Statement in Gardiner pension file, NA.

45. Belton to Dade, December 26, 1835, Orderly Book; Belton to Clinch, December 22, 1835, Orderly Book.

46. Belton to Clinch, December 22, 1835, Orderly Book; Belton to the adjutant general, January 1, 1836, Order and Letter Book.

47. Clinch to commanding officer, Fort Brooke, November 13, 1835, NA.

48. Belton to Clinch, December 22, 1835, Orderly Book; Manucy, *Artillery through the Ages*; Peterson, *Round Shot and Rammers*. Valuable information and pictures were supplied by the staff of the Ft. Sill Museum, Ft. Sill, Oklahoma; Belton to the adjutant general, January 1, 1836, Order and Letter Book; Prince, Diary, June 1, 1836; Belton to Dade, December 26, 1835, Orderly Book; Belton to the adjutant general, January 1, 1836, Order and Letter Book.

49. Belton to Clinch, December 22, 1835, Orderly Book.

50. McReynolds, *Seminoles*, 97; Boyd, *Florida Aflame*, 12; Cohen, *Notices*, 174; Belton to the adjutant general, January 1, 1836, Order and Letter Book; Belton to Clinch and Dade, December 23, 1835, Orderly Book.

51. *General Regulations*, 1835, 25–26.

52. Ibid., 221–33; Hickox, *Collector's Guide*, 1; Hickox, *Edged Weapons*, 33; Duncan, Diary, February 20, 1836.

53. Heiskell to Lovell, November 23, 1835, Heiskell Papers, SGO, NA; Alvord

to Buchanan in Cohen, *Notices*, 77; Nourse letter, January 5, 1836, NA; Bemrose, *Reminiscences*, 62–63; Theodorus Bailey to Honorable Smith Thompson, secretary of the navy, January 26, 1822, SGO, NA.

54. Lt. John Gardinier to Lt. Duncan, January 11, 1836, Record Group 107, Adjutant General's Office (AGO), NA; J. Parker to Lt. John Gardinier, March 31, 1836, Record Group 107, AGO, NA; Bemrose, *Reminiscences*, 63.

55. Bemrose, *Reminiscences*, 93, 94.

56. Kyle to Basinger, February 25, 1836, Frances Basinger to Elizabeth Basinger, March 12, 1836, both in Basinger, *Personal Reminiscences*, appendices 5 and 6, in P. K. Yonge Library of Florida History; Heiskell to Lovell, February 18, 1834; Heiskell to J. A. Kearney, medical director, Army of the South, May 8, 1837; Heiskell to Lovell, December 19, 1834, Heiskell Papers, SGO, NA; Lawton, *Saga*, 134; Statistical Report, SGO, NA, 296.

57. Hugh H. McGuire, M.D., to John H. Eaton, secretary of war, June 15, 1829, Heiskell Papers, SGO, NA; [Name illegible] to Lewis Cass, secretary of war, June 14, 1832, Heiskell Papers, SGO, NA; *University of Pennsylvania Alumni Catalog*, University of Pennsylvania Archives, Philadelphia, Penn.; James, *Life of Andrew Jackson*, 76–79.

58. Robert Allen to Eaton, June 10, 1829, Heiskell Papers, SGO, NA; Heiskell to Lovell, February 24, 1834, Heiskell Papers, SGO, NA.

59. Heiskell obituary, Heiskell Papers, SGO, NA; Bemrose, *Reminiscences*, 94; Heiskell to Lovell, November 23, 1835, Heiskell Papers, SGO, NA.

60. Heiskell to Lovell, November 23, 1835, Heiskell Papers, SGO, NA; Heiskell to Lovell, January 9, 1836, Heiskell Papers, SGO, NA; Statement in Frances Gardiner pension file, NA.

61. Heiskell to Lovell, November 23, 1835, Heiskell Papers, SGO, NA.

62. Statistical Report, SGO, NA, 299; Heiskell to Lawton, November 23, 1835, Heiskell Papers, SGO, NA.

63. Heiskell to Lovell, January 9, 1836, Heiskell Papers, SGO, NA.

64. Heitman, *Historical Register* 1:143; Oil painting in the possession of Dr. Joseph D. Cushman, University of the South, Sewanee, Tenn.; Prince, *Diary*, February 20, 1836; Belton to Jones, March 25, 1836, Orderly Book; *Army and Navy Chronicle* 2 (January 1-June 30, 1836): 56.

65. *General Regulations*, 1835, Article 9, no. 34; *General Regulations*, 1825, Article 31, no. 250; Covington, *Southwestern Florida*, 335; Robinson, *History of Hillsborough County*, 104–5; *Army and Navy Chronicle* 3, no. 23 (1836): 368; Hickox, *Armament*, 2.

66. *General Regulations*, 1835, Article 4, no. 1; Nourse to [unknown, but assumed to be the surgeon general], January 5, 1836, NA; Alvord to Clinch, January 23, 1836, Orderly Book.

67. Jesup to Dade, December 16, 1842, and Dade to Jesup, January 10, 1843 (both in *Pensacola Gazette*, February 11, 1843); text with map of Dade battleground, Senate Document Number 33, 67-1 (faces p. 10), NA; Alvord to Jesup, January 4, 1836, Orderly Book; "List of Officers Requiring Caps," signed by Col. George M. Brooke, Fort Brooke (judged to be 1823–24), NA; *General Regulations*, 1835, 224; Duncan, Diary, February 20, 1836; Farr, *Tampa's Earliest Living Pioneer*, 11; Statement in Frances Gardiner pension file, NA.

68. Frances Kyle Basinger to Mrs. Peter Basinger, March 12, 1836 (in Lawton, *Saga*, 140–41); Monthly Post Returns (Fort Brooke), NA, December 1835, states "8 horses . . . killed." Assuming this represents all horses with the detachment, and four drew the gun, it is assumed that four officers rode. At the start, however, Gardiner had not joined with horses for the gun.

69. Basinger, *Personal Reminiscences*, 42, 61; Cullum, *Register*, 361.

70. Lawton, *Saga*, 133; *Georgian*, December 27, 1833; Lawton, *Saga*, 140–41; Monthly Post Returns (Fort Brooke), NA, November 1835; Lawton, *Saga*, 133.

71. Lawton, *Saga*, 140; Cullum, *Register*, 225; Heitman, *Historical Register* 1:522.

72. Heitman, *Historical Register* 1:586, 734; Cullum, *Register*, 223, 225; Peterson, *Round Shot and Rammers*, 88–89; *System of Artillery Discipline*, plate 2, figures 1–7; *System of Exercise and Instruction*, plate 4; Manucy to Laumer, personal communication, September 7, 1984; Peterson, *Round Shot and Rammers*, 60, 74.

73. Belton to Clinch, December 22, 1836, Orderly Book.

74. A basic source of information on enlisted men of the U.S. Army during this period is their personal file in the Registers of Enlistments, NA. These files were created for a man when application was made in his name for bounty land, for example, and sometimes contain much personal information. In the case of the men with Dade's command I have found such a record only on those few who survived, as well as those whose widows filed a claim. In this case, a letter in the file of Sgt. John Vailing, written to Vailing's widow by Major (John Lane?) Gardner on April 8, 1836, mentions in passing that Mrs. (Benjamin) Chapman "had just arrived from Tampa Bay." Hence, I feel that it is not too great a leap to assume that Mrs. Chapman would have been in the little group that watched the passing of the command. Registers of Enlistments, 1833, p. 39, no. 162; personal file on Clark in NA. Further sources on Clark will be given as they pertain to the text. Blanchard, *Narrative*, 16; Registers of Enlistments, 1832, p. 230, no. 83; *General Regulations*, 1825, Article 31, no. 249; NA personal file on Michael Kenny.

75. Carter, *Territorial Papers* 24:949.

76. Grismer, *Tampa*, 65; Carter, *Territorial Papers* 25:89; Grismer, *Tampa*, 61; Farr, *Tampa's Earliest Living Pioneer*, 7–10; Prince, Diary, June 1, 1836.

77. *Pensacola Gazette*, April 15, 1826, quoted in McKay, *Pioneer Florida* 1:15; Davis, "Early Orange Culture"; Carter, *Territorial Papers* 23:428; Interview with Louis Pacheco in the *Florida Times-Union*, October 30, 1892.

78. Covington, "Life at Fort Brooke."

79. Belton to the adjutant general, January 1, 1836, Order and Letter Book; Author interviews with Leroy Ford, July 27, 1987, and August 28, 1993; Klinkenborg, "If It Weren't for the Ox."

80. Belton to the adjutant general, January 1, 1836, Order and Letter Book.

81. Belton, Order Number 2, December 23, 1835, Orderly Book; Belton to Clinch and Dade, December 23, 1835, Orderly Book.

82. "A Short Sketch of the Life of the Only Survivor of 'Dade's Massacre,'" *Sunland Tribune* 5, no. 9 (May 6, 1880); Petition of Joseph Elzaurdi, April 1, 1842, HR Document 472, 27 Cong., 2 sess., *United States Congress Serial Set*, Washington, D.C.; Petition of Joseph Elzaurdi, February 9, 1848, HR Document 187, 30 Cong., 1 sess., *United States Congress Serial Set*, Washington, D.C.

83. Bunce to "The Commander of the U.S. Troops—Tampa," December 22, 1835; HR Document 472 (see note 82); Mathews, *Edge of Wilderness*, 74–80, 87; Belton to Clinch, December 22, 1835, Orderly Book; Porter, "Louis Pacheco."

84. *Portsmouth (N.H.) Journal*, January 13, 1849, p. 2, cols. 2 and 3; *Times-Union*, October 30, 1892.

85. *Times-Union*, October 30, 1892; Prince, Diary, June 1, 1836; Belton to Clinch and Dade, December 23, 1835, Orderly Book; Belton to the adjutant general, January 1, 1836, Order and Letter Book. This letter is assumed to have been carried by Pacheco, since Belton had no plan at this time for anyone else to join the command. Though Belton indicates that Pacheco has already left at 9:00, it seems likely that, in fact, he would have had him stand by for the completion of the letter (only three more lines); Belton, Order Number 2, December 23, 1835, Orderly Book.

86. Prince, Diary, June 1, 1836.

87. Author interview with Leroy Ford, July 27, 1987.

88. Carter, *Territorial Papers* 23:428; McCall, *Letters*, 188; Carter, *Territorial Papers* 23:129.

89. Meek, "Journal," March 14, 1836; Clinch to Zantzinger, January 18, 1835, Record Group 391, NA.

90. McCall, *Letters*, 192.

91. Belton to the adjutant general, January 1, 1836, Order and Letter Book.

92. Senate Document Number 33, 67-1 (faces p. 10). This resume of Dade's battle states, "The writer of this accompanied the Detachment to their first encamp-

ment." No record found identifies this person, but circumstances strongly indicate that Alvord was the man; Alvord, *Address*, 33–56.

93. Motte, *Journey into Wilderness*, 190; Senate Document Number 33, 67-1.

94. Nourse to surgeon general, January 5, 1836, SGO, NA; Bemrose, *Reminiscences*, 63; Gardenier to Duncan, January 11, 1836 (2 letters), Duncan Papers, U.S. Military Academy Library.

95. Belton to the adjutant general, January 1, 1836, Order and Letter Book. The number of men assumed to have taken up the cannon is explained in appendix 3. As to Gardiner leading these men, it is clear that the gun was returned to Dade and that Gardiner rejoined. Only the conjunction of the two is in question, and a study of the circumstances and timing (departure of the *Motto*, Alvord's return, and so on) indicate that such is the logical conclusion.

96. Young, *Knickerbocker's Almanac*, 16; *Hutchins' Improved Almanac*, 16.

97. Belton to the adjutant general, January 1, 1836, Order and Letter Book; Motte, *Journey into Wilderness*, 190.

98. Cullum, "Recollections"; Bemrose, *Reminiscences*, 63.

99. Clinch to Jones, December 23, 1835, Orderly Book, italics added; Clinch to commanding officer, U.S. Troops, Fort Brooke, December 23, 1835, Orderly Book.

Chapter Two: The Second Day

1. Dade to Macomb, March 28, 1834, Record Group 94, AGO, NA; *Florida Times-Union*, October 30, 1892.

2. *Florida Times-Union*, October 30, 1892; *Sunland Tribune* 5, no. 9 (May 6, 1880).

3. *Florida Times-Union*, October 30, 1892.

4. Ibid.

5. Ibid.

6. Ibid.; *Sunland Tribune*, May 6, 1880.

7. *Florida Times-Union*, October 30, 1892.

8. McCall, *Letters*, 141; Motte, *Journey into Wilderness*, 306; Robinson, *History of Hillsborough County*, 104.

9. McCall, *Letters*, 189; Belton to Clinch, December 22, 1835, Orderly Book; *Florida Times-Union*, October 30, 1892; McCall, *Letters*, 189–90; Clinch to Zantzinger, January 18, 1835, Orderly Book.

10. Covington, *Seminoles*, 48; McCall, *Letters*, 141; Robinson, *History of Hills-*

borough County, 105; Gaylord, *Life in Florida*, 3; *General Regulations*, 1835, Article 22, no. 14.

11. Bemrose, *Reminiscences*, 42–43. This description is taken from another group of regulars, marching from Fort Drane toward the Withlacoochee on December 29, 1835. Made up of about the same proportion of foreign and American troops, their dialects and tongues must have been much the same as those of Dade's men.

12. Registers of Enlistments, NA; Latrobe, *Rambler*, 319.

13. Dade Chronology (compiled by the author, the chronology lists every date and event that can be verified in Francis Dade's life).

14. Latrobe, *Rambler*, 319.

15. *General Regulations*, Article 16, no. 3.

16. Mahon, *Second Seminole War*, 77; Mahon in Bemrose, *Reminiscences*, 14.

17. Eby, "Memoir," 155–57, 162–63; Heitman, *Historical Register* 1:555, 1065; McCall, *Letters*, 158–59.

18. Carter, *Territorial Papers* 23:682–83, 856–57; *Niles' Weekly Register*, January 13, 1827; Mahon, *Second Seminole War*, 123–25; Call-Brevard Papers, M 92-1, Box 2, Folder 21, Florida State Archives; Mahon, *Second Seminole War*, 120.

19. *Florida Times-Union*, October 30, 1892; Covington, *Seminoles*, 25; Mahon, *Second Seminole War*, 10, 24; Porter, "Bill Bowlegs"; Porter, "Cowkeeper Dynasty."

20. Porter, "Bill Bowlegs," 220; *Army and Navy Chronicle* 1 (January 1835): 304, 331.

21. Kanapaha Pond is in the vicinity of present-day Gainesville; Boyd, *Florida Aflame*, 55; Patrick, *Aristocrat in Uniform*, 85–86.

22. Clinch, December 21, 1835, Order Number 1, Orderly Book; Patrick, *Aristocrat in Uniform*, 97.

23. Carter, *Territorial Papers* 25:214; Call to Macomb, August 3, 1837 (in Boyd, *Florida Aflame*, 81); Carter, *Territorial Papers* 25:216.

24. Patrick, *Aristocrat in Uniform*, 44, 61; Bemrose, *Reminiscences*, 33.

25. Bemrose, *Reminiscences*, 59.

26. Patrick, *Aristocrat in Uniform*, 70–83; Carter, *Territorial Papers* 25:129–31. The date here given is accepted as written, yet the date handwritten in Clinch's letterbook appears to be the twentieth—presumably an error.

27. Patrick, *Aristocrat in Uniform*, 71; Clinch to the adjutant general, January 22, 1835, Orderly Book; Bemrose, *Reminiscences*, 37; Patrick, *Aristocrat in Uniform*, 86.

28. Simmons, "Recollections," in *National Atlas and Sunday Morning Mail*, July 1836, p. 14.

29. Ibid., in *Saturday Evening Post*, August 20, 1836.

30. Ibid.; Bemrose, *Reminiscences*, 17–21; Porter, "Negro Guides," 174–78.

31. Simmons, "Recollections," in *National Atlas and Sunday Morning Mail*, July 1836, p. 19.

32. Ibid.

33. Ibid.

34. Ibid.; Bemrose, *Reminiscences*, 17–21.

35. Motte, *Journey into Wilderness*, 283; Sprague, *Florida War*, 97; Cohen, *Notices*, 239.

36. Bemrose, *Reminiscences*, 17–21; Simmons, "Recollections," in *Saturday Evening Post*, August 20, 1836.

37. Bemrose, *Reminiscences*, 17–21.

38. Ibid., 19.

39. Ibid.

40. Ibid.

41. Patrick, *Aristocrat in Uniform*, 77–78; Clinch to the adjutant general, April 20, 1835 (in Carter, *Territorial Papers* 25:129–31).

42. Simmons, "Recollections," in *Saturday Evening Post*, August 20, 1836.

43. Mahon, *Second Seminole War*, 95–96; Clinch to the adjutant general, April 20, 1835 (in Carter, *Territorial Papers* 25:129–31); Sprague, *Florida War*, 84–85; Patrick, *Aristocrat in Uniform*, 76–78; Clinch to the adjutant general, April 1, 1835 (in Carter, *Territorial Papers* 25:129–30).

44. Simmons, "Recollections," in *Saturday Evening Post*, August 20, 1836.

45. Clinch to the adjutant general, April 20, 1835 (in Carter, *Territorial Papers* 25:129–31).

46. Sprague, *Florida War*, 21.

47. Patrick, *Aristocrat in Uniform*, 10.

48. Clinch to the adjutant general, January 22, 1835, Clinch Letter Book, AGO, NA; Sprague, *Florida War*, 51.

49. Clinch to the adjutant general, October 8, 1835, Clinch Letter Book, AGO, NA.

50. Bemrose, *Reminiscences*, 31; McReynolds, *Seminoles*, 152; Carter, *Territorial Papers* 25:186–87.

51. Clinch to Dade, October 17, 1835, Clinch Letter Book, AGO, NA.

52. Cass to Clinch, October 22, 1835 (in Carter, *Territorial Papers* 25:188).

53. Ibid.

54. Clinch to the adjutant general, November 3, December 16, 1835 (in Carter, *Territorial Papers* 25:192–93, 213–14); Clinch to commanding officer, Fort Brooke, November 13, 1835, Clinch Order Book, AGO, NA.

55. Clinch to the adjutant general, November 29, 1835 (in Carter, *Territorial Papers* 25:199); Fanning to Clinch, November 27, 1835 (in Carter, *Territorial Papers*

25:200); Fanning to Clinch, November 28, 1835 (in Carter, *Territorial Papers* 25:203–4).

56. Clinch to Macomb, December 1, 1835 (in Carter, *Territorial Papers* 25:203).

57. Clinch to Walker, December 1, 1835 (in Carter, *Territorial Papers* 25:207–8).

58. Mahon in Bemrose, *Reminiscences*, 32–35; McReynolds, *Seminoles*, 235; Clinch to the adjutant general, December 9, 1835 (in Carter, *Territorial Papers* 25:209–10); Sprague, *Florida War*, 88; Clinch to Macomb, December 1, 1835 (in Carter, *Territorial Papers* 25:207–8).

59. Clinch spelled it Newlandsville. Clinch to Walker, December 5, 1835 (in Carter, *Territorial Papers* 25:208); Boyd, *Florida Aflame*, 71; Mahon, *Second Seminole War*, 46.

60. Patrick, *Aristocrat in Uniform*, 96; Clinch to Walker, December 5, 1835 (in Carter, *Territorial Papers* 25:208).

61. Bemrose, *Reminiscences*, 32.

62. Heitman, *Historical Register* 1:382.

63. Mahon in Bemrose, *Reminiscences*, 35; Mahon, *Second Seminole War*, 33, 173; Carter, *Territorial Papers* 25:209–10.

64. Bemrose, *Reminiscences*, 32.

65. Dade Memorial in "Dade Papers," prepared by Judge W. A. G. Dade, in the author's collection.

66. "The Dade Family," *Tyler's Quarterly Magazine* (July 1935-April 1936): 49–59; Application for bounty land, Amanda Dade, Dade pension files, NA.

67. Parton, *Andrew Jackson*, 507–13; Heitman, *Historical Register* 1:248; Dade to John Bruce, 25 November 1818, author's collection; Andrew Jackson, Memorandum, August 22, 1821, in Library of Congress, Manuscript Division; Parton, *Andrew Jackson*, 620; James, *Life of Andrew Jackson*, 322–23; *Sunland Tribune*, vol. 1, no. 1, p. 14.

68. Monthly Post Returns (Fort Brooke), NA, February 1824; Thomas Fay to Jesup, December 4, 1827, Jesup, Letters, AGO, NA.

69. McCall, *Letters*, 15; U.S. Census, 1840, 1850 (Pensacola); T. T. Wentworth, Jr., to Laumer, January 27, 1964.

70. *Army and Navy Chronicle* 1 (January 1-June 30, 1835): 409; Browne, *Key West*, 77; ibid., map (facing Index); *United States Military Reservations*, 59, 60; Quarterly Report of the Sick and Wounded at Key West, Florida, for the Quarter Ending December 31, 1835, SGO, NA.

71. Browne, *Key West*, 84; *Enquirer* (Key West), January 16, 1836; Dade to Macomb, March 28, 1834, Record Group 94, AGO, NA; *Enquirer* (Key West), November 29, 1834; Kearney, "Autobiography," 198–99.

72. Browne, *Key West*, 157, 173; Kearney, "Autobiography," 199; Browne, *Key West*, 156; *Army and Navy Chronicle* 1 (January 1-June 30, 1835): 279–80, 295, 302, 305, 315, 324.

73. Heitman, *Historical Register* 1:350; *General Regulations*, 1835, 194, 198.

74. Heitman, *Historical Register* 2:584.

75. Ibid., 1:555; McCall, *Letters*, 145–48; Carter, *Territorial Papers* 23:683; Brooke to Brown, August 14, 1825, Office of the Adjutant General, Letters Received, AGO, NA; Sprague, *Florida War*, 29; Eby, "Memoir," 157–62.

76. Clark, in *Portsmouth (Maine) Daily Advertiser*, January or February 13, 1836.

77. Ibid.; Carter, *Territorial Papers* 23:130–31.

78. Belton to the adjutant general, January 1, 1836, Order and Letter Book; Registers of Enlistments, roll 19, p. 100, no. 67.

79. Goggin, "Osceola," 181–85; McCall, *Letters*, 161–91; Unless otherwise noted, all Seminole vocabulary is taken from Smith, *Sketch of the Seminole War*, 90–109; Williams, *Territory of Florida*, 89; Sprague, *Florida War*, 281.

80. Cohen, *Notices*, 239; Sprague, *Florida War*, 97.

81. Giddings, *Exiles of Florida*, 3.

82. Cohen, *Notices*, 31; Mahon, *Second Seminole War*, 1, 2, 7; Carter, *Territorial Papers* 23:549; Sprague, *Florida War*, 19.

83. Williams, *Territory of Florida*, 276; Carter, *Territorial Papers* 23:549.

84. Peithmann, *Unconquered Seminole Indians*, 21.

85. Mahon, *Second Seminole War*, 43–50.

86. Carter, *Territorial Papers* 23:550.

87. Sprague, *Florida War*, 20–24; Cohen 57–58; *American State Papers* 1:524.

88. Carter, *Territorial Papers* 23:202–3.

89. Boyd, *Florida Aflame*, 208, 251; Sprague, *Florida War*, 90.

90. Belton to Dade, December 26, 1835, Orderly Book.

Chapter Three: The Third Day

1. Belton to the adjutant general, January 1, 1836, Order and Letter Book.

2. Belton to Mountfort, December 25, 1835, Orderly Book.

3. Belton to the adjutant general, January 1, 1836, Order and Letter Book; *Herald* (New York), January 28, 1836; *Niles' Weekly Register* 49 (September 1835-March 1836): 368.

4. *Herald* (New York), January 28, 1836.

5. Belton to Dade, December 26, 1835, Orderly Book.

6. Belton to the adjutant general, January 1, 1836, Order and Letter Book.

7. Duncan, Diary, February 16, 1836.

8. Government Survey, Township 26 S, Range 21 E, and field notes, 1848, Florida Department of Agriculture; *Florida Times-Union*, October 30, 1892.

9. Duncan, Diary, February 18, 1836 (Duncan describes Gaines's crossing of the Withlacoochee River nearly two months later, but the use of a pole to find the highest footing in that case seems to indicate a customary method of fording unknown streams). *General Regulations*, 1835, Article 9, no. 25.

10. Cohen, *Notices*, 167.

11. Registers of Enlistments, NA, roll 19, p. 201, no. 70 (John Thomas); Surgeon's Certificate for Pension (John Thomas), May 26, 1837, Thomas pension file, NA.

12. Surgeon's Certificate for Pension (John Thomas), May 26, 1837, Pension Files, NA.

13. Belton to the adjutant general, January 1, 1836, Order and Letter Book.

14. *General Regulations*, 1835, Article 53, no. 6; Prince, Diary, May 31, 1836; Gatlin to Lovell, September 12, 1835, Gatlin pension file, NA; *Army and Navy Chronicle* 5 (January 1-June 30, 1837): 127.

15. Johnson and Holloman, *Heritage*, 8–14; *Army and Navy Chronicle* 3 (July 1-December 31, 1836): 48; Heitman, *Historical Register* 1:450.

16. Hammond to Laumer, May 14, 1983; Gatlin to surgeon general, August 22, 1834, SGO, NA; *United States Military Reservations*, 307–8.

17. Gatlin to surgeon general, November 30, 1834, SGO, NA; Latrobe, *Rambler*, 319.

18. *Army and Navy Chronicle* 1 (January 1-June 30, 1835): 206; Gatlin to surgeon general, April 1, September 12, 1835, SGO, NA.

19. Gatlin to surgeon general, November 12, 1835, SGO, NA.

20. Ibid., September 12, 1835.

21. Ibid., November 30, 1835; Heiskell to surgeon general, January 9, 1836, SGO, NA.

22. McCall, *Letters*, 193.

23. Ibid., 196.

24. Smith, *Sketch of the Seminole War*, 152–53.

25. Motte, *Journey into Wilderness*, 90–91.

26. Long, *Florida Breezes*, 170–71.

27. Ibid., 52–54.

28. Jarvis, Diary, entry dated October 1837, P. K. Yonge Library of Florida History.

29. Heitman, *Historical Register* 1:445.

30. Cullum, "Recollections."

31. Cullum, *Register*, 16; Thayer to Gibson, August 21, 1820, Gardiner Papers, U.S. Military Academy Library; *Centennial of the United States Military Academy*, 377, 382.

32. Gardiner to Calhoun, February 2, 1822, AGO, NA; *Biographical Directory*, 1194; Schoonmaker, *History of Kingston*, 451; Brink, "Ulster Congressman," 129–136.

33. [Unknown] to Calhoun, February 14, 1822, AGO, NA; Bailey to Thompson, January 26, 1822, AGO, NA; Sarah Gardinier to Van Buren, February 26, 1823, AGO, NA.

34. Bailey to Thompson, January 26, 1822, AGO, NA; S. Gardinier to Van Buren, February 26, 1823, AGO, NA.

35. Heitman, *Historical Register* 1:445; Cullum, *Register*, 181; J. Gardinier to Duncan, January 11, 1836, Pension Files, NA.

36. Cullum, *Register*, 131; Frances Gardiner pension application, Gardiner pension file, NA.

37. Bemrose, *Reminiscences*, 50; Cullum, *Register*, 107–8; Clinch to Jones, October 17, 1835 (in Carter, *Territorial Papers* 25:187–200); Fanning letter, December 2, 1835 (in Frances Gardiner pension file, NA).

38. Fanning to Jones, April 29, 1835 (in Carter, *Territorial Papers* 25:132–33).

39. Ibid., 203–5.

40. Ibid., 186–87.

41. Fanning letter, December 2, 1835, Pension Files, NA.

42. Frances Gardiner pension file, NA.

43. Boyd, *Florida Aflame*, 71; Fanning to Clinch, November 23, 1835 (in Carter, *Territorial Papers* 25:203–4).

44. Frances Gardiner pension file, NA, italics added; Fanning to Clinch, November 27, 1835 (in Carter, *Territorial Papers* 25:200–201).

45. Heitman, *Historical Register* 1:628; Boyd, *Florida Aflame*, 71–72.

46. Ott and Chazel, *Ocali Country*, 22–24; Archer to Lovell, November 17, 1835, SGO, NA; Carter, *Territorial Papers* 25:200; Potter, *War in Florida*, 98; White, "Macomb's Mission," 161.

47. Simmons, "Recollections," in *National Atlas and Sunday Morning Mail*, August 1836; Potter, *War in Florida*, 109–11; *Ocala (Fla.) Star Banner*, October 20, November 3, 1968.

48. Potter, *War in Florida*, 109; Boyd, *Florida Aflame*, 50; Patrick, *Aristocrat in Uniform*, 98.

49. Malone, *Dictionary of American Biography*, 474–75; Carter, *Territorial Papers* 24:876, 916–17; ibid., 25:39–40, 61; McReynolds, *Seminoles*, 128; *Biographical Directory*, 1915–16; Knight, *Memoirs and Memories*, 401; McIntosh, *History of Elbert*

County, 87–89; *Tampa Tribune* (by McKay, September 10, 1950); Governor Rabun to Calhoun, February 17, 1819, Governor Rabun Correspondence, Georgia Department of Archives; Thompson, Floyd, and Blackshear to Rabun, February 20, 1819 (ibid.); Carter, *Territorial Papers* 24:876, 917.

50. Carter, *Territorial Papers* 24:917.

51. Ibid.; *Tampa Tribune* (McKay, May 21, 1960.)

52. Cohen, *Notices*, 50; Mahon, *Second Seminole War*, 373, 380.

53. Mahon, *Second Seminole War*, 49.

54. Sprague, *Florida War*, 70–71, 76–78.

55. Mahon, *Second Seminole War*, 47.

56. Sprague, *Florida War*, 76; Cohen, *Notices*, 53–63; *American State Papers* 6:58–59, 65–69.

57. Sprague, *Florida War*, 77; Cohen, *Notices*, 57–58; McReynolds, *Seminoles*, 126 (italics added).

58. *American State Papers* 6:67–68; Cohen, *Notices*, 57–63.

59. McCall, *Letters*, 141; Boyd, *Florida Aflame*, 55.

60. McReynolds, *Seminoles*, 147; Cohen, *Notices*, 67; Boyd, *Florida Aflame*, 51–53; Boyd, "Osceola," 275; Mahon, *Second Seminole War*, 95–96.

61. Smith, *Sketch of the Seminole War*, 12; Carter, *Territorial Papers* 25:200; Boyd, "Osceola," 277–78; Mahon, *Second Seminole War*, 101; Thompson to Gibson, November 30, 1835, Office of Indian Affairs, NA.

62. Smith, *Sketch of the Seminole War*, 5; Boyd, "Osceola," 250–53; Carter, *Territorial Papers* 25:59; Sprague, *Florida War*, 100–101; Boyd, "Osceola," 202–4; Boyd, *Florida Aflame*, 48.

63. Smith, *Sketch of the Seminole War*, 5; Goggin, "Osceola"; Thompson to Gibson, June 3, 1835, Office of Indian Affairs, NA.

64. Mahon, *Second Seminole War*, 91; Goggin, "Osceola," 181–87; Smith, *Sketch of the Seminole War*, 5.

65. Simmons, "Recollections," in *National Atlas and Sunday Morning Mail*, July 1836, p. 15.

66. Smith, *Sketch of the Seminole War*, 10; Boyd, "Osceola," 274–75; Williams, *Territory of Florida*, 216; Cohen, *Notices*, 56; Potter, *War in Florida*, 80; Thompson to Gibson, June 3, 1835, Office of Indian Affairs, NA; Peithmann, *Unconquered Seminole Indians*, 27.

67. Thompson to Walker, June 23, 1835; Thompson to Gibson, June 3, 1835 (both in Office of Indian Affairs, NA).

68. Thompson to Gibson, June 3, 1835, Office of Indian Affairs, NA; Smith, *Sketch of the Seminole War*, 10.

69. Thompson to Gibson, June 3, 1835, Office of Indian Affairs, NA; Smith, *Sketch of the Seminole War*, 5; Boyd, "Osceola," 275; *Army and Navy Chronicle* 2

(1836): 199; *Tampa Tribune* (McKay, September 10, 1950); *American State Papers* 2:76.

70. Carter, *Territorial Papers* 25:200.

71. Cohen, *Notices*, 62; Thompson to Gibson, November 30, 1835, Office of Indian Affairs, NA; McReynolds, *Seminoles*, 152.

72. Fort King Weather Diary, December 25, 1835, Environmental Science Services Administration; Jones to Cass, February 9, 1836; Harris to Gibson, December 30, 1835; Thompson to Gibson, June 3, 1835, Office of Indian Affairs, NA.

73. A map was found by Gardiner's body, and the assumption is that he carried it day by day.

74. Carter, *Territorial Papers* 23:129–31.

75. Smith, *Sketch of the Seminole War*, 10; Carter, *Territorial Papers* 23:129.

76. Morris, *Florida Handbook*, 348.

77. *Florida Times-Union*, October 30, 1892. Pacheco recalled that Dade had sent him to "Istowatchotka" on the morning of December 25. Believing that Istowatchotka was the area still known as Toadchudka (west of Dade City), Pacheco must have been sent there (as related) the morning of December 24 in order to have rejoined Dade at Hagerman's Hole the same evening, having made the swing north and west from the area of present-day Zephyrhills to Toadchudka and back east to Hagerman's Hole on the south and west of present-day Dade City.

78. Ibid.

79. Ibid.

80. Ibid.

81. *General Regulations*, 1835, 39–47.

82. Belton to the adjutant general, January 1, 1836, Order and Letter Book.

83. This message carried by Jewell has not been found. However, Belton wrote (Belton to the adjutant general, January 1, 1836, Order and Letter Book) that Jewell had carried his message informing Dade of Mountfort's arrival and planned departure with ammunition and rations. He further stated that "a duplicate of this was sent the next day [the 26th]." We have the letter of December 26, and hence, the information given (see note 1, chapter 4).

84. Ibid.

Chapter Four: The Fourth Day

1. Belton to Dade, December 26, 1835; Mountfort to Rea, January 1, 1836 (both in Order and Letter Book).

2. Belton to Dade, December 26, 1835, Order and Letter Book.

3. Casey to Basinger, January 2, 1836, Order and Letter Book.

4. Belton to Dade, December 26, 1835, Order and Letter Book.

5. Ibid.

6. Ibid.; Belton to the adjutant general, January 1, 1836, Order and Letter Book.

7. Smith, *Sketch of the Seminole War*, 8; Cohen, *Notices*, 69, 236; Boyd, "Osceola," 261, 280; *Florida Times-Union*, October 30, 1892.

8. Smith, *Sketch of the Seminole War*, 5–8.

9. Sprague, *Florida War*, 90–91. This is an account of Dade's battle by Halpatter Tustenuggee ("Alligator"), assumed to have been given to Sprague in person after Halpatter Tustenuggee's capture in March 1838.

10. Wickman, *Osceola's Legacy*, 1–21; Boyd, "Osceola," 252–59; Sprague, *Florida War*, 100–101; Boyd, *Florida Aflame*, 20.

11. Sprague, *Florida War*, 100–101; Wickman, *Osceola's Legacy*, 27–31; Boyd, "Osceola," 255–63; Mahon, *Second Seminole War*, 91.

12. Cohen, *Notices*, 65, 234–35; Potter, *War in Florida*, 11; Mahon, *Second Seminole War*, 10; Boyd, "Osceola," 261.

13. Cohen, *Notices*, 234–35.

14. Cohen, *Notices*, 236; Smith, *Sketch of the Seminole War*, 10; Boyd, "Osceola," 262.

15. Cohen, *Notices*, 57–59; *American State Papers* 6:66–67.

16. Sprague, *Florida War*, 80; Boyd, *Florida Aflame*, 48; Potter, *War in Florida*, 48–69; Mahon, *Second Seminole War*, 89–93; Cohen, *Notices*, 57–63; *American State Papers* 6:63–68.

17. Boyd, "Osceola," 161–75.

18. Potter, *War in Florida*, 53–54.

19. Ibid., 54.

20. *American State Papers* 6:66.

21. Potter, *War in Florida*, 60; *American State Papers* 6:67.

22. *American State Papers* 6:68.

23. Ibid.; Cohen, *Notices*, 234; Potter, *War in Florida*, 66; Boyd, "Osceola," 269–70.

24. Cohen, *Notices*, 62–63; Boyd, "Osceola," 269–70.

25. Simmons, "Recollections," in *National Atlas and Sunday Morning Mail*, July 1836.

26. Ibid.

27. Sprague, *Florida War*, 86.

28. Bemrose, *Reminiscences*, 50; Boyd, *Florida Aflame*, 76.

29. *Florida Times-Union*, October 30, 1892.

30. Ibid.; *Portland (Maine) Daily Advertiser*, 1836 (exact date unknown).

31. Mudge, *Memorials*, 222; Lieutenant Child to secretary of war (Porter), December 29, 1828, Navy and Military Service Branch, NA; Mudge to secretary of war, March 16, 1829, Navy and Military Service Branch, NA; Cullum, *Register*, 185; Mudge, *Memorials*, 385; Prince, Diary, February 20, 1836; Duncan, Diary, February 20, 1836.

32. Blount letter, February 15, 1830; Bryant to Eaton, October 13, 1829; Calhoun to Gratiot (undated); Keais to Johnston, August 11, 1835, Keais Papers, U.S. Military Academy Library.

33. Keais to Johnston, August 11, 1835; Keais to Johnston, November 3, 1835 (both in Keais Papers, U.S. Military Academy Library).

34. Keais to Johnston, November 3, 1835, Keais Papers, U.S. Military Academy Library; "riddle"—a coarse-meshed sieve.

35. Keais to Johnston, November 3, 1835, Keais Papers, U.S. Military Academy Library.

36. Keais to Johnston, August 11, 1835; Keais to Johnston, November 3, 1835 (both in Keais Papers, U.S. Military Academy Library).

37. *Portland (Maine) Daily Advertiser*; Motte, *Journey into Wilderness*, 11.

38. Louisa Vailing pension application, 1837, NA; Registers of Enlistments, p. 2, no. 136, NA; Austin Farley pension file, NA.

39. *Sunland Tribune* 1, no. 1 (July 1974): 10; Sprague, *Florida War*, 20–24 (italics added).

40. Carter, *Territorial Papers* 23:226–27, 233, 246, 328, 366, 428.

41. Boyd, *Florida Aflame*, 41; McCall, *Letters*, 145–60.

42. Carter, *Territorial Papers* 23:428, 25:164, 227; McCall, *Letters*, 185.

43. *Florida Times-Union*, October 30, 1892.

44. McCall, *Letters*, 191.

45. Ibid.; Clinch to Zantzinger, January 18, 1835, Clinch Letter Book, AGO, NA; *Portland (Maine) Daily Advertiser*; Carter, *Territorial Papers* 23:130.

46. *Portland (Maine) Daily Advertiser*; Carter, *Territorial Papers* 23:130.

47. *Portland (Maine) Daily Advertiser*.

48. Ibid.

49. Duncan, Diary, February 18, 1836.

50. Sprague, *Florida War*, 90.

51. Motte, *Journey into Wilderness*, 214, 306–7; Smith, *Sketch of the Seminole War*, 99. Motte's description of an Indian encampment at night may be taken as typical, though he was not, of course, writing of Ote Emathla's camp in the Wahoo Swamp.

52. Cohen, *Notices*, 57, 61.

53. Sprague, *Florida War*, 20, 29; Mahon, *Second Seminole War*, 49.

54. Mahon, *Second Seminole War*, 55, 58.

55. Ibid.; Mahon, *Second Seminole War*, 73; Sprague, *Florida War*, 28, 36–37. A law enacted by the governor and legislative council of the Territory of Florida: "if any Indian . . . venture . . . beyond the boundary . . . it shall . . . be lawful for any person . . . to apprehend, seize and take [him] before some justice of the peace, who is . . . *required*, to direct . . . that there shall be inflicted not exceeding thirty-nine stripes . . . on the bare back of said Indian"; Boyd, *Florida Aflame*, 55.

56. Lankford, *Native American Legends*, 140–41.

57. Ibid.

58. McCall, *Letters*, 160.

59. Sprague, *Florida War*, 51

60. Ibid., 20–22; *American State Papers* 2:203–5.

61. Sprague, *Florida War*, 50, 51.

62. *American State Papers* 2:203, 204; Mahon, *Second Seminole War*, 75.

63. Cohen, *Notices*, 60–61; *American State Papers* 6:67; McReynolds, *Seminoles*, 123–28; Sprague, *Florida War*, 73–84; *American State Papers* 2:208–9; Mahon, *Second Seminole War*, 74–86.

64. Cohen, *Notices*, 58–59.

65. Sprague, *Florida War*, 76; Cohen, *Notices*, 57–58.

66. *American State Papers* 6:65–67; Mahon, *Second Seminole War*, 83.

67. *American State Papers* 6:66; Cohen, *Notices*, 58.

68. *American State Papers* 6:67; Cohen, *Notices*, 62.

69. Sprague, *Florida War*, 90; Smith, *Sketch of the Seminole War*, 4; Boyd, "Osce-ola," 251. The latter is a thorough explication of the name commonly known as "Osceola."

70. Smith, *Sketch of the Seminole War*, 4; Boyd, *Florida Aflame*, 12, 13.

Chapter Five: The Fifth Day

1. *Historic Livingston County* (pamphlet).

2. Probate proceedings on Will of Benjamin Clark, recorded in Livingston County Courthouse, vol. 2 of Wills, beginning p. 399 (citation was published in the *Albany Argus*, November 17, 1843).

3. Ibid.

4. *Livingston (N.Y.) Register*, May 12, 1830; Registers of Enlistments, NA; Clark, *Narrative*, 4.

5. Clark, *Narrative*, 5.

6. Ibid., 7; Monthly Post Records, Fort Morgan, February 1834, Roll 805, no. 617, NA; Prucha, *Military Posts*, 92–93; Heitman, *Historical Register* 1:295; Cullum, *Register*, 182.

7. Clark, *Narrative*, 7; John Friend, Jr., to Laumer, October 8, 1989; Monthly Post Records, Fort Morgan, January 1835, Roll 805, no. 617; *Columbus (Ga.) Enquirer*, February 20, 1835?; Fort Morgan Weather Diary, January 1835, National Weather Records Center.

8. *Columbus (Ga.) Enquirer*, February 20, 1835; John Friend to Laumer, October 8, 1989; Meteorological data, Dauphin Island Sea Lab, January 1982–86. The temperature of air and water off Dauphin Island (west of Fort Morgan, directly across the bay) on January 25 for 1982–86 was given in Celsius. Transposing these figures to Fahrenheit gives almost identical readings: 49.06 air, 49.60 water. There is no reason to believe that these figures would have been significantly different 150 years ago.

9. Clark, *Narrative*, 7.

10. *Florida Times-Union*, October 30, 1892.

11. Duncan, Diary, February 18, 1836; Belton to the adjutant general, January 1, 1836, Order and Letter Book.

12. Carter, *Territorial Papers* 23:328; *Florida Times-Union*, October 30, 1892.

13. McCall, *Letters*, 193; Prince, Diary, 117; Duncan, Diary, February 19, 1836. Duncan states "all cross on log . . . horses ford." Obviously the bridge had been burnt at this time, and given that there is clear mention of fire damage to the bridges across the Big Hillsborough and Big Withlacoochee at the time of Dade's passage, it seems very likely that this bridge, too, was beyond repair.

14. Prince, Diary, 117.

15. McCall, *Letters*, 193.

16. Clark, *Portland (Maine) Daily Advertiser*; Duncan, Diary, February 19, 1836.

17. Christopher Laumer, taxidermist and a lifetime student of Florida fowl with personal knowledge of this particular body of water (now known as Lake Bowling), provided the author with information on the probable inhabitants of the lake at this time.

18. Bemrose, *Reminiscences*, 42–43.

19. McCall, *Letters*, 192.

20. Duncan, Diary, February 19, 1836; Sinclair et al., *Sinkholes*, 1; McCall, *Letters*, 197; Barr, *Authentic Narrative*, March 16, 1836.

21. Luecke, *Feeding the Frontier Army*, 9.

22. Boyd, *Florida Aflame*, 75–76; Bemrose, *Reminiscences*, 39; Ott and Chazel, *Ocali Country*, 29–30; Knetsch, *Fort Drane*, 2, in author's collection.

23. Boyd, *Florida Aflame*, 76–82; Bemrose, *Reminiscences*, 38–40; Call-Brevard Papers, M 92-1, Box 2, Folder 21, Florida State Archives.

24. Sprague, *Florida War*, 143.

Chapter Six: The Final Day

1. Belton to Greyson, December 28, 1835, Orderly Book; Belton to the adjutant general, January 1, 1836, Order and Letter Book.

2. *Portland (Maine) Daily Advertiser; Dade City (Fla.) Banner*, June 1, 1923.

3. *Dade City (Fla.) Banner*, June 1, 1923 ("Nephew Described Major Francis Dade"); Hitchcock, *Fifty Years*, 56–57; Roberts, "Dade Massacre," 124–25; *Florida Times-Union*, October 30, 1892.

4. Hitchcock, *Fifty Years*, 86–87; Roberts, "Dade Massacre," 124–25; *Florida Times-Union*, October 30, 1892.

5. Boyd, *Florida Aflame*, 12–13; Cohen, *Notices*, 174; McCall, *Letters*, 148, 160, 303; McReynolds, *Seminoles*, 97.

6. Belton to adjutant general, March 25, 1836, AGO, NA; McCall, *Letters*, 299–300, 303–8; Clark, *Narrative*, 13.

7. *Florida Times-Union*, October 30, 1892; *Sunland Tribune* 5, no. 9 (May 6, 1880).

8. *Army and Navy Chronicle* 4, no. 24 (June 15, 1837): 369; *Daily National Intelligencer*, June 14, 1837; *Charleston (S.C.) Courier*, July 27, 1836.

9. McCall, *Letters*, 148.

10. Sprague, *Florida War*, 90–91; Prince, Diary, February 20, 1836, 12.

11. Sprague, *Florida War*, 90–91; Mahon, *Second Seminole War*, 123; Sprague, *Florida War*, 112. This reference is in connection with Gaines's battle two months later but involves Osceola and Ote Emathla in the process of counting bundles of sticks; this is assumed to have been the customary method of determining the number of warriors before engaging in battle; McCall, *Letters*, 307.

12. Heintzelman, March 18, 1836, Library of Congress, Manuscript Division; McCall, *Letters*, 303–4; *Pensacola (Fla.) Commercial*, March 13, 1888; *Georgian* (Savannah), May 18, 1837 (exact title unknown); *Florida Times-Union*, October 30, 1892.

13. Sprague, *Florida War*, 330; Alvord to Benjamin Mudge, January 3, 1836, in Mudge, *Memorials*, 383–84; *Portland (Maine) Daily Advertiser*.

14. *Florida Times-Union*, October 30, 1892.

15. *Portland (Maine) Daily Advertiser*; Cohen, *Notices*, 151; Mahon, *Second Seminole War*, 120; *General Regulations*, 1835, 160; Clark deposition, March 11, 1836, M 221, Roll 116, 5321(39), NA.

16. Sprague, *Florida War*, 90–91.

17. Scott, *Infantry Tactics*, 37–44; Raymond Giron, interviews with author, 1992–93.

18. *Daily National Intelligencer*, June 14, 1837.

19. *Portland (Maine) Daily Advertiser*.

20. Peterson, *Round Shots and Rammers*, Preface, 89.

21. Scott, *Infantry Tactics*, 14–158.

22. On March 6, 1964, with permission of the Florida Board of Parks and Historic Memorials, this site was excavated by members of the Florida Historical Society. Material found left no reasonable doubt that this spot is in fact the location of the last stand and, later, the graves of the enlisted men. The site is presently enclosed with cement reproductions of the original logs, though roughly half the circumference of the original and open to the west and closed on the east, the reverse of the original.

23. *System of Exercise and Instruction*, 13–25.

24. Ibid.

25. Peterson, *Round Shot and Rammers*, 89; conversations with Raymond Giron, April and May 1990; Simmons, "Recollections," in *Saturday Evening Post*, August 20, 1836. For several years the author has taken part in the annual reenactment of Dade's battle and can attest to the stunning sound and fury of the replica cannon's firing.

26. Sprague, *Florida War*, 90–91.

27. Mahon, *Second Seminole War*, 120; Bemrose, *Reminiscences*, 51–52; Smith, *Sketch of the Seminole War*, 96, 280; Motte, *Journey into Wilderness*, 11.

28. *Georgian* (Savannah), May 18, 1837; *Portland (Maine) Daily Advertiser*.

29. *Florida Times-Union*, October 30, 1892; *Sunland Tribune*, May 6, 1880.

30. *Sunland Tribune*, May 6, 1880.

31. Motte, *Journey into Wilderness*, 10; Simmons, "Recollections," in *Saturday Evening Post*, August 20, 1836.

32. Sprague, *Florida War*, 108–9; McCall, *Letters*, 305–6; Simmons, "Recollections," in *Saturday Evening Post*, August 20, 1836; "Sketch of Major Dade's Battleground taken upon the spot by E. Rose, U.S. Army," January 18, 1837, Record Group 77(b), File L75, NA; Dade battleground map, Senate Document Number 33, 67-1 (faces p. 10, no. 3), believed to have been drawn by Lt. Benjamin Alvord.

33. *Portland (Maine) Daily Advertiser*; *Daily National Intelligencer*, June 14, 1837; Tampa Bay Arms Collectors Association, *En Garde!*, 3.

34. McCall, *Letters*, 304; *Portland (Maine) Daily Advertiser*.

35. Duncan, Diary, February 20, 1836; Clark deposition, January 8, 1836, M 221, Roll 116, 5321(39), NA; McCall, *Letters*, 304.

36. Belton to the adjutant general, March 25, 1836, Belton Letter Book, AGO, NA; *Portland (Maine) Daily Advertiser.*

37. *Portland (Maine) Daily Advertiser.*

38. *System of Exercise and Instruction*, 17.

39. Alvord, *Address*, 35; *Georgian* (Savannah), May 18, 1837; *Portland (Maine) Daily Advertiser; Niles' Weekly Register*, August 20, 1836; *Army and Navy Chronicle* 4, no. 24 (June 15, 1837): 369; Bemrose, *Reminiscences*, 42.

40. Alvord, *Address*, 35–36; Cohen, *Notices*, 76; McKay, *Pioneer Florida* 2:346.

41. *Portland (Maine) Daily Advertiser;* Coe, *Red Patriots*, 61. (Coe here refers to an account in the *Charleston [S.C.] Courier*, August 20, 1836. Boynton in his *History of West Point* [p. 294], cites the same paper, the same month. The microfilm of the paper for that date showed no interview with Clark. Reading every issue for July and September was equally fruitless. While searching other sources for the solution to the mystery of the missing interview I found a reference in Boyd [p. 91] to an interview with Clark "published in the *Charleston Courier* [noted in *Niles' Weekly Register* of August 20, 1836]." After obtaining a copy of the *Niles' Weekly Register* for that date I found [pp. 419–20] an article titled "The Last of Major Dade's Command, From the Charleston Courier." Evidently Coe had accidentally taken the article from the *Courier* and the *date* from *Niles'.* But the correct issue of the *Courier*, with the entire original interview with Clark, was still to be found. Back to the Courier microfilm. I first went forward through September: no luck. I began reading every issue of July. There, on July 27, was the elusive article, titled "The Last of the Denoted" (no page numbers); author interview with Raymond Giron, May 25, 1990.

42. McCall, *Letters*, 304–6; *Niles' Weekly Register*, August 20, 1836.

43. Clark, *Narrative*, 14.

44. Djavaheri, Protocol, in author's collection; *Portland (Maine) Daily Advertiser;* Statement in Gardiner pension file, NA.

45. *Portland (Maine) Daily Advertiser; Daily National Intelligencer*, June 14, 1837; Belton to the adjutant general, March 25, 1836, Belton Letter Book, AGO, NA; Statement in Gardiner pension file, NA; Cullum, *Register*, 112.

46. Cullum, *Register*, 361; *Niles' Weekly Register*, August 20, 1836; *Daily National Intelligencer*, June 14, 1837; *Army and Navy Chronicle* 4, no. 24 (June 15, 1837): 369; Djavaheri, Protocol, in author's collection.

47. *Portland (Maine) Daily Advertiser;* Djavaheri, Protocol, in author's collection.

48. *Florida Times-Union*, October 30, 1892; McCall, *Letters*, 307; *Portland (Maine) Daily Advertiser.*

49. *Portland (Maine) Daily Advertiser.*

50. Sprague, *Florida War*, 90–91.

51. Ibid.

52. *Charleston Courier*, March 11, 14, 1836; Cohen, *Notices*, 74; Duncan, Diary, February 20, 1836; *Portland (Maine) Daily Advertiser*; Potter, *War in Florida*, 106.

53. Simmons, "Recollections," in *Saturday Evening Post*, August 20, 1836; Belton to the adjutant general, January 1, 1836, Order and Letter Book; ibid., March 25, 1836; Duncan, Diary, February 20, 1836; McCall, *Letters*, 304.

54. Boyd, *Florida Aflame*, 71, 72.

55. Ibid.; Sprague, *Florida War*, 101.

56. Sprague, *Florida War*, 89; Potter, *War in Florida*, 111.

57. *Sunland Tribune*, May 6, 1880.

58. Boyd, *Florida Aflame*, 71, 72.

59. Sprague, *Florida War*, 91.

60. Simmons, "Recollections," in *National Atlas and Sunday Morning Mail*, July 1836.

61. McCall, *Letters*, 306; Clark, *Narrative*, 15; *Daily National Intelligencer*, June 14, 1837; Duncan, Diary, February 20, 1836; Belton to the adjutant general, March 25, 1836, Order and Letter Book; *Niles' Weekly Register*, August 20, 1836.

Epilogue

1. *Niles' Weekly Register*, August 20, 1836.

2. Weather Diaries for Fort Brooke and Fort King, December 29, 1836, Environmental Science Services Administration.

3. Bemrose, *Reminiscences*, 68; Clark, *Narrative*, 16; *Daily National Intelligencer*, June 14, 1837.

4. *Pennsylvanian*, April 12, 1836; *Daily National Intelligencer*, June 14, 1837; *Florida Wildlife* 41, no. 3 (May-June 1987): 7–8.

5. Belton to the adjutant general, January 1, 1836, Order and Letter Book.

6. Ibid.

7. Heiskell to Lovell, November 23, 1835, SGO, NA; Heiskell statement, November 16, 1843 (in White, *Private Joseph Sprague*, 65).

8. Bemrose, *Reminiscences*, 65.

9. *Boston Post*, June 6, 1837; Surgeon's certificate for a pension, John Cuyler, assistant surgeon, SGO, NA; *New York Times*, July 16, 1836, statement of Maj. James Harvey Hook.

10. McCall, *Letters*, 307.

11. Belton to the adjutant general, January 1, 1836, Order and Letter Book.

12. Barr, *Authentic Narrative*, March 16, 1836; Belton to the adjutant general,

January 1, 1836, Order and Letter Book; Mountfort to Rea, *Herald* (New York), January 28, 1836.

13. Belton to the adjutant general, January 1, 1836, Order and Letter Book; Boyd, *Florida Aflame*, 97, 104; Ayers MS 210, Newberry Library, Chicago; Mahon, *Second Seminole War*, 111.

14. Lt. Timothy Paige (misspelled Parge) in the *Charleston (S.C.) Courier*, January 20, March 14, 1836.

15. *Daily National Intelligencer*, January 26, 1836; *New Orleans Bee*, January 11, 1836; Belton to Eaton and Clinch, January 5, 1836, Belton Letter Book, AGO, NA.

16. Mahon, *Second Seminole War*, 316; Sprague, *Florida War*, 486.

Appendix Three

1. Duncan, February 20, 1836; Belton to Jones, March 25, 1836, Belton Letter Book, SGO, NA.

2. Cooper to Reeve, June 6, 1842, NA; *Florida Herald*, August 15, 1842.

3. Covington, "Final Years"; *Sunland Tribune*, November 1981, 42; Schuppert to Laumer, September 30, 1982.

4. Statement by Fanning in Gardiner pension file, NA.

5. Heitman, *Historical Register* 1:412–13.

6. McIntosh, *History of Elbert County*, 89.

7. Ibid.

8. Miles to Kearney, November 26, 1843 (in White, *Private Joseph Sprague*, 65); Sprague to secretary of war, April 5, 1845 (in White, *Private Joseph Sprague*, 65); Statement by Porter (secretary of war), January 12, 1844 (in White, *Private Joseph Sprague*, 66).

9. Boyd, "Osceola," 218–34; Wickman, *Osceola's Legacy*, 121, 122; Boyd, "Osceola," 193–201; Wickman, *Osceola's Legacy*, 89–101.

10. Wickman, *Osceola's Legacy*, 105–14, 144–53.

11. Ibid., 105–14.

12. Foreman, *Indian Removal*, 354–58; Peters, *Florida Wars*, 153; Porter, "Cowkeeper Dynasty," 346–47.

13. Foreman, *Indian Removal*, 356, 364; Peters, *Florida Wars*, 153.

14. Foreman, *Indian Removal*, 362; Peithmann, *Unconquered Seminole Indians*, 39–43; McReynolds, *Seminoles*, 226; Foreman, *Indian Removal*, 380; Neill, *Florida's Seminole Indians*, 120.

Bibliography

Manuscript Sources

AUTHOR'S COLLECTION

Dade Memorial. In "Dade Papers," prepared by W. A. G. Dade. No date.
Djavaheri, Amir A. Protocol for the author on examination of the remains of Ransom Clark. December 4, 1977.
Knetsch, Joe. *Fort Drane: In the Whirlwind But Briefly.* December 1986.

ENVIRONMENTAL SCIENCE SERVICES ADMINISTRATION, NATIONAL WEATHER RECORDS CENTER, ASHEVILLE, N.C.

Fort Brooke Weather Diary, 1824–42
Fort King Weather Diary, 1832–43
Fort Morgan Weather Diary, quarter ending March 31, 1835

FLORIDA DEPARTMENT OF AGRICULTURE, FIELD NOTE DIVISION, TALLAHASSEE

Township 26 S, Range 21 E, and field notes, 1848.

FLORIDA STATE ARCHIVES

Call-Brevard Papers, *Incidents of the Seminole War: 1835–42.*

GEORGIA DEPARTMENT OF ARCHIVES AND HISTORY

Governor Rabun Correspondence, 1819

LIBRARY OF CONGRESS, MANUSCRIPT DIVISION

Jackson, Andrew, Papers, Reel 34; Memorandum, August 22, 1821.
Heintzelman, 1st. Lt. Samuel Peter, Papers. Reel 2 of 13, March 18, 1836.

NATIONAL ARCHIVES AND RECORDS SERVICE, WASHINGTON, D.C.

Adjutant General's Office. Re: John R. B. Gardinier. Record Group 94, U.S. Military Academy Application Papers; Record Group 107, Letters Received by the Secretary of War; Clinch Letter Book; Clinch Order Book; Jesup, Letters Received; Records of the War Department, Office of the Attorney General, Letters Received.
Monthly Post Records. Microfilm no. 805, roll 617 (Fort Morgan).
Monthly Post Returns. Microcopy no. 617, rolls 147–49 (Fort Brooke).
Navy and Military Service Branch.
Office of Indian Affairs. Letters Received, 1824–81, rolls 234, 286.
Pension Files. Belton, Francis S., WC-7737; Clark, Ransom, OWF-48471; Dade, Francis L., OWW-27581; Farley, Austin, BLW 114, 110-160-55; Gardiner, George W., OWW-17939; Kenny, Michael, OWWF-9769; Thomas, John, OWIF-6224; Vailing, John, OWWR-10818.
Records of U.S. Regular Army Mobile Units, 1821–1942. Order and Letter Book, November 24, 1834-March 27, 1838; Record Group 391, Records of 2nd U.S. Artillery Regiment, Orders of Battery B, 1834–38; Orderly Book, Company B, Record Group 391, December 1835, January 1836.
Registers of Enlistments in the U.S. Army, 1798–1914. Microcopy no. 233, rolls 19–20.
Surgeon General's Office. Archer, Robert, Papers; Heiskell, Henry, Papers; Quarterly Report of the Sick and Wounded at Key West, Florida, for the Quarter Ending December 31, 1835; Quarterly Returns of the Sick and Wounded at Fort King, East Florida, December 21, 1835, George R. Clark, Assistant Surgeon; Statistical Report on the Sickness and Mortality in the Army of the United States, January 1819-January 1839.

THE NEWBERRY LIBRARY, CHICAGO

Handwritten message from Gov. John H. Eaton in Tallahassee to General Clinch at Fort Drane, received January 22, 1836. Ayer MS 210.

P. K. YONGE LIBRARY OF FLORIDA HISTORY, GAINESVILLE

Basinger, William Starr. *The Personal Reminiscences of William Starr Basinger, 1827–1910.*

Jarvis, Nathan S. "Diary Kept While a Surgeon with the Army in Florida, 1837–1839." New York Academy of Medicine. Microfilm.
Prince, Lt. Henry. Diary.

UNIVERSITY OF PENNSYLVANIA ARCHIVES, PHILADELPHIA

Jenkins, John H., ed. *Texas Revolution 1835–36.* Vols. 1 and 2. Austin: Presidial Press, 1973.

U.S. MILITARY ACADEMY LIBRARY, WEST POINT, N.Y.

Duncan Papers; Gardenier Papers; Gardiner Papers; Keais Papers.
Duncan, Lt. James. Diary, February-March 1836.

Published Sources

NEWSPAPERS

Albany Argus, 1843.
Army and Navy Chronicle (Washington, D.C.), 1835–42.
Boston Post, 1837.
Charleston (S.C.) Courier, 1836.
Columbus (Ga.) Enquirer, 1835.
Dade City (Fla.) Banner, 1923.
Daily National Enquirer (Washington, D.C.), 1836–37.
Daily National Intelligencer (Washington, D.C.), 1837.
Enquirer (Key West, Fla.), 1834–36.
Florida Herald (St. Augustine), 1842.
Florida Times-Union (Jacksonville), 1892.
Georgian (Savannah), 1833, 1837.
Herald (N.Y.), 1836.
Livingston (N.Y.) Register, 1830.
Lynn (Mass.) Mirror, 1836.
National Atlas and Sunday Morning Mail (Philadelphia), 1836.
New Orleans Bee, 1836.
New York Commercial Advertiser, 1835.
New York Times, 1836.
Niles' Weekly Register (Baltimore), 1827–36.
Ocala (Fla.) Star Banner, 1968.

Pennsylvanian (Philadelphia), 1836.
Pensacola (Fla.) Gazette, 1826.
Pensacola (Fla.) Commercial, 1888.
Portland (Maine) Daily Advertiser, 1836.
Portsmouth (N.H.) Journal, 1849.
Saturday Evening Post, 1836.
St. Petersburg (Fla.) Times, 1978.
Sunland Tribune (Tampa, Fla.), 1880.
Tampa Tribune, 1880, 1950–60.

BOOKS, ARTICLES, AND PAMPHLETS

Alvord, Benjamin. *Address before the Dialectic Society of the Corps of Cadets*. New York: Wiley and Putnam, 1839.

American State Papers: Documents, Legislative and Executive of the Congress of the United States. Vol. 2: *Treaties*. Vols. 6 and 7: *Military Affairs*. Washington, D.C.: Gales and Seaton, 1861.

Barr, James. *A Correct and Authentic Narrative of the Indian War in Florida*. New York: J. Nabine, 1836.

Bemrose, John. *Reminiscences of the Second Seminole War*. Edited by John K. Mahon. Gainesville: University of Florida Press, 1966.

Biographical Directory of the American Congress, 1774–1949. Washington, D.C.: U.S. Government Printing Office, 1950.

Blanchard, D. F. *An Authentic Narrative of the Seminole War*. Providence and New York: Blanchard and Others, 1836.

Boyd, Mark F. *Florida Aflame*. Tallahassee, 1951. Reprinted from *Florida Historical Quarterly* 30, no. 1 (July 1951).

Boyd, Mark F. "The Complete Story of Osceola." Reprinted in *Florida Historical Quarterly* 33, nos. 3 and 4 (Osceola Issue) (January-April 1955): 249–305.

Boynton, Edward C. *History of West Point*. New York, 1863.

Brink, Benjamin M. "An Ulster Congressman Fights a Duel." *Olde Ulster, an Historical and Genealogical Magazine* (May 1912): 129–36.

Browne, Jefferson B. *Key West: The Old and the New*. Gainesville: University of Florida Press, 1973.

Carter, Clarence Edward, ed. *The Territorial Papers of the United States*. Vols. 22–25. Washington, D.C.: U.S. Government Printing Office, 1956–62.

The Centennial of the United States Military Academy at West Point, New York, 1802–1902. Vol. 1. Washington, D.C.: U.S. Government Printing Office, 1904.

Clark, Ransom. *Narrative of Ransom Clark.* Binghamton, N.Y.: Johnson and Marble, 1839.

Coe, Charles H. *Red Patriots: The Story of the Seminoles.* Gainesville: University Presses of Florida, 1974.

Cohen, M. M. *Notices of Florida and the Campaigns.* Gainesville: University of Florida Press, 1964. Reprint of 1836 edition.

Covington, James W. "The Final Years of Fort Brooke." *Sunland Tribune* (Journal of the Tampa Historical Society) 7, no. 1 (November 1981): 41–42.

———. "The Hackley Grant." *Sunland Tribune* 6, no. 1 (November 1980): 4–9.

———. "Life at Fort Brooke, 1824–1836." *Florida Historical Quarterly* 36, no. 4 (April 1958): 319–30.

———. *The Seminoles of Florida.* Gainesville: University Press of Florida, 1993.

———. *The Story of Southwestern Florida.* Vol. 1. New York: Lewis Historical Publishing Company, 1957.

Cullum, George Washington. "Recollections of the Cadet Life of George D. Ramsey." In *Biographical Register of the Officers and Graduates of the U.S. Military Academy at West Point, N.Y.* Vol. 3, p. 624. Cambridge, Mass.: Riverside Press.

———. *Register of Graduates and Former Cadets of the United States Military Academy.* West Point, N.Y.: West Point Alumni Foundation, 1960.

"The Dade Family." *Tyler's Quarterly Magazine* 17 (July 1935-April 1936).

Davis, Frederick. "Early Orange Culture in Florida and the Epochal Cold of 1835." *Florida Historical Quarterly* 15 (April 1937): 232–39.

Documents, Legislative and Executive, of the Congress of the United States. Vol. 3: *Military Affairs.* Washington, D.C.: Gales and Seaton, 1861.

Eby, Cecil D., Jr., ed. "Memoir of a West Pointer in Florida: 1825." *Florida Historical Quarterly* 41, no. 2 (October 1962): 154–64.

Farr, Cynthia K. *Tampa's Earliest Living Pioneer . . . A Sketch from the life of Mrs. Nancy Jackson.* Tallahassee, Fla., 1900.

Foreman, Grant. *Indian Removal.* Norman: University of Oklahoma Press, 1932.

Fort Morgan, 1833 Bastion of American History. Brochure distributed by Alabama Historical Commission, Montgomery.

Gaylord, Emma N. *Life in Florida since 1886.* Miami: Hurricane House Publishers, 1969.

General Regulations for the Army of the United States. Washington, D.C.: U.S. Department of War, 1825/1835.

Giddings, Joshua R. *The Exiles of Florida*. Columbus, Ohio: Follett, Foster, and Co., 1858.

Goggin, John M. "The Complete Story of Osceola." *Florida Historical Quarterly* 33, nos. 3–4 (January-April 1955): 161–92.

Goza, William. "The Ft. King Road—1963." *Florida Historical Quarterly* 43, no. 1 (July 1964): 52–70.

Grismer, Karl H. *Tampa: A History of the City of Tampa and the Tampa Bay Region of Florida*. St. Petersburg, Fla.: Tourist News Publishing Co., 1950.

Guild, J. C. *Old Times in Tennessee*. Nashville, 1878.

Heard, Norman J. *The Black Frontiersmen*. New York: John Day, 1969.

Heitman, Francis B. *Historical Register and Dictionary of the United States Army from Its Organization, September 29, 1789 to March 2, 1903*. 2 vols. Washington, D.C.: U.S. Government Printing Office, 1903.

Hickox, Ron G. *The Armament of Major Dade's Last Command*. Tampa: Tampa Bay Arms Collectors Association, March 1979.

——— . *Collectors' Guide to Ames U.S. Contract Military Edges Weapons: 1832–1906*. Brandon, Fla.: Ron G. Hickox, 1984.

——— . *U.S. Military Edged Weapons of the Second Seminole War, 1835–1842*. Brandon, Fla.: Ron G. Hickox, 1984.

Historic Livingston County. Brochure distributed by the Office of the Livingston County Historian. Geneseo, N.Y., 1972.

Hitchcock, Ethan Allen. *Fifty Years in Camp and Field*. New York: G. P. Putnam's Sons, 1909.

Huntington, R. T. *Accoutrements of the United States Infantry, Riflemen, and Dragoons, 1834–1839*. Alexandria Bay, N.Y.: Museum Restoration Service, 1987.

Hutchins' Improved Almanac and Ephemeris for 1835. New York: R. Bartlett and S. Raynor, 1836.

James, Marquis. *The Life of Andrew Jackson*. New York: Bobbs-Merrill, 1938.

Jenkins, John H., ed. *Texas Revolution 1835–1836*. Vols. 1–2. Austin, Texas: Presidial Press, 1973.

Johnson [first name unknown], and Holloman, Charles R. *The Heritage of Lenoir County*. Kinston, N.C.: Lenoir County Historical Society, 1981.

Klinkenborg, Verlyn. "If It Weren't for the Ox, We Wouldn't Be Where We Are." *Smithsonian* 24, no. 6 (September 1993): 82–93.

Knight, Lucian Lamar. *Georgia's Bi-Centennial Memoirs and Memories*. First Series. N.p.: Published by the author, n.d.

Lankford, George E. *Native American Legends*. Little Rock, Ark.: August House, 1987.

Latrobe, Charles. *The Rambler in North America: 1832–1833*. Vol. 2. London: Sweeley and Burnside, 1835.

Lawton, Edward P. *A Saga of the South*. Ft. Myers Beach, Fla.: Island Press, 1965.

Long, Ellen Call. *Florida Breezes*. Gainesville: University of Florida Press, 1962.

Luecke, Barbara K. *Feeding the Frontier Army, 1775–1865*. Eagan, Minn.: Grenadier, 1990.

McCall, George A. *Letters from the Frontier*. Philadelphia: Lippincott, 1868.

McIntosh, John H. *The Official History of Elbert County, 1790–1935: Supplement, 1935–1939*. Atlanta: Cherokee Publishing Co., 1968.

McKay, D. B., ed. *Pioneer Florida*. 2 vols. Tampa, Fla: Southern Publishing Co., 1959.

McReynolds, Edwin C. *The Seminoles*. Norman: University of Oklahoma Press, 1957.

Mahon, John K. *History of the Second Seminole War, 1835–1842*. Gainesville: University Presses of Florida, 1967.

Malone, Dumas. *Dictionary of American Biography*. Vol. 9. New York: Charles Scribner's Sons, 1964.

Manucy, Albert. *Artillery through the Ages*. Washington, D.C.: U.S. Government Printing Office, 1949. Reprint 1962.

Mathews, Janet Snyder. *Edge of Wilderness*. Sarasota, Fla.: Coastal Press, 1983.

Meek, A. B. "The Journal of A. B. Meek and the Second Seminole War, 1836." Edited by John K. Mahon. *Florida Historical Quarterly* 38 (April 1960): 302–18.

Morris, Allen. *The Florida Handbook*. Tallahassee, Fla.: Peninsular Publishing Co., 1961.

Motte, Jacob Rhett. *Journey into Wilderness*. Gainesville: University of Florida Press, 1963.

Mudge, Alfred. *Memorials: Being a Genealogical, Biographical, and Historical Account of the Name of Mudge in America, from 1638 to 1868*. Boston: Alfred Mudge and Son, for the Family, 1868.

Murray, Elizabeth Dunbar. *My Mother Used to Say: Memories of Mary Conway Shields Dunbar*. Norwell, Mass.: Christopher Publishing House, 1959.

Neill, Wilfred T. *Florida's Seminole Indians*. St. Petersburg, Fla.: Great Outdoors Association, 1976.

The Official History of Elbert County, 1790–1935. Atlanta: Cherokee Publishing Co., 1968.

Ott, Eloise Robinson, and Louis Hickman Chazel. *Ocali Country, Kingdom of the Sun*. Ocala, Fla.: Marion Publishers, 1966.

Parton, James. *Life of Andrew Jackson*. Vol. 2. New York: Mason, 1860.

Patrick, Rembert W. *Aristocrat in Uniform: General Duncan L. Clinch*. Gainesville: University of Florida Press, 1963.

Peithmann, Irvin M. *The Unconquered Seminole Indians*. St. Petersburg, Fla.: Great Outdoors Association, 1957.

Peters, Virginia B. *The Florida Wars*. Hamden, Conn.: Shoestring Press, 1979.

Peterson, Harold L. *Round Shot and Rammers*. South Bend, Ind.: South Bend Replicas, n.d.

Porter, Kenneth W. "Bill Bowlegs (Holata Micco) in the Seminole Wars." *Florida Historical Quarterly* 45, no. 3 (January 1967): 219–42.

———. "The Cowkeeper Dynasty of the Seminole Nation." *Florida Historical Quarterly* 30 (April 1952): 341–49.

———. "Louis Pacheco: The Man and the Myth." *Journal of Negro History* 28 (January 1943): 65–72.

———. "Negro Guides and Interpreters in the Early Stages of the Seminole War." *Journal of Negro History* 35 (April 1950): 174–82.

Potter, Woodburne. *The War in Florida*. Baltimore: Lewis and Coleman, 1836.

Powell, William H. *A History of the Origin and Movement of the Fourth Regiment of Infantry U.S.A., May 30, 1796 to Dec. 31, 1870*. Washington, D.C.: McGill and Withrow, 1871.

Prucha, Francis Paul. *A Guide to the Military Posts of the United States, 1789–1895*. Milwaukee: North American Press, 1966.

Richardson, James D., ed. *A Compilation of the Messages and Papers of the Presidents, 1789–1902*. Vol. 2. Washington, D.C.: Bureau of National Literature and Art, 1904.

Roberts, Albert H. "The Dade Massacre." *Florida Historical Quarterly* 5 (January 1927): 123–38.

Robinson, Ernest L. *History of Hillsborough County*. St. Augustine, Fla.: Records Co., 1928.

Schoonmaker, Marius. *The History of Kingston, New York, from Its Early Settlement to the Year 1820*. New York: Burr Printing House, 1888.

Scott, Winfield. *Infantry Tactics*. Vol. 1. New York: Harper and Brothers, 1840.

Simmons, James. "Recollections of the Late Campaign in East Florida." *National Atlas and Sunday Morning Mail*, July and August 1836.

———. "Recollections of the Late Campaign in East Florida." *Saturday Evening Post*, August 20, 1836.

Sinclair, William C., J. W. Stewart, R. L. Knutilla, A. E. Gilboy, and R. L. Miller. *Types, Features, and Occurrence of Sinkholes in the Karst of West-Central*

Florida. Tallahassee, Fla.: U.S. Department of the Interior Geological Survey, 1985.

Smith, W. W. *Sketch of the Seminole War, and Sketches during a Campaign.* Charleston, S.C.: Dan J. Dowling, 1836.

Sprague, John T. *The Origin, Progess, and Conclusion of the Florida War.* New York: Appleton, 1848.

The Story of Kinston and Lenoir County. Kinston, N.C.: Lenoir County Historical Association, 1981.

A System of Artillery Discipline. Boston: Munroe and Francis, 1817.

System of Exercise and Instruction of Field-Artillery. Boston: Hillard, Gray, Little, and Wilkins, 1829.

Tampa Bay Arms Collectors Association. *En Garde!* St. Petersburg, Fla.: Ron Hickox Publishers, 1979.

United States Military Reservations, National Cemeteries, and Military Parks. Washington, D.C.: U.S. Government Printing Office, 1916.

University of Pennsylvania Alumni Catalog. Class of 1829.

White, Frank F., ed. "Macomb's Mission to the Seminoles." *Florida Historical Quarterly* 35 (October 1956): 161.

White, Nathan W. *Private Joseph Sprague of Vermont: The Last Soldier-Survivor of Dade's Massacre in Florida.* Ft. Lauderdale, Fla., 1981.

Wickman, Patricia R. *Osceola's Legacy.* Tuscaloosa: University of Alabama Press, 1991.

Williams, John Lee. *The Territory of Florida.* New York: Goodrich, 1837.

Wood, Don A. "The Realities of Extinction." *Florida Wildlife* 41, no. 3 (May-June 1987).

Young, David. *Knickerbocker's Almanac for the Year of Our Lord 1835.* New Haven: Yale University Library, 1835.

Index